Cape York Peninsula

Cape York Peninsula

A History of Unlauded Heroes 1845-2003

Lennie Wallace

First published in 2004 by Central Queensland University Press

Second published in 2012 by Boolarong Press, Salisbury, Brisbane, Australia.

National Library of Australia Cataloguing-in-Publication entry

Author:	Wallace, Lennie.
Title:	Cape York Peninsula / Lennie Wallace.
ISBN:	9781921920677 (pbk.)
Subjects:	Pioneers--Queensland--Cape York Peninsula.
	Country life--Queensland--Cape York Peninsula.
	Cape York Peninsula (Qld.)--History.
	Cape York Peninsula (Qld.)--Discovery and exploration.
Dewey Number:	994.38

Cover design and typesetting by Jane Dorrington

Cover painting: *End of the Wet* by Mark Burton

Chapter image: Unloading cattle from the *Clara Clausen*

Printed and bound by Watson Ferguson & Company, Salisbury, Brisbane, Australia.

Preface

All four of my books have been about life on the Cape York Peninsula. I began with comic autobiographical confessions of what life was like on a cattle station on the Peninsula in the 1950s or thereabouts. There was *Bitten by the Bull Bug* and there was *Bow Waves in the Bull Dust (formerly Leaves from the Peninsula)*. Then my publisher at Central Queensland University Press accepted my comic stories about family life on a Peninsula cattle station and named it *Dad and Joey in Possum Gully*, dedicated to R.M. Williams who first published my stories in *Hoofs and Horns* and who sent me a new typewriter when my old one packed it in.

Gradually I moved from the autobiographical to the historical and began to enjoy my research. I even found a hero: the Scottish immigrant, Dr Jack Hamilton, pugilist, gold prospector, physician of the goldfields and finally Queensland politician. I celebrated him and other FNQ heroes in *Nomads of the Queensland Goldfields.*

My love of Butcher's Hill re-asserted itself. It wasn't just that my husband Bill and I gave the best part of our lives to developing our cattle station there. It was the romance of the region with its dark, volcanic soil and its tropical lakes and the sequence of bold adventurers whom it attracted. This history was called simply *The Battlers of Butcher's Hill.*

Now in this fifth book, I have, under orders from my irascible publisher, broadened my perspective and my painting. I have attempted, in an informal and personal way, to pen a history of all the regions in Cape York Peninsula. It is not an academic history and I make no claim that it is exhaustive. But I do hope that it full of life and atmosphere and tells many of the stories that make up our frontier history, from the sandalwood cutters and the pearl divers to the cattle station owners and the drovers. My heart will always be in the Peninsula, so you shouldn't be surprised if my history is also a celebration of the explorers, dreamers, settlers, developers, drovers, mailmen and stockmen who gave their lives to Cape York Peninsula.

Lennie Wallace
October 2003

Publication of this book was generously supported by a RADF grant from Cook Shire Council

Contents

Introduction

Cape York Peninsula is such a vast area with so few residents compared to the rest of the continent that it is difficult to tell its story and to do it justice. Stories abound of very early visitors from overseas but if these mariners left any clues to their occupancy, they are extremely hard to trace all these hundreds of years later. At least Capt. James Cook did leave easily recognisable signs of his sojourn on the banks of the Endeavour River, named for his ship.

Other sea visitors came and the land explorers followed. William Hann's surveyor, Frederick Warner, won a prize of tobacco for washing some gold from the banks of the Palmer River but the discovery was slight and the area so isolated that Hann didn't like to publicise the find. His caution was not taken into consideration by miner James Venture Mulligan. When he heard the news, Mulligan and his mates hastened to the field, and with their expertise, discovered what was more than just 'payable gold.' It was a bonanza.

Cattlemen followed with their stock, first to sell as food to the miners, and later to establish cattle runs to provide for future settlers. By the time the gold was no longer payable, other goldfields were discovered and tin mines worked in the Cooktown Hinterland. Many of the Chinese who flocked in to get what gold they could, remained as successful gardeners and local businessmen. Timber was cut and milled for housing and also for export. Timber of another kind, sandalwood, also proved a very lucrative export to the Orient.

With population growth, a Telegraph Line was extended from an existing one servicing the Palmer Goldfield, to the tip of Cape York where the Colony's government had established a Residency. Great hopes were held for trade from there to Asia and Europe but that was not to be. The Residency, relegated in importance, was a shifted to Thursday Island which had a thriving trade itself in pearl and trochus shell, trepang and, of course, the lustrous pearl. On the mainland, the cattle industry and the farms around Cooktown were the only bases of settlement until World War 2. Then the whole place came alive with the threat of Japanese invasion.

Airfields were quickly assembled, the Telegraph Line upgraded and large numbers of troops, both Australian and American, were stationed in the far north. The cattle industry also benefited with a wartime market for beef. At the war's end people clamoured to have a road put through to connect Cooktown and the Peninsula with the more-settled south. Approval was finally given and a road was built, the Mulligan Highway, from Mareeba to Cooktown and later extended to the north. Laura lost its little weekly railmotor soon after but the future seemed bright.

A new and lucrative industry began after the war, croc-shooting, but this did not last. The crocodile became protected and the harvesting was stopped in 1972. The road brought the Peninsula cattle country to the notice of foreign investors and some Americans moved onto the better cattle runs. Their interest did not endure and most accepted the Government's offer to buy their leases for National Parks. The Land Council acquired grazing land and Aboriginal cattle stations were encouraged. However, as neither National Parks nor Aboriginal Title pay rates, this has become a problem for the Cook Shire with a vastly reduced rate base from which to raise finance for maintenance of infrastructure.

1

Early Mariners and Castaways in the Torres Straits

Speculations on early Asian Mariners · Spanish Galleons and the Santa Barbara 1596 · The Rattlesnake in the Torres Strait 1848 · Barbara Thompson, Taken in by the Kaurareg 1845-1848 · The Charles Eaton, Europeans wrecked in the Torres Strait, 1834 · Rescue of two boys by the Isabella on Murray Island, 1836 · Rescue of Joseph Forbes from Timor in 1838 · Cabin Boy Narcisse Pellatier rescued near Cape Direction by the John Bell, 1875, after being marooned seventeen years previously · William Bligh after the Mutiny on the Bounty · Convict William Bryant and party to Timor · Flinders' charts of the Torres Strait · Captain Jeffreys of the Kangaroo, 1815 · Wickham in the Beagle,1839 · The Wild White Woman of the Normanby, 1887

Atlantis, that fabulous Great Southland, inspired navigators to sail off from settled countries in search of the legendary riches of the unknown. Egyptians, Phoenicians and later the Europeans, sailed in primitive vessels across the oceans in search of the new continent. Did one, or some of them, land on what is now Australia? Lucian, writing in about 170A.D. speaks of outlandish animals 'that use their bellies like a pouch; it opens and shuts; there is nothing in it, but it is shaggy and hairy, so that their young creep into it when cold.'[1]

According to pyramid-researchers, Rex and Heather Gilroy, Chinese knowledge of Australia, their *Chui Hiao,* dates back almost 3000 years. Ancient Chinese records recount solar eclipses witnessed near present-day Darwin on two occasions in the sixth century B.C. Two hundred years later, *Shi Tzu* tells of the introduction of strange pouched animals to China. The Emperor sent out a fleet to procure more of these bizarre marsupials for the Peking zoo. The Gilroy's say the name for these exotic animals was *Shuti*, 'leaping hare', and after many years of dedicated research they are sure that many daring navigators visited our northern coasts. They even go further in proposing, not without convincing evidence, that the Phoenicians and Egyptians were more permanent residents who mined and exported the metals back to their homelands.

The Japanese claim that their seamen circumnavigated the Southern Continent well before Tasman. The Chinese maintain that their mariners also sailed around what is now Australia and were familiar with the northern coasts. Centuries after their first exploratory voyages, the Chinese of the fifteenth century possessed a 'porcelain map' showing the west coasts of both American continents and the eastern coastline of Australia. Other island groups including New Zealand could be recognised in what must have been their depiction of the Pacific Ocean.[2] Some of the sailors died during the voyage and were said to have been buried on the North Queensland mainland.

Spanish Galleons and the Santa Barbara

The unpredictability of both the weather and the Great Barrier Reef created insurmountable difficulties for the early visitors from the sea. Stories abound of the remains of galleons lying under sand and water along the length of the Reef. A brass cannon with *Santa Barbara 1596*[3] inscribed on it was said to have been found on an island near Port Curtis. It was recovered and sent to Sydney but failed to reach its destination. Hector Holthouse explains the finding of the *Santa Barbara* cannon in his book. A Captain Jensen, at one time a pilot working out from Gladstone, had earlier been a seaman on a coastal sailing ship, the *Marina,* when it struck a reef in 1859. The crew escaped in the ship's boats and after a couple of anxious days made a safe landfall on 'one of the Sir Charles Hardy Islands off Cape Melville.' Here there were the remains of two wrecks. One appeared to have met its fate relatively recently but the other showed obvious signs of having been there a great deal longer.

High up on the beach were two cannons. One was of iron, the other was brass. The brass cannon bore the marking *Santa Barbara.* The sailors took both cannons on board as ballast as the boat wasn't handling the seas as well as hoped. In a patch of particularly rough seas, the iron cannon was jettisoned, but the *Santa Barbara* cannon was retained and later deposited by them on Facing Island. Nearby was an ancient wreck believed to have been an early Spanish galleon and when the cannon was later discovered it was understandably assumed that there was a link between the two.

Such was the rivalry between Portuguese, Dutch, Spanish and English mariners in the pre-Cook days that maps were vigilantly guarded from other observers and were even, at times, falsified to mislead competitors.

The indigenous Australians came south over the landbridge from neighbouring Asia. They brought no livestock — if you don't count their dogs, the dingoes, related to the non-barking Indian dhole. At that time, the very deep Wallace Trench in the sea to the north of New Guinea acted as a barrier to migratory animals. Marsupials and monotremes were isolated from

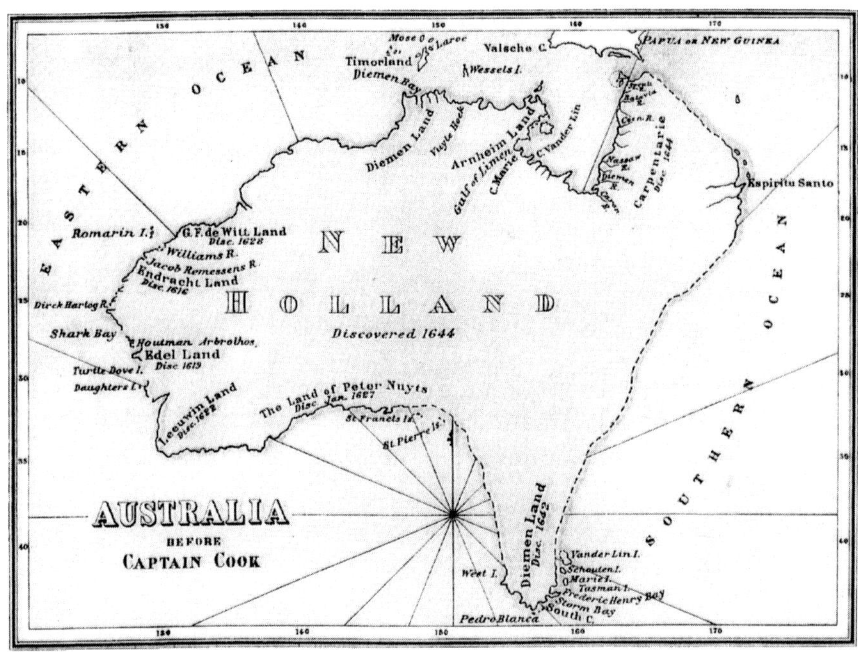

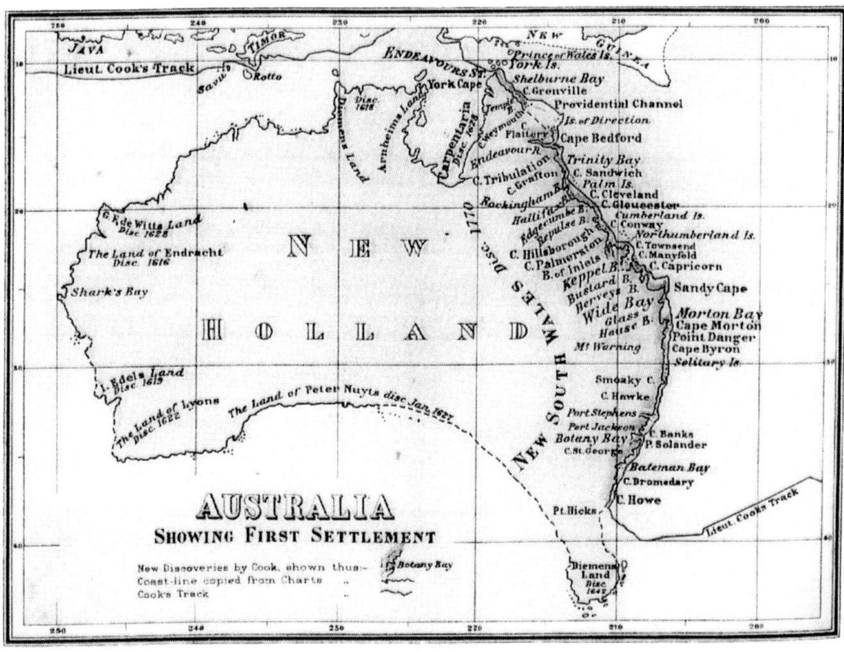

Australia before and after Captain James Cook

Courtesy *Our First Half Century* — Queensland Government

the rest of the world's placentals with a few species of both their fauna and flora existing also in neighbouring New Guinea. A smaller race of dark-skinned people was probably here before the Aborigines. They were short in stature, darker in complexion and had tightly curled hair. Sometimes these people are referred to as Negritas. Sightings of small people in the wild were still reported in the North during the early twentieth century, on the coast near Silver Plains, 'in the mangroves' near Hopevale and on the Atherton Tableland and the adjacent coast.

Other Visitors from the Sea

There were other visitors who came by sea. Malaccamen often visited the coasts of the Gulf and the Peninsula in their search for trepang and other items that they could use in trade. Spanish and Portuguese navigators left maps of voyages showing their interest in northern Australia. The Jardine family is said to have had an elegant cutlery set made from coins thought to be of Spanish origin which were found off the coast from Somerset where another ship was apparently claimed by the hidden reefs of the Torres Straits. Ion Idriess's Wild Man of Badu — Wini, Weenie or Wongai — was considered by Oswald Brierly to be the survivor of an Indonesian or a Dutch ship wrecked in Torres Strait. Brierly met Wini when he was on the survey vessel *Rattlesnake* in 1848. He wrote in his log that Wini could speak no English and was 'dark skinned and pock-marked'. McGillivray, who also saw him, thought he was an escaped convict from Norfolk Island but his lack of English cast some doubt on this. It was thought he had been on the island with the Badulaig 'from about 1840' and remained with them until his death.

The *Rattlesnake* (with its 28 guns) was sent on a routine surveying expedition around the coasts of Cape York in 1848. Later on its voyage there was an unexpected visitor. Near Cape York, at Evans Bay, on 16th October 1849[4], a white woman met up with a party from the ship. She spoke to them in English saying, 'I am a Christian. I am ashamed.' Incredulous, the sailors helped her on board the ship. In 1845 she had watched helplessly as the *H.M.S. Fly* and the *Bramble* passed by. The castaway did not want a repetition of that disappointment. To her tribal friends she gave the excuse that she needed to board the vessel to get white man's medicine, '*uperi*', for a sore knee and a nasal problem that were worrying her. She was Barbara Thompson, 'a native of Aberdeen' who had migrated to N.S.W. on the *John Barry* with her parents from their home in Scotland in the 1830s. Once in N.S.W. she married at an early age and soon afterwards accompanied her husband in the *America*, a speedy cutter, to salvage oil from a whaling ship which had come to grief on Brampton Shoal. Unfortunately, the guide whom they took on for the purpose of locating the treasure trove could not find the wrecked vessel. This led to 'recrimination and quarrelling.' In the course of the resulting turmoil two men were accidentally drowned and a third was marooned on a small islet.

The *America* sailed on for Torres Strait where it was itself wrecked 'on the eastern Prince of Wales Island' thought by Robert Logan Jack to be Entrance Island. Of the three left on the boat, Barbara's husband, a sailor and Barbara herself, only Barbara reached the shore. The other two drowned. Barbara owed her rescue to intervention by the local indigenous people. Once ashore she almost immediately gained the protection of a very powerful chief, Peaqui, on Murulug (Prince of Wales Island). He believed her to be, with her fair skin, the reincarnation of his daughter Gi Om.

Though Barbara must have mourned the loss of her husband and family, she appears to have lived a harmonious life with the Kaurareg people for several years. The *America* was thought to have been wrecked in 1845. Brierly of the *Rattlesnake* was extremely interested in the lives of the Aborigines and Islanders and made the most of his opportunity to interview Barbara or 'Mrs. T.' as he referred to her, recording what she told him and reading it back to her for confirmation. She still spoke English with a Scots brogue but Kaurareg had become her first language.

Coincidentally, one of the officers on the *Rattlesnake* was a Dr. Thompson. Thomas Huxley was the assistant surgeon, McGillivray the ship's zoologist and Brierly the official artist. Huxley, through his nephew Julian, published accounts of the *Rattlesnake's* voyages. Strangely, considering Brierly's interest and his vocation as an artist, there is no painting of Barbara.[5] Owen Stanley, the Captain, and Huxley were also talented artists.

Barbara was twenty-one when she boarded the *Rattlesnake*. She must have been a young woman of only sixteen when she was rescued earlier by the Kaurareg. Her skin was tanned to a credible Aboriginal brown with a large scar on one side of her face. She had rolled onto the ashes of a fire while asleep and almost, much more seriously, lost the sight of one eye. Burns were one of the hazards that accompanied sleeping by the side of a fire. Jacky Jacky a.k.a Galmarra, Kennedy's loyal henchman, while droving through the Albury district in 1854 'falls into the campfire, and is burned to death.'[6]

Coming from the mostly uneducated working class of that era, Barbara was illiterate but she was intelligent, resourceful and pleasant looking. Huxley, too, was impressed with her 'perfect truth and sincerity and no little intelligence'. Being interested in Mrs.T, Brierly and Huxley found out all that they could of her earlier life. At sixteen[7], the young Barbara Crawford, daughter of a respectable tinsmith, ran off with a young sailor, William Thompson. They were married at Moreton Bay on the way north to seek their treasure. Barbara sent her father a letter from there telling him of their marriage but received no reply. She told Brierly that her new husband was given the opportunity to accompany the unfortunate Leichhardt to Port Essington but decided to try his luck with Barbara in his own salvage operation. The *America* left Moreton Bay in September 1844, about two weeks after the ill-fated Leichhardt party set out.

After striking trouble when the wreck could not be located and two men were accidentally drowned when a dinghy overloaded with firewood turned turtle and sank, the survivors were left to live on whatever fish and shellfish they could find. In December, the *America,* caught in a savage tropical storm, was washed onto a reef near Horn Island. It was here that Thompson and the sailor drowned trying to swim for help and where Barbara, clinging to the wreckage, was rescued by a party of Kaurareg hunting for turtle. They took her in their canoe to Prince of Wales Island where she was presented to Peaqui. Some accounts of Barbara's sojourn with the Islanders say that she married one of her rescuers, Boroto. Brierly was given no hint of this in his conversation with Barbara although he reported that she was remarkably candid about all aspects of her life. Alikia and Tomagagu were her co-rescuers with Boroto and she referred to them all in conversations with Brierly as her 'brothers'. Tomagagu was a mainland Aborigine and was very sympathetic to Barbara's plight. He promised her that he would help her to return to her people.

On the other hand, the Kaurareg, because of the prestige her fair skin brought to the island, wanted to keep her. Boroto made quite a scene on the *Rattlesnake* and, quite vociferously, demanded her return. Barbara was never ill-treated and as a ghost or a Marki, the tribe would never have forced her to marry. Brierly wrote, 'they treated her as a pet'. A Marki was something very special. Although polygamy was accepted practice, it was not compulsory and Boroto already had one wife, Yuri, a widow.

Brierly's record of his talks with Mrs. T. also throws doubt on the villainous character of the man Idriess wrote of as Wongai, the Wild White Man of Badu. Badu or Mulgrave Island was to the north of Murulug (Prince of Wales Island). According to what the Kaurareg told Brierly, he considered that Wini had arrived on Badu and lived with the Badulug 'from about 1840'. He remained with them until his death. Barbara told Brierly[8] how, at one time, a large Badu party came in sixteen canoes to take her back to 'Weenie' to be his wife. The groom-to-be, according to Barbara, did not accompany them. Although accounts of him paint Wini as a bloodthirsty savage, Barbara found him a 'mild mannered middle-aged man'. The Badulug called the stranger Wini or Weenie but Barbara told her rescuers that he referred to himself as Gienow. Like her, he had been 'adopted' by 'brothers' whom he assisted in repairing canoes and in their usual round of activities. One of Barbara's adopted kinsmen corroborated her opinion of Wini. Manu, a Kaurareg leader, told Brierly that Wini was a Kopi/Garki — a 'good man'.

Once aboard the *Rattlesnake*, Barbara quickly regained her health and, given sewing needles, cotton and calico made 'feminine toggery' to replace the sailor's shirts she was given to wear when she boarded the ship. The *Rattlesnake* arrived in Sydney on 5th February 1850, four months after Barbara was picked up. Her parents were both alive and thankfully welcomed her back to the bosom of the family.

Back at Prince of Wales Island, Barbara's influence was still felt and in 1863 two missionaries Messrs Jagg and Kennett who were stationed at Somerset were asked by a deputation from the Kaurareg which included Mrs. T's protector Peaqui, to establish a school for the children of the Kaurareg. Unfortunately, Somerset was itself struggling for existence at that time and nothing permanent came from the request.

Europeans Living With Tribal People

One of the first records of white people co-existing with tribes of the Torres Strait was that of the survivors of the *Charles Eaton*. The *Charles Eaton* was a 313 ton barque skippered by Captain Moore. It left Sydney on 29th July 1834 bound for Ceylon (Sri Lanka). Sailing from England with 'calicoes and lead'[9] it arrived in Sydney by way of the Cape of Good Hope. There were '26 crew including two apprenticed boys', John Sexton and John Ireland. Other passengers were a Mr. Armstrong and Capt. D'Oyley 'of the Artillery', together with his wife, their son of about two years, another boy of 'about ten' and their female Bengalese servant.

On 15th August the ship's look-out saw breakers which indicated a reef ahead but because of extremely strong winds, the crew could do nothing to avoid the reef and the following disaster. The Torres Strait was always dangerous for shipping and the Captain had prudently decided not to enter these dangerous waters until dawn the following day but the treachery of The Detached Reef put an end to his carefully-laid plans. They had four boats — a long-boat, two cutters and a dinghy. The Captain ordered that provisions be put aboard these boats in readiness for a flight to Timor, the closest European settlement. Unfortunately, while lowering the boats, the long- boat was swamped, as was the smaller cutter. The dinghy was smashed when the ship keeled over on her side, crushing it beneath her. The surviving cutter, the largest, was lowered successfully and some of the company made their escape in it, hoping to get help. The Captain and other survivors including the D'Oyleys spent six days making a raft but it wasn't bouyant. The weight of all the survivors combined caused it to sink and the crew returned to the stricken ship. The Captain, the

D'Oyleys and their amah plus three others, nine in all, refloated the raft and remained on it. During the night, with them on board, the raft pulled out from the ship. A week later, a second raft was launched for the remaining survivors, one of whom was tragically drowned in the launching process.

Of the first raft, Robert Logan Jack writes 'little is known with certainty'. The only survivors were the two very shocked and shaken little boys who said that all the adults had been killed. The boys were taken by canoe, to Aureed. The second raft carried seventeen persons including the two apprentices Ireland and Sexton. They were intercepted by a canoe of apparently friendly natives who escorted them to the island of Boydan about 40 miles (64 k) northwest of the Charles Hardy Group. Here there was neither food nor water and, in their weakened condition, the survivors, with the exception of the two lads, were beaten to death. The heads of the victims were taken along with the two young hostages by canoe to Aureed where the two survivors were thankfully reunited with the D'Oyley boys. There were about fifty people on the island and, after about two months[10] they split into two parties. The first included Ireland and the two-year old boy. The second took with them Sexton and the older D'Oyley boy. Sexton and the boy were never heard of again but Ireland and the younger boy were taken to Marsden Island to the north of Aureed. After some time, a 'native named Dappar and his wife' landed on the island and took Ireland and the little boy to Murray Island (Mer). Here, they were 'kindly treated' until their rescue by the *Isabella.*

Stories circulated among the crews of the ships traversing the Strait of a 'white boy' living on one of the Torres Strait islands and soon evidence was found of the wrecked *Charles Eaton.* Hoping that the stories bore some grains of truth, Captain Lewis of the *Isabella* detoured in anticipation of finding some survivors of the tragedy. At Murray Island, natives came out to meet the *Isabella* in canoes. Parleying began. John Ireland 'two years older than when he shipped as Steward's Boy on the *Charles Eaton'* was brought out and exchanged for tomahawks. Little William was also presented. He spoke the Murray Island dialect fluently but knew no English. After two years it was not unexpected that 'the chief difficulty' in ransoming him was his 'reluctance to part with his black foster mother'. He cried bitterly at being separated.[11]

Other islands were visited and keenly searched but no other survivors were found although an impressive display of human skulls and turtleshell was. The skulls were taken to Sydney where 'a sufficient number were pronounced to be of European origin' to fit the majority of the shipwreck victims. With its mission accomplished, the *Isabella* left for Timor through the Prince of Wales Channel and Booby Island on 3rd August 1836. From Timor, the *Isabella* returned to Sydney.

Young William was claimed by his relatives, Mr. and Mrs. Slade, who soon nursed him back to robust health despite a lingering cough. He eventually returned to England under the care of the same Captain Lewis from the *Isabella.* Ireland had no friends or relations to help him although he also wished to return to England. Sadly, it was a long time before 'this wish was gratified'.[12] The skulls were interred by Governor Bourke in the Sydney Cemetery and an impressive memorial was erected there.

The *Isabella*[13] came upon the scene again as a rescue vessel in late 1838. She had been re-fitted and re-named, the *Essington.* With a new Captain, Thomas Watson, she was sailing to the new settlement of Port Essington on Coburg Peninsula with the material to build a church. A call at Timor alerted Watson to the fact that a white youth was with the natives there. He was Joseph Forbes, a cabin boy from the ill-fated *Stedcombe* which had come to grief there. Forbes' older brother, a sailor, together with the rest of the crew, had been massacred. Joseph was the sole survivor. Several Dutch ships sailed past, at least one of which was offered the castaway in return for a modest ransom but the Dutch did not wish to be involved. It was left to Capt. Watson of the new *Essington* to do the rescuing. Forbes was taken to Sydney where he spent a few months re-gaining his strength. A public subscription raised enough money for his passage back to England in October 1841.

Lloyds of London awarded Watson a Silver Medal in recognition of his 'highly praiseworthy proceedings' in rescuing Joe Forbes. The *Brittomart* also travelling with a shipment for Port Essington made contact with an 'elderly man' at Oleillet on Timor who gave the Captain some papers, clothing and relics which the Captain considered to have come from survivors of the *Charles Eaton.* In appreciation of Captain Lewis's part in the rescue of the *Charles Eaton* survivors he was made the first Harbour Master of Port Phillip (Sydney).[14]

Narcisse Pellatier

Narcisse Pierre Pellatier[15] was the son of a shoemaker of 'St. Gillies near Bordeaux'. In 1858 he was cabin boy on the ship the *St. Paul* on a voyage bringing 350 Chinese immigrants to Australia. The *St. Paul* was wrecked on a reef in the Louisiade Group. The crew managed to reach an island in the ship's very overcrowded boats but the unfortunate Chinese were abandoned. The crew battled the elements for almost a thousand kilometres to First Red Rocky Point just south of Cape Direction near the mouth of the Lockhart River. Here Pellatier was also abandoned when he failed to turn up in time to embark. Fortunately, he did not suffer the fate of the Chinese who abandoned. They were said to have appeared regularly on the natives' menus until the last sixteen were finally rescued. On the contrary, the Aborigines of Cape Direction

Narcisse Pellatier

treated the cabin boy exceedingly well. He was marooned there, weak and dying of malnutrition. The Aborigines took him into their camp and into their hearts. He recovered his strength, learnt their language, Makadamas, and lived there apparently quite happily for seventeen years until 'rescued' by the crew of the *John Bell,* a pearl schooner anchored at Night Island, south east of Cape Direction on 11th April 1875. When found, like his adopted family, Pellatier was completely naked and the sun had burnt his skin 'a rich red colour'. On his breast he had raised tribal markings and he carried the pierced ear-lobes of a tribal warrior. He was very proud of the marks on his chest made, he explained, by cutting with a sharpened piece of quartz and pinching manually during the healing process to acquire the desired raised effect. His ear-lobe was decorated with a piece of wood about one centimetre in diameter and about ten centimetres long when he went aboard the *John Bell.*

He told his rescuers, that in the early years of his new life his thoughts constantly reverted to home and family but, as he was accepted into the tribe, the 'memories faded' and he 'thoroughly identified with the blacks'. He was not particularly overjoyed to be rescued nor was his adopted family happy to see him go. Although he was very young when abandoned by the crew of the *St. Paul* he 'retained his knowledge of reading and writing and counting with ease up to one hundred and he drew some excellent sketches of the animals he had hunted.'[16] A few months after he was found on the east coast of the Peninsula, he was reunited with his family in France. One can barely imagine their joy at seeing him alive and restored to them after all those years but a story is told how, after some time elapsed, Pellatier is said to have disappeared from the family circle. It was thought that he returned to his Aboriginal friends.

Spencer Browne who worked on one of Cooktown's newspapers in the Palmer River days, wrote of a white woman living with the Aborigines near Cape Grenville. This story was corroborated by miner Willie Webb. Searches were made to 'rescue' her but the men of the tribe always managed to get her away out of sight of the search party. A Captain Pearn also reported sighting the woman in 1878 and assumed she was the survivor of a shipwreck. Miners at the Bowden wolfram field inland from Cape Grenville were told in 1918 of this white 'queen' with fair skin, fair hair and bright blue eyes who 'ruled' over the tribe there.

William Bligh and the Bryants

The sea route up the eastern coastline, through the Torres Strait to the then Dutch East Indies was used not infrequently by ships heading for India or Europe. After the mutiny on the *Bounty* when William Bligh and the eighteen men from the ship who remained loyal to him were cast adrift in a twenty-three feet (approximately seven metres) long boat, the castaways in 1789 made for the haven of the East Indies by way of the passage through Torres Strait. An excellent seaman, and certainly not a man who would cower under a bed to hide from Rum-trader MacArthur, Bligh found a passage through the Barrier Reef east of Cape Direction. He thought that it was Cook's Providential Channel but he was a little out in his calculations. Though Bligh and his fellow castaways landed on several coastal islands they did not visit the mainland. He named Restoration Island near Cape Weymouth as it was the anniversary of the Restoration of the Stuart dynasty in 1660. The sight of land also 'restored' their own spirits. Puddingpan Hill, a flat-topped tableland between Cape Grenville and Cape York was also named by Bligh. The castaways made it safely through the Strait, turning west near four rocky islets that Bligh called The Brothers, passing through Cook's Endeavour Strait and Booby Island to reach Timor safely. They had covered the 3600 miles (almost 6000k) in an incredible forty-one days.

In 1891, two years after Bligh reached Timor another small group of escapees made the voyage to Timor. They were convicts who stole a six-oared fishing boat and fled, hugging the coast and rowing inside the Reef from Sydney. The leader, William Bryant must have been a very skilful boatman but he didn't keep a log nor make any charts so that his experience was of little benefit to those who followed — except to show that it could be done in a rowboat. Bryant's wife, Mary, accompanied them and shared their hardships. Sadly for them, once in Timor, fever struck and left very few survivors.

Flinders, the man who gave the continent its name, Australia, circumnavigated it at the turn of the nineteenth century but, cognisant of Cook's fate and the dangerous reefs skirting the coast, the *Investigator* sailed through Flinders Passage to the east of Townsville to the waters outside the Reef until he reached the seas to the north of Cape York. He veered westward here at a dangerous array of reefs, the Eastern Fields, and sailed through Flinders Entrance to the 'Indian

Seas'. In a remarkable feat, he made the transition from the Pacific Ocean to the 'Indian Seas' in an astounding three days. Even Bligh took over two weeks to accomplish the dangerous passage. Other vessels followed both him and his mentor, Cook, in charting the coasts of Australia and taking the route within the Reef.

Naval Surveys

Captain Jeffreys (or Jeffries) negotiated the inner route successfully in the *Kangaroo* in 1815. He sailed close to the shoreline and named some of the features that are well known today, Princess Charlotte Bay and the Flinders Group of islands are among them.[17] Jeffrey was not popular with the authorities, Governor Macquarie in particular. His habit of not always obeying orders did not endear him to his superiors. On one voyage he took on board an 'undischarged bankrupt indebted to the Crown for two thousand, three hundred and eighty-five pounds, eight shillings and ninepence unpaid Customs duties.'[18] He was also suspected of carrying escaping convicts and illegal grog. He may have been a 'bit of lad' but Jeffrey was a great navigator. He left seafaring to bcome a farmer in Tasmania.

Phillip Parker King, born on Norfolk Island, completed the remainder of the marine surveying, a task in which he excelled. He was the son of Governor Phillip Gidley King. In 1819 in the *Mermaid* he carried out an accurate survey of the eastern coast of what is now Queensland . He is credited with naming Mt. Cook on the Endeavour in honour of the Great Navigator and also naming the Bloomfield River. His botanist was a man who later made a name for himself as a land explorer — Alan Cunningham. As a favour to Cunningham, King named Bellenden Kerr Range near Babinda for a longtime botanist friend of Cunningham's.[19]

Wickham in the *Beagle* made a further survey in 1839 accompanied by John Lort Stokes. Wickham unsuccessfully attempted to find survivors of the *Charles Eaton*. Captain Carr of the *Mangles* reported sighting a white youth — Ireland — and a small boy, William D'Oyley, on Murray Island but his negotiations with the Islanders to hand them over failed. Stokes later continued coastal surveys in the *Beagle* sailing down the western shores of Cape York Peninsula. In from the south-east corner of the Gulf of Carpentaria he named the Plains of Promise and forecast a glowing future for the land there. Blackwood in the *Fly* and Yule in the *Bramble* made more surveys. In 1844 Blackwood erected a 70 feet (23 metre) high beacon on Raine Islet near Cape Grenville to mark a safe passage through the Reef there. Other non-official mariners travelled the coast, some with success, some with tragic results, before Stanley sailed by in the *Rattlesnake* to find Barbara Thompson.

Wild White Woman of the Normanby

A 'wild white woman' story that didn't have a happy ending was the story of the woman buried in the Cooktown Cemetery, the Wild White Woman of the Normanby. She had been seen on several occasions by miners and travellers near Earlton, a tiny goldmining settlement on the headwaters of the West Normanby River, inland from Cooktown and part of the legendary Palmer River Goldfield. Finally, when she was seen close to the Earlton settlement, she was 'rescued'. She was thought to have been about sixty years of age and could speak only three words of English — Black Mary and potato.[20] Her rescue entailed her being put on a quiet police horse and led by a mounted constable with an armed police officer as escort. Some distance from Earlton the party was intercepted by a group of Aborigines — not the ones with whom she had been living — who made threatening gestures and threw at least one spear. The police officer fired a shot to deter them but the shot frightened the woman's mount. It reared and plunged, knocking over the constable's mount. Unused to horses and possibly with her hands tied, the woman couldn't control the animal, fell off over its rump and was dragged a short distance.

Although they made every effort to sustain her, with Chinese recruited from the neighbouring cattle station, The Springs (Springvale), carrying her to Cooktown on an improvised litter, she died soon after her arrival there. The very experienced and practical Dr. Korteum of Palmer River fame, gave the opinion that she died as a result of the head injuries received in the fall. The tragic part was that he considered that she was not a 'wild' white woman but rather an albino Aborigine.

At about the same time a 'wild white man' led natives in forays around the Bloomfield region and it was believed that he and the woman were brother and sister, white children survivors of a shipwreck who were adopted by the tribes. It sounded logical but for Dr. Korteum's finding and the fact that there are, today, in the Bloomfield and Daintree area, indigenous people possessing albino characteristics. Christie Palmerston, the legendary Pathfinder, was said to have shot a 'native leader, a man with long fair hair and fair skin' in the Daintree area.[21]

2

The Land Explorers

Kennedy's tragic journey 1848 · Frank and Alec Jardine with cattle to Somerset, 1864 · Transfer of the Residency from Somerset to Thursday Island, 1879 · William Hann, Frederick Warner, 1872, and Mulligan — the Palmer Gold Rush · Firth takes sheep to Mt. Surprise and disposes of them at the Palmer, other cattlemen follow · Pastoralists and Aborigines 1880s · Cooktown booms as port for the goldfield · Economic Depression, drought and tick fever hits cattlemen — 1890s · From cattle tick to footrot. Trials for drovers · Women pioneers — Rebecca Armbrust.

The explorers came onto the scene after the early navigators. The ill-fated twenty-nine year old, Edmund Kennedy, had sheep for rations and cumbersome, heavy-wheeled wagons for transport when he landed at Tam o' Shanter Point near Cardwell in May, 1848, some years after the wreck of the *Charles Eaton* and not long before Barbara Thompson's rescue. It was a journey doomed from the start as the officials who planned it had no practical experience of the area. Kennedy, as a member of Sir Thomas Mitchell's party had made two expeditions towards the Gulf. They didn't reach any further than the Belyando River but the young Kennedy was hopeful of striking on to the Gulf[1] and then, from there, making his way in a more easterly direction to Cape York.

The men who planned the expedition depended upon the logs of earlier navigators, Phillip Parker King and Lort Stokes who traversed the east coast on survey exercises between 1820 and 1841. These had described the ranges north of Rockingham Bay as 'wooded hills and green vallies'.[2] After trying to find a way through the rain forest with his clumsy wagons and obstinate sheep, Kennedy himself wrote that 'a viler looking country never looked me in the face before.' The ranges contain the highest mountain in Queensland and the covering of almost impenetrable vine jungle made his task virtually impossible. He was severely handicapped before he had a chance to begin.

Because of the need to take their food with them, the land explorers found themselves cast also in the role of drovers with horses, cattle and sheep accompanying the exploratory party. As the expeditions took place relatively soon after the establishment of the settlement at Botany Bay, it was a seller's market. This probably accounts for the explorers taking with them mares either with foals or due to foal, and cows heavy in calf. The resulting babies added to their problems though a few later contributed to the party's meagre menu during the second leg of their journey.

Kennedy, or 'Poor Kennedy' as his old mentor Sir Thomas Mitchell referred to his late assistant when Kennedy's waterlogged and useless field sketches were given to him after Kennedy's tragic death, was expected to do more than to reach Cape York on this expedition. It was the era of exploration for pastoral and other expansion and there was an urgent desire to link the tip of the Cape by an appropriate route to the lower Gulf. In those days Governments fervently believed in the future and the worth of the furthest north.

Kennedy wrote to another of his mentors, the Reverend W. B. Clarke, the 'Father of Australian Geology', a precis of his instructions.

> 'To proceed with party and equipment in the Tam o' Shanter to Rockingham Bay, 180 degrees south (if ready on[3] the 26th Inst. under the convoy of the *Rattlesnake*) to travel thence by Land to Princess Charlotte Bay and Cape York keeping the most convenient distance from the coast. After communicating with the *Rattlesnake* or *Bramble* at Pt. Albany near Cape York and receiving a supply of provisions to be provided by the Government in four months time — To move down the East Shore of the Gulf of Carpentaria to the Water Plaets, ascertain whether that be an Estuary of the Mitchell or the Leichardt (sic) and, if so, follow it up to the junction of the "Lynd". From the junction of the Lynd with the Mitchell River strike off in a W.S.W. direction to the "Flinders", determine whereabouts the river has its source and connect my way with Sir T.L. Mitchell's discoveries in 1846 on the Belyando or other convenient point and thence by the most convenient route to Sydney.'

From Tam O'Shanter Point to the Belyando was estimated to be a distance of over 3000 k and the trip from there to Sydney a mere weekend hike at 1600k.

The task set was of titanic proportions and undertaken without any of today's prior feasibility studies before the commencement of expedition. It was doomed before it started. The number of sheep taken is confusing but there were probably 250, with approximately half off-loaded at Rockingham Bay and the rest to be landed from the store-ship at Albany Passage. Trying to make progress through the dense rainforest with the sheep and the ponderous wagons must have been a heartbreaking task. Although Kennedy twice left the weakened members of his party at Camp KLXXX, near Weymouth Bay and further north at the Shelburne Bay Camp KLXXXIV, that didn't help. They daily expected relief from the arrival of the *Ariel* and the *Rattlesnake* but these ships failed to appear. Kennedy was speared at Escape Creek and Jackey alone made it to Cape York. On 23rd December he met the *Ariel* and was taken on board. Of the parties left to await the supply ships only Carron and Goddard survived. It was written that Carron was so emaciated that his bones were all but poking through his skin.[4]

Like most of the ill-fated party, none of Kennedy's sheep survived, nor did the explorers' horses.

The Jardine Brothers

The next overlander/explorers to enter the Peninsula were the Jardine brothers. They also came from the south and headed for the northernmost tip but Frank and Alec were *bona fide* drovers. They were bushmen and possessed practical skills. All these and more were needed on their long, arduous trek.

The brothers were the sons of John Jardine, Police Magistrate of Rockhampton. Burketown on the Gulf, Mackay, Bowen, Townsville and Cardwell on the eastern coast were already settled when Somerset, at the very top of Cape York Peninsula, was opened in the optimistic hope that it would become an international port. The Singapore of the South. The British Government sent out a detachment of marines to make the settlement official and Queensland looked set to be developed systematically from the North down.

The Jardine Brothers

The man selected to take charge of this new outpost was John Jardine.[5] He proposed establishing there a cattle herd to provide fresh beef for the passengers and crews of the vessels expected to use the port, as well as for local consumption. He arranged for his two sons, Frank, 22 years of age and Alec, two years his junior, to overland the nucleus herd. As no explorer except the ill-fated Kennedy had traversed the northern end of the Peninsula, the Government welcomed the idea as what would now be termed a 'fact-finding mission' and wished to contribute.

The Dutch navigators of the 17th century named some of the rivers flowing into the Gulf but very little was known of them as they flowed further inland. Leichhardt traversed the western fall in 1845, turning back south of the mighty Mitchell River after Gilbert was speared. From the Walsh River, a tributary of the Mitchell, Kennedy kept more to the eastern side.

John Jardine had every confidence in his sons with their practical bush background. The Government supplied 'a qualified surveyor, fully equipped,' A.J.Richardson 'to act as Geographer',[6] three other men, Scrutton, Binnie and Cowderoy and four natives with 'horses, arms and equipment'. With hindsight it would have been better if the young Jardines had marked out a suitable route to Somerset and then returned for the stock. It was an almost impossible task to drive cattle over such an unknown interminable route. Another case for the much-maligned feasibility study.

Alec Jardine left Rockhampton in May 1864 with most of the party and the thirty-one horses that they'd purchased. Frank and Surveyor Richardson went by boat to Bowen (Port Denison) in July and set about purchasing suitable cattle and eleven extra horses. Undoubtedly they had little choice in the matter as herds were small but baby calves and foals added to the general difficulties and, in Jardine's case, cows began to calve at Camp 13, not two weeks out from Carpentaria Downs. At the time, an outbreak of bovine pleuro-pneumonia was rife, making the choice of stock for the road even more limited.

In the 1860s Carpentaria Downs, owned by J.G. MacDonald, was the most northerly settled property. On their way to Carpentaria the party was joined by a Charters Towers district cattleman, Harry Bode, who was looking for suitable pastoral country for his own herd and who was of great practical assistance to the brothers.

Alec and the horse plant arrived before Frank and the cattle and he spent the interval exploring the country ahead to find the best route for the stock. Usually he travelled alone but for his native stockman, Eulah, but on this occasion Bode and his native stockmen accompanied him. With two packhorses to carry provisions they were able to make a comprehensive survey.

Despite this precaution, they made a serious mistake which compounded the problems they later experienced. The river on which Carpentaria Downs was situated was thought to be Leichhardt's Lynd. It wasn't. It was a tributary of the Gilbert, the Einasleigh. Leichhardt's Lynd, a tributary of the Mitchell, was much further north. The party followed the pseudo-Lynd for nearly 300k before they were convinced that it wasn't what it purported to be. The Government surveyor was sure Leichhardt's naming was correct but the brothers were doubtful even after just a few days out from their base camp. The country didn't match up with Leichhardt's description of the terrain around his Lynd.

Alec returned to Carpentaria on 11th October and the combined party left with their 42 horses and 250 head of cattle with Cowderoy in charge of the cattle. The brothers scouted out ahead to try to find the best route.

The trip, planned to avoid the flood rains of the Wet Season, was disastrously delayed by the error of the rivers. Their journey was no tourist trip. They met with inhospitable country and with shortages of forage and water early in their trip. Their camp was burnt out because of 'the carelessness of some of the party'. Half of the food and equipment was lost in the fire but Scrutton heroically 'snatched' the gunpowder cannisters from the flames even as the solder was melting from the extreme heat. A bit over a third of their flour, almost all of the tea, 50kgs of rice, jam, dried apples and currants, a box of cartridges and caps, two tents, a pack saddle and twenty-two packbags plus numerous items of saddlery were lost. In addition, most of the men's clothing and four blankets went up in the blaze. Poison plants and even snake bite, took a toll of their horses. The fashionably-bred grey stallion, Maroon, selected to breed horses for Somerset, died from plant poisoning. When the Wet began, flooded rivers inundated the coastal plains making movement almost impossible. All the while, the party was followed by Aborigines, possibly of the same tribe that killed Gilbert and who did not welcome the intrusion of the overlanders. Eternal vigilance was kept and although there were narrow escapes from their encounters, the drovers got through.

On March 13th they were met by John Jardine about 12k from Somerset, not far from where the unfortunate Kennedy met his end. The men, about a dozen horses and approximately a fifth of their precious cattle, had arrived. In five months they had travelled about two and a half thousand kilometres, the last 400 of which were done on foot — and mostly barefoot, as the fire destroyed the spare boots they had brought with them. Their hats also disintegrated and makeshift ones were contrived from emu skin and other raw materials to hand. They also tried moccasins fashioned from different types of skin and even of bark, as the cuts in their bare feet were prone to infection and swelling. For the last month they lived, except for a small supply of dried strips of veal, 'off the land'.

Once a permanent camp was established at Vallack Point, named for Dr. Vallack of the *Ariel*, 'the weary horses and cattle at length found rest, while their drivers were able to indulge in the unwonted luxuries of regular feeding and uninterrupted sleep'.[7]

As a financial venture, the project was a costly loss. The Government offered to reimburse Jardine to recoup his expenses in recognition of the part the overland trip played in exploration but Jardine magnanimously declined their offer. After all, in his view, it had been a private enterprise.

Had the brothers and their men perished like Burke and Wills, Kennedy or Leichhardt they would have been heroes — admittedly, only Second Class, not Sporting Heroes. As it was, they merely accomplished the almost-impossible without loss of human life.

Some of the cattle which had to be abandoned, recovered and became the ancestors of Peninsula Cleanskins, the subject of many station disputes and a few courtcases in later years.

Residency Transferred from Somerset to Thursday Island

Sadly, Somerset didn't live up to expectations. Few ships made it their port of call. The narrow channels between the Torres Strait islands were too dangerous. By 1866, the garrison was recalled. The Residency was moved to nearby Thursday Island, then known as Port Kennedy, in 1879 and Somerset carried on simply as the Jardines' home and as the base of their cattle enterprise. The Hon. John Douglas, Resident at Thursday Island in 1885 had also been Premier of Queensland in 1877 when the North's future looked rosier. 'I have often thought'[8] Douglas wrote, 'that a good deal was lost to us when we left Somerset and the mainland. We abandoned with it the chance of occupying some twenty or thirty thousand acres of fine rich scrub soil.... And we abandoned also the chance of a railway which might have pushed through the Peninsula and made our starting-point for the East, for India, China and even the Old Country.' Not only were they keen on transcontinental railways in those days, they also believed in trade with Asia.

Fred Warner, seated right, discoverer of gold on Palmer with Hann (leaning), Tate (standing left) and Taylor.

William Hann

William Hann's expedition of 1872 began the next phase. Hann, a pastoralist from near Charters Towers, was asked by the Colonial Government to conduct an expedition into Cape York Peninsula. He was to investigate both the mining and the pastoral potential of the area as far north as the present Port Stewart. Hann reported 'fair second-class pastoral country' but he was also personally interested in minerals. As an incentive, he offered half a pound, about 225 gms, of tobacco to whoever of his party discovered gold. The reward was claimed by his surveyor, Fred Warner, at a spot called Warner's Gully on the Palmer River which was itself a tributary of the Mitchell. Hann was far from confident that the field would be payable and considering the extreme isolation and the rough terrain, he tried not to broadcast the discovery.

Mulligan Finds Payable Gold on Palmer

Prospectors, however, have always an eye to the ground looking for traces of mineral and an ear to the ground, strained for reports of other men's finds. It did not take long for experienced miner James Venture Mulligan and his mates to leave Georgetown on the Etheridge Field to check out this new prospect. If a surveyor could find gold, surely veteran gold-seekers could improve on the yield. Also mindful of the inconsistencies of gold-mining and the great difficulties involved, once Mulligan discovered gold in payable quantities, he tried not to promote a rush. In that, he was not at all successful but the results gained by him and his party were extremely so. Miners flocked to the field.

James Venture Mulligan discovered gold in the Hodgkinson

Being so far away from the closest settlement, the supply of food was an immense and immediate problem. The closest station was Ezra Firth's Mt. Surprise, many kilometres to the south. Firth and his partner James Atkinson came north from Geelong, picking up sheep in the Ipswich district en route. Their massive droving trip of over 3000 kilometres took them two years to accomplish. They arrived at their destination in 1864, just in time for the depression of 1866 which was fortuitously relieved the following year by the discovery of gold at Gympie.

Graziers Take Sheep and Cattle to Goldfield

Firth had a flock of sheep at Mt. Surprise which, in the tropical conditions, weren't doing as well as he'd hoped. Dingoes which ravaged the sheep, and grass seed which drastically downgraded the value of the fleece and caused often fatal infections, added to his problems. When he received news of the gold strike he quickly drafted off a mob of sheep and hurried with them to the Palmer. The miners dined well on the mutton and Ezra returned with enough gold to enable him to buy cattle and eventually to restock Mt. Surprise as a cattle station.

Other intrepid cattlemen hastily took mobs of cattle to the goldfield for immediate consumption and many selected runs near there on which to breed a continuous supply of beef for the miners. A.C. Grant, formerly Captain Grant, Commander of the Queensland Rifles, the Colony's own army, left Havilah near Bowen with 300 head of cattle with which to establish a pastoral run and to try to corner the butchery market on the Palmer. Almost on arrival he sold his 300 head at the previously unheard of price of $24 head. Returning to Havilah, he formed a partnership with the property's owners, Skene and Henderson, who agreed to supply him with cattle for his new run near the Palmer, Wrotham Park. Held there for a period until they freshened-up and fattened, they could then be converted into beef for sale on the goldfield. Beef was bringing as much as 25c/kg. William Hann recommended the Wrotham Park country to Grant after his return from the Stewart River.

Cattle Stations Established

The word soon spread. The Earl brothers, also from the Bowen district, had experience in supplying miners on the Ravenswood and Charters Towers goldfields. James Earl put together a mob from the family property of Yacamunda and overlanded them to the Palmer. The cattle were readily sold and Earl returned with more to replace them. On his second trip he decided to take up the run at the head of the Laura River which he called Butcher's Hill. From a herd there, he could regularly supply cattle to the Palmer market.

William Hann, D'Arcy Uhr and Charlie Scrutton, the man who bravely rescued the gunpowder from the Jardine campblaze, all became drovers, bringing cattle from Ravenswood, Mt. McConnel, Havilah and Salisbury Plains to the goldrush. Cattle were also droved from Maryvale and properties along the Clarke River to the north of Charters Towers. A mob of 200 fat cattle were sent from as far distant as Lawn Hill on the Northern Territory border.[9] W.H. Corfield, then a cattleman/carrier but later a Queensland Parliamentarian, bought thirteen steers newly arrived on the Palmer for a princely $32 per head. He wanted them for use in his bullock wagon and the long trip to the field had educated them so well that he was able to yoke the bullocks straight onto his wagon behind his old, experienced leaders. He would complete their education on the way into Cooktown to bring out another load of supplies.

As diggers spread out to prospect further north of the Palmer, cattlemen followed suit and took up grazing runs. In 1881 Donald Mackenzie took up Lakefield, now a National Park, where, although he did not take a hardline attitude with the natives, he was killed by a native he'd considered friendly.

The beginnings of Cooktown — early in 1874

Henry Jones was also killed by an Aborigine after selecting and establishing Koolburra in 1884. Further north, out from the gold finds of the Coen region Ebenezer Knott took up Langi in 1883. The previous year, the Massey brothers selected Lalla Rookh on the Stewart River and later took a nucleus breeding herd to Rokeby. One brother, Charles, lost his life at Pine Tree, a property then recently acquired by Pat Fox. There had been a gathering of Aborigines who staged a corroboree. Jack Boyd intended staying there too with his wife Louisa but Louisa, recently arrived from England, was disturbed by the wild goings-on of the corroboree. They rode on to the Mein Telegraph Station. In the middle of the night the Aborigines attacked. Eddie Watson died of a wound to the throat. Jim Evans suffered tomahawk gashes to his head and neck, a Chinaman was grazed by spears but one man, Nicholls, escaped and frightened the attackers off with his revolver.

The young Aboriginal horse-tailer cleared out as fast as he could to where he could hear the bells on the Boyds' horses. Jack and Louisa immediately returned to offer what help they could. Louisa dressed Evan's deep wounds as best she could with what little was available — soap and neats foot oil. The Watson brothers settled with their herd at Merluna in 1888. It had been first settled by Cox and Sefton as Pioneer Downs, four years earlier. Most of the cattlemen, hoping to make their stay permanent, made an effort to co-exist with the Aborigines but in Edwin Watson's case it wasn't enough. He was speared.

Pearling Prospers but Gold Declines

After the Residency was established at Thursday Island, the port didn't assume the importance of Singapore but it did become a thriving pearling centre. Beef was needed to supplement the seafood diet and cattle properties in the far north found a ready market there for their cattle. Cooktown prospered both as a port for the Palmer goldfield and as a point of entry for the thousands of Chinese miners who landed there legally. Those who chose to arrive illegally landed in sheltered coves away to the north of the port. Cooktown was also a base for trochus, beche de mer and pearl seekers. It was officially proclaimed as a port for exporting pearlshell in July, 1892, thanks to representations from the local Member, 'Dr.' Jack Hamilton.[10] With the rapidly increased population, all looked well for the cattlemen until the gold became less easy to find and miners left in droves for the new Hodgkinson Field behind the then non-existent Cairns. Others drifted further north to the Coen prospects.

The cattlemen's market collapsed. Thursday Island still utilised the meat from small drafts of cattle killed on the mainland at Red Island Point (known locally as R.I.P.) but the population on the Palmer townships of Maytown, Palmerville, Uhrstown and Byerstown all but disappeared completely. Most of Cooktown's population followed suit.

Drought, Depression and the Dreaded Cattle Tick

Even worse was to come. There was a general economic depression in the Colony, an extremely severe drought and, to cap it all, the appearance of a tiny creature that decimated both the herds and the luckless bullock teams. The cattle tick had arrived and brought with it the usually fatal Red Water Fever. It took some time for the cattlemen to associate their devastating losses with the tiny, almost insignificant parasitic tick brought in with travelling cattle from the Northern Territory. It had recently been introduced there unknowingly on bovine imports.

In 1888, two brothers overlanding 270 head of cattle west from Townsville to stock a northern Gulf run, lost over half the herd before reaching their destination. By 1894, a property near Croydon had lost 3000 of its herd of 9000. At first the Government applied a quarantine,[11] North of 20 degrees South and West of 144 degrees East, but this lapsed as the ticks crawled undaunted through the boundaries set on Governmental paper. The more fortunate runs lost only a third of their total herd. Some small holders, bullock teams and dairies were completely wiped out and the once-profitable trade in cattle to the southern states was closed down.

Australian bushmen are resilient and those in the Far North are even more so. They tightened their collective belts and set their minds upon riding out their difficulties. In time, the reduced herds gained immunity to the cattle tick's fever-carrying tendency and the herds re-built. However, there was still one major problem — the lack of markets.

In an attempt to combat this, some cattlemen established holding paddocks closer to civilisation and the markets it supported, or diversified into butchery businesses in the townships springing up to the south. The Masseys of Rokeby took the former alternative and set up a fattening depot at Southedge near Mareeba. They also bought a half-share in a butcher shop on Thursday Island, overlanding cattle to the Tip and holding them on Prince of Wales Island to ensure a steady supply for the shop. Ned Earl, a son of James Earl of Butcher's Hill, established butcher shops in the expanding Cairns hinterland. The Lawrences, then owners of Wrotham Park did the same.

Small mobs of cattle made their way regularly from the far-out runs to service the butcher-shop demand. Usually these mobs were small, about 80 head, sometimes a little less, at times a little more. They could be handled by a minimum of drovers, usually one white drover and one or two Aboriginal assistants. Despite the smallness of the mob, the problems were much the same as with the big herds. Sufficient grass and water had to be found to sustain the stock and to keep them in reasonable condition. The route was still long and difficult and the problems experienced then were those that beset later drovers, flooded rivers, lameness from the stony terrain and what every drover fears, a 'rush' — a 'stampede' in the terms of the American Wild West.

Horses strayed off-camp despite being hobbled and the cattle's hoofs became damaged, especially on the rocky 'road', the Byerstown Range, that climbed from the Laura valley to the western fall of the Palmer River. Once the outer hoof covering was broken, germs entered and a crippling condition known as 'footrot' developed. It was a very painful affliction. The affected beast could not put any weight on the swollen limb and was unable to proceed. There was no cure until antibiotics came upon the scene many decades later.

Tin Mining and Meatworks Operational

As the tin mines around Herberton and its hinterland prospered and the port of Cairns expanded, the demand for beef increased but it wasn't until 1897 that a meatworks producing mostly tallow, hides and fertiliser, was opened at Biboohra out from Mareeba, by the Barron Meat and Export Company. They did not export much meat but the hides and tallow sales were some compensation for walking cattle down from the Peninsula. Unfortunately, the meatworks' life was short, but by then butchers were looking to the northern herds to supply their growing clientele. These cattle were brought down the stock route either by drovers engaged by the stations or by the butcher's own 'plant', his drovers with their horses and gear.

Women, though present in smaller numbers than the corresponding men, were always held in high regard in the Peninsula. As early as its first century of white settlement, the nineteenth, the Peninsula had its women drovers. Some of the Aboriginal women were skilful 'stockpersons' but a white woman, Rebecca Armbrust, accompanied her husband on his droving trips.

Nicholas and Rebecca Armbrust

Nicholas Armbrust[12] was one of the early European settlers in the Peninsula. He was a Danish immigrant who gradually worked his way north to the Palmer. In doing so he quickly became a competent bushman and a very capable horseman. He was one of those enterprising men who overlanded cattle to the Palmer River miners. Cooktown was the port and the metropolis for the goldfield. Cairns barely existed. The best hotel in Townsville was, at that time, 'a bark-roofed hut'.

It was in 1875 that a young Rebecca Harris arrived from Exeter in Britain, disembarking at Brisbane hoping to seek a new life, a life of adventure in the new Colony. She achieved what she sought. Moving north to Cooktown in early 1876 she met Nicholas Armbrust. They were married in Cooktown's Church of England on June 15th that same year. Nicholas took his cattle on to the goldfield while Rebecca remained in Cooktown. She was expecting their first child and attacks on travellers by the dispossessed Aborigines were not uncommon occurrences, as the murder of the Strau family illustrated.

In Cooktown, Rebecca and Nicholas's son Archie was born. Soon after the birth, Nicholas saddled a horse for his wife, and Rebecca and their new-born son accompanied Nicholas on his next trip. Prospectors had moved further north in their search for gold and he was taking cattle up to the Coen district.

Not long after they reached the outpost of Coen, Archie's brother, Coen, was born. He was the first white child born in the tiny settlement. There was another married woman, Mrs. H. Kuzner, living there and she acted as midwife to Rebecca but Coen was only four days old when the family moved on again with the cattle. Archie, now eighteen months old rode behind his mother, clutching her about the waist for support. Baby Coen was cradled in her arms. In those days, babies were often carried in a large sling similar to the ones used for broken arms. It is possible Rebecca used this method. (I carried our firstborn home from Cooktown hospital in a sling but only for one very long day's ride.) The sling provided reasonable comfort for the baby and left the mother's hands free to hold the reins.

The natives around Coen were no more welcoming to strangers than those of the Palmer. The baby wasn't yet a fortnight old when they attacked the Armbrust camp, spearing almost all the horses and carrying off large quantities of the party's precious food supply. To help her with the children, Rebecca had a twelve-year-old indigenous maid. Nicholas's partner, Lachlan Kennedy was also with them.

On their way back to Cooktown they made a detour of nearly a hundred kilometres in an attempt to reach a cattle station — either Lakefield or Koolburra — in the hopes of replenishing their stores. They found the station deserted and 'their sole gain was a tin of jam'. Retracing their steps to where they'd branched off, they made camp, leaving Rebecca there with her maid and the small children, while the men took the horses to water about two kilometres downstream. The men were scarcely out of sight when two mobs of armed natives 'converged on the camp'. They seized the young native girl and a tall warrior advanced on Rebecca with an up-raised waddy. She had the baby in her arms — and no gun. She was 'frigid with fear'. At that moment a dramatic entrance by Lach Kennedy, shouting and firing shots from his galloping horse put the intruders hurriedly in retreat. They dropped their spears as they ran but the young 'maid' was never seen again.

Nicholas decided they'd best move on as soon as possible and headed for Laura Station on the banks of the Laura River. Normally the trip would have taken at least three days but, in the emergency, they made it in a day. Rebecca's droving days were over for the time being, although later she did again help her husband and Lach Kennedy on trips from Coen to Cape York to supply cattle for Thursday Island.

1889 saw the Armbrusts as proprietors of the Bristol and Exeter Hotel in Laura. The longed-for railway had by then connected that township to Cooktown. Later they re-located to Cooktown being licencees in turn of the Black Eagle, the White Horse and the Captain Cook hotels. Lach Kennedy, when the partnership ended, moved on to York Downs and Pioneer Downs. The Watson brothers later purchased it. While in Laura, the Armbrust family expanded (9 sons and 4 daughters) and eventually, around the turn of the century when Coen had become quite an important gold mining centre, they returned there and played an important part in the business and social life of that township.

Courtesy Burns Philp

Charlotte St Cooktown with Burns Philp Store

3

Enter the Peninsula Drover

A day — and a night — in the life of a drover · Women drovers · Pig droving at its best · The China Camp road to Daintree · Possible sighting of thylacines · Alternate route to Daintree through Mossman streets · Road transport opens up a bright future · The Wewak pioneers transport of cattle by sea

Because of the nature of their work, drovers were on call twenty-four hours a day. An unexpected noise or movement could start a 'rush', something to be dreaded and avoided at all costs. Cattle were more likely to 'jump up' on some camps than on the usual run of night-camps. Various theories were bandied about. Hollow ground making hoof-beats echo. Hollow trees inhabited by animals or birds which scuttled about in the hours of darkness. On one occasion spanning a few days, three separate mobs travelling to Mareeba and being yarded in the Font Hill dip-yards awaiting dipping the next morning, 'took the yards'. They rushed, forced open the gates of the receiving yard and galloped, panic-stricken, down and through the barbed wire 'wing', the fence that helped funnel a mob into the yards.

The culprit was thought, probably correctly, to have been an earlier drover who saw fit to kill and butcher a beast for rations under a shady tree near the gate. Though it was thought to have happened a week or more previously, the cattle sensed or smelt the blood and took fright. I was among those trying to catch up on sleep the night when one lot ran amok and it was a frightening thing to hear three thousand or more hoofs pounding towards the camp. On the long Peninsula stockroutes, there were few yards in which cattle could be held overnight and drovers allowed the opportunity of a quiet night's rest in their swags. Yards were a luxury to dream about.

Cattle were usually double-watched at night early in the trip or in expected trouble spots. Two drovers took the watch at the same time, quietly riding around the resting cattle and singing. Their song helped dull the impact of a sudden noise, lulling cattle into a sense of security. The Hopevale Mission drovers were, almost without exception, excellent singers and harmonised beautifully. It was easy, with this backdrop, for the rest of the team to drift off to sleep too. The Boss Drover usually took the midnight watch as that was the time the cattle stirred, stood up to relieve themselves, and awakened, were more likely to re-act to sudden movement or sound. Once the cattle became used to the night-time routine, the watch was changed to a single watch, one man at a time and with the time spent by each drover reduced accordingly. When I gave my husband a hand with the cattle, I took the first watch, the easiest. It began when the cattle were put 'on camp' and the droving team, finished with the day's chores, were having tea. When that was done, the first watch was relieved.

The Working Day of the Drover

The drover's day began at first light, 'picanninny daylight', before the sun rose completely above the horizon. The horse-tailer's day began even earlier. It was his job to supervise the horses and to have them mustered and in the camp ready for a daylight start. With an average mob of eight hundred head, six men were a minimum. Eight were preferable. Two, the cook and the horse-tailer, only helped with the cattle in an emergency. Their responsibilities were the meals and water, the camp and the horses. Usually each man was allotted two horses with maybe a couple of spares, the night-horses and packhorses. The night-horses were superior animals that could be relied upon to turn and hold a runaway mob in the hours of darkness should the cattle take fright and rush. Each evening the night-horses were tethered to a night-line stretched between two convenient trees so that they could be quickly caught and saddled if the need arose. The other saddle-horses, with the pack-horses, were hobbled out to graze. Pack-horses, at about one per man, carried the tucker, shoeing and saddlery gear for emergencies, and, as 'top-loads' across the two packbags slung from the pack-saddles, the folded tent — a berkmyre fly, really — and the rolled swags. The billycans, in a nest of diminishing sizes, in their own leather or greenhide case, were also part of the top-load. Billycans were carried only on the most reliable pack-horse. They had a nasty habit of being shaken free and lost. Water could be carried to a dry camp in 'canteens', metal containers shaped to fit comparatively comfortably against the packhorse's ribs when slung from the hooks of the pack-saddle. Dry camps weren't all that rare. As long as the cattle (and horses) had a good long drink each day, the men could make do with carried water that night.

Once the horses were brought in and the men breakfasted, they hastily saddled and mounted their horses. The cattle would be beginning to get to their feet and the Boss Drover had to count them as they strung off camp. He

Courtesy Ray Evans

Packing Up

took the count as they led off camp in a line kept moving steadily in the right direction. The count had to be accurate as it must tally with that of the previous day — or else! Missing cattle must be sought out and, if at all possible, returned to the mob. Legally an owner could demand an account of every beast given over at the delivery.

On the average, cattle were travelled eight miles or about thirteen kilometres a day. That was the optimum. At times, the mob could barely travel a quarter of that distance. Camps were spaced at the eight mile/thirteen kilometre rate. Here could usually be found a ridge pole between two trees and accompanying 'side' rails for erecting the 'tucker' tent, a sapling rail saddle-rack between two more obliging trees on which pack- and riding-saddles were placed at night and sometimes there was a wire stretched between two more trees for the night-horses. If the horse-tailer were lucky, there'd be enough wood left around for the fire. As 'wood and water joey,' he was responsible for supplying wood for the fire and water for the camp. He also took the pack- and saddle-horses to water before hobbling them out for the night with a bell on one or two of the leaders. Cattle came to know the bells and when they heard them, they brightened up. Night camp was close. Time to rest. No more walking.

Unless it were raining, drovers rolled their swags out around the fire or on some other relatively comfortable patch of ground. A billy of coffee simmered all night to refresh the nightwatch and to keep them awake and alert. The saddles on the rack were always covered with packcovers, two-metre lengths of berkmyre canvas to keep any rain, dew or any other stray moisture from the leather. If the Wet set in, and the weather was rainified, a second tent was often put up so the men would have a dry-ish camp, too.

After an early breakfast of tea, stew, rice and damper, the drovers cut 'dinners' or 'cribs', slabs of damper with jam and a hunk of cooked salt beef. Tinned butter was sometimes available but it usually turned quickly to oil and was omitted from the menu. Syrup and jam were carried in tightly-lidded tins enclosed in leather-strapped cases for safety. A busted tin of syrup in a packbag is not calculated to make a cook happy. Cribs were wrapped only in a double sheet of newspaper, usually the old 'bushman's bible', the *North Queensland Register*. The comic and puzzle pages were eagerly sought after. Each drover carried his own saddlebag and a quartpot for boiling-up tea, slung from his saddle-dees.

At the start of the trip there were usually carefully-wrapped fruit cakes, biscuits in a tin and maybe plum puddings cooked and stored in syrup tins. Unfortunately, these didn't last. Some drovers' cooks created desserts of rice, custard made with powdered milk and stewed dried apples, while the really expert ones sometimes came across with a currant brownie cooked in the camp oven, but these were rare treats. Dampers made in the camp oven were the rule. A camp oven hole was usually to be found beside the site of the fire, which would have, with a bit of luck, its wire hooks hanging from a horizontal rod for the billycans. Coals from the fire were placed under, over and around the camp oven to provide heat for cooking.

At times of extreme wetness, when 'the sugar turned to water and the flour turned to glue' as one bush poet described it, the camp oven was sometimes placed above ground level inside a hole dug into the side a convenient antbed. There were usually plenty of these to be found. For a change, or if the damper hole was too full of water to make a damper, Johnnie Cakes were cooked on a bed of coals. These were something like miniature dampers the size of a puftaloon or fried scone. Some bush cooks could turn them out beautifully, a tantalising golden brown all over with nary a piece of black charcoal embedded in them. If a damper had to be cooked in very wet conditions the 'oven' dug in the side of the ever-present antbed made a more than acceptable 'damper hole'.

Stew alternated with curry and at times, if a good creek was passed and the horse-tailer had time to spare, small fish (perch) or yabbies (freshwater crays) featured on the menu. At times, when a largish mob crossed a stream, they churned up the water in the process and fish floated, temporarily stupefied, to the top. Again, if the cook and his offsider were quick, there was fish for tea.

In the Peninsula the drovers' road followed the Telegraph Line, a clearing from memory two chains or forty metres wide that ran in an almost straight line to the very top of the Peninsula. In places, you could almost see a whole day's droving ahead of you. Main Roads, when they came along, were also designated as stock routes. When the Telegraph Line cut out at Laura, the stock route followed the Laura River almost to its source, climbed the dreaded Byerstown Range by way of the old wagon road and followed Mulligan's and the teamsters' tracks to Mareeba.

Advent of Motor Road and Watering Facilities

After the road was pushed through from Mareeba to Cooktown, then to Laura and further north in the 1950s, a few Government dams and bores were put down in strategic places along the very dry stretches to aid the travelling stock. A Government dip was also installed in Laura and all cattle passing through were dipped there (for a fee) under the supervision of the local Police Sergeant. With the dipping completed to the Sergeant's satisfaction, the drover was given another stock permit to travel which took him as far as Font Hill, the MacDowall's family property near Mt. Molloy. Here, the Mt.Molloy policeman presided over a second dipping treatment and wrote out a further permit to allow the cattle to move on to the Mareeba saleyards.

Courtesy Meridith Monro

Government Dip Yard, Laura — July 1965

When entering a station property, 'notice' was required to be given to the leaseholder by the drover. Usually, the horse-tailer was the one assigned to the job, a popular one that usually brought with it tea, cake and homemade biscuits. The forward notice allowed the station owner to ride out to inspect the travelling mob and to assure himself that the drover wasn't making up for any losses by annexing station cattle along the way. Sometimes there were problems when cattle dropped off by the drover were appropriated by the station owner. A lame bullock, once spelled and allowed to fatten would made a good killer — and save killing one of the station beasts. Cows left behind could provide a calf to pay for its board before it was generously handed back the following season — or the next. At times, drovers tended to even the score, killing a beast for rations without depleting their own numbers. Mostly station folk were sympathetic to the drovers' plight. '*Let them spread, their thousand head, For we've been droving, too.*'[1] The kind-hearted station missus invariably sent back with the notice-bearer welcome gifts, a boiled fruitcake, a tin of biscuits, a cooked roast as a change from the eternal saltbeef and even eggs carefully wrapped in paper and protected in a lidded powdered milk tin, if the chooks were laying. Needless to say, the gift was always met with whole-hearted appreciation.

There were other much more humble gifts that were also well-appreciated. Old half-worn-out horseshoes. These were hung up in tree forks at drovers' camps or suspended as visibly as possible along the stock route. Cut in halves, they were used to 'cue' or shoe cattle afflicted with badly abraded hoofs. Cattle, so lame that they preferred not to travel with their mates in the mob, often lay down to get some ease. This is when the alert Boss Drover would act. Greenhide ropes soon secured the animal and the discarded shoes, cut in half to fit the outsides of the patient's cloven hoof, were quickly tapped on using the finest of horseshoe nails. Cattle have a very narrow 'wall' to their hoof, much less substance to hammer nails into than a horse's hoof offers. Once the old 'piker' — a recalcitrant bullock — received his shoes and was freed, he would struggle to his feet. The relief was immediate and plain to see. The tiniest fragment of stone could no longer hurt his shod hoofs. Rejuvenated, it took him little time to rejoin the mob.

The Byerstown Range was notorious for causing lameness. Until the mob reached that rocky range, the stock route traversed sandy country, almost devoid of stone. The sand gradually abraded the hoofs, especially if they'd become softened by the effect of mud, water or rain. The sharp stones on the Range cut easily into the softened hoof and the microbes that caused footrot were then free to do their worst on any wound, however slight.

If cueing wasn't possible and cattle couldn't keep up, they were left behind on grass and water in the hope that some other drover would pick them up and bring them on if they had recovered sufficiently. It worked out fairly evenly for the drovers. Cattlemen, though generous in many ways, were never agreeable for mobs affected with footrot to use their yards or small holding paddocks over night. Without fail, the bacteria would be passed on to some of the next draft of station cattle that used the same facility and there is no need to go looking for trouble.

The wagon road up the Byerstown Range was steep, winding and narrow. Bullock- and horse-teams didn't lay claim to the higher standards that motor vehicles require, although the old bullock route served as a motor route for many years until an upgraded version was in use. In 2001, a new Byerstown Range road was opened. One wonders what the old teamsters would think of its wide, tarred surface, its bridges and its gentle grades. To move a large mob of cattle up the Range, they were taken up in 'cuts'. This meant that though they went up in the same large mob, the task was done in sections of about a hundred head of cattle, with one man ahead and another behind. In this way, if a beast did venture, or was shouldered, over the side, it was comparatively easy to get around to it and poke it back up onto the road. With the whole mob strung out, the escapee could be almost at the bottom again before a drover could get to it.

Crossing flooded streams caused some headaches both to drovers and to the droved. 'Ringing' was something to be avoided at all costs. This happened when the lead cattle, which seemed to be proceeding without trouble from bank to bank suddenly veered about and began circling. The rest of the mob soon followed and there was a circular mass of seething cattle making no forward progress at all. Somehow, the ringing movement had to be broken and the leaders encouraged to strike out for the far bank. On most occasions it could be avoided by two drovers riding close on either side of the lead to keep them on the straight and narrow but, as in the best regulated of families, accidents did happen.

River crossings, when the water was above packbag height, were also a problem to the cook and horse-tailer. The horses were unpacked and a makeshift 'boat' contrived from one of the berkmyre tent covers. Both ends were gathered up as tightly as possible and fastened with straps and pack-saddles laid carefully in the body of the canoe-like 'boat'. These gave support and some shape to the canvas sides as the packbags and other gear was stowed as the next layer. Leather surcingles passed under and around the canvas 'boat', held it together and added a little to the stability and waterproofing. The 'boat' was then propelled across the stream by a two-man motor as the cook and horse-tailer swam beside it and directed its movement. At Font Hill, the MacDowalls had a refined version. They kept a large, circular galvanised washtub in readiness when Rifle Creek came up. This could be used as a boat with swimmers holding on to each of the tub's two handles to propel and to navigate it safely across.

Until the advent of motor or sea transport, many mobs of cattle made it down from the Peninsula each year. Some properties, such as Rokeby and Lakefield, sent several smaller mobs through the season, but most used the route for an annual turnoff. At times, several smaller stations combined to put a mob on the road. From ten to twenty thousand came down each year as the dipping records for Laura revealed. Quite often, mobs were camped close enough for neighbouring bells to be heard. Some drovers, like Dick Linklater, specialised in very small mobs such as delivering to the stations bulls railed up to Cairns and then to Mareeba from southern studs.

The 1930s, 1940s and 1950s were perhaps the heydays of the Peninsula drovers. This was to take advantage of the Cairns meatworks and the new Mareeba Sale Yards. With the advent of World War 2, a Fifteen Year Meat Agreement was entered into with Britain and this created a feeling of optimism

Courtesy Bowie Gostelow

Peninsula cattle, with Bowie Gostelow in charge (on horse in front) crossing the Daintree River en route to Mossman, 1955

among the cattlemen as they did their bit for the war effort by producing more beef for the soldiers. Large numbers of cattle moved down along the stock routes during the earlier part of the year when there was sufficient grass and water available for their sustenance.

Some properties had a regular drover who took their cattle over while some used their own station plant to shift them. Others, with smaller turnoffs, combined with neighbours to put a composite mob on the road. Bowie Gostelow took regular delivery of cattle from Yarraden, Violetvale and Musgrave. He also took cattle, on occasion, from Lakefield and Laura. His biggest mob, possibly one of the largest walked down the route, was 1500 head. He, too, had problems with lame bullocks and had to cue a fair number in each mob. His solution to the lame ones keeping up with the others was simple and successful. Each night his Aboriginal helper, Barney, would take them an extra two miles (3 kilometres) at their own pace after the main mob pulled up at the camp. He left them when they'd settled for the night and they were again absorbed in with their fellow travellers the following day.

Women Drovers

Billy Wallace from Bald Hills north of Cooktown, or Old Billy as he was known to distinguish him from his nephew, my husband Billy, was another of the earlier drovers. Billy sometimes took the Rokeby cattle to their Southedge depot but was the regular drover of stock from Kalpowar, then owned by his brother Arthur, and Lakefield. He also took mobs from the Cooktown and coastal side, from Kings Plains, Springvale and Butcher's Hill. Old Billy married when in his sixties to a very enterprising woman named Sadie. After their marriage Sadie accompanied him on all his droving trips. Living close to Hopevale Mission, Old Billy had very good relations with the people there and was able to select capable men from the Mission as his assistants. The same ones usually did each trip with him.

To take delivery of the cattle, Old Billy often took a shortcut with his plant through Starcke, north of Bald Hills and over through Kalpowar to where the cattle were waiting. Old Bill died in harness on one of these shortcuts. He and Sadie were heading up to take delivery of a mob when he had a fatal heart attack. He was giving himself a routine shave, squatted by the campfire, when he fell over dead. Sadie was left with him while one of the men rode for help. Another drover took the cattle down that year.

After Old Billy's death, my husband bought his plant and took over some of his contracts. His horse-tailer from Hopevale, Archie Gibson, went with the young Bill on every trip and was invaluable. It began a friendship that carried on until Archie's death.

Peninsula women had long had a reputation for being hardworking, innovative and multi-skilled. When Bowie Gostelow was shorthanded on a droving trip, his wife Vivian rolled her swag and went with him. With small children to care for she was torn both ways but on at least two occasions she was able to help Bowie out of a difficult position. Bowie's mother, Roseanne, didn't go droving but her presence was readily seen in everything that concerned the work of the station and the stock route. There was very little that she could not do. And she did it all with excellent results. Not only did she supply the food for the drovers' catering arm, she kept all the saddles, both pack and riding, in exemplary order, counterlining them with curled hair collected when bang-tailing station cattle, repairing and making bridles and other leather gear. She tanned hides, converting them into the hobbles so necessary for the plant horses and she made packbags.

Roseanne tried to initiate me into some of her skills. Some of my lessons had a favourable outcome but my first attempt at tanning hide was no success. My husband, Bill, was away droving for several months each year and, in his absence, I tried to keep the leather gear in order. The batch of hobbles I hoped to make from what I recalled of Roseanne's directions was to be a surprise. It was — but not a pleasant one. Our neighbours, Jock and Glady Christensen, rode over. As an expert tanner, Jock was curious to view my efforts. Confidently I drew the prepared hide from its bath of tan. Shock! Horror! Instead of being soft, pliable and beautifully tanned, it came out rigid and hard, with tidal waves and deep, broad hollows alternating along its length.

"Oh," said Jock, in a disarmingly polite voice, "I didn't know you were making corrugated iron."

I'd made the mixture too strong and burnt the hide. Maybe the fact that I'd used ironwood bark contributed to its metallic outcome. The next batch, made under Jock's eagle eyes, was much more successful. I soaked the hide first — as directed — in water infused with a collection of the white bits occurring in chook manure, before putting it into a tan of weaker strength than my first brew. Some chemical property in the white chook manure was, according to Jock, supposed to make the hide more receptive to the tanning process. It worked. For my trouble, I had a bag of hobble straps, each secured with a specially tied knot to be inserted, like a button, through a strategically-placed slit. They really were a pleasant surprise for Bill on his return.

A generation later than Rebecca Armbrust and her ilk there were other droving wives. In the early 1950s it became necessary for me, temporarily, to join the ranks of the female drovers. The cattle, over twelve hundred of them, were from Hardy and Iris Wallace's Merluna, near Weipa. Hardy, having a Telegraph Office near him on the O.T. Line, sent us a telegram advising the delivery date. He wanted to catch the first sale of the year in Mareeba in late January. We had no Telegraph Office handy. Our telegram came out with the monthly pack-horse mail three weeks after Hardy sent it. As it meant that the mob would be on the road over Christmas, the recruitment of men was a little harder. Bill's regular cook John Barry and Archie the horse-tailer were ready to go, a couple of young tin miners decided to try droving as a new experience but Bill was still left short-handed. His mother offered to take our eldest, young Johnnie, and a friend in Cooktown with a toddler four days younger than Nancy, said she'd look after her for us.

I don't know if my going was such a bright idea — from my point of view at least. The mob was one of the worst ones ever to come down the stock route. There had been none of the expected early storms. The grass was brown and short except where some grazier, fooled by promising dark storm clouds, had set fire to it hoping for rain — and blackened it. The cattle had been in hand for several months and weren't in very good condition. To cap it all, they'd 'taken' the yard just before we took delivery and some had horn wounds as a result. A few cows were already calving and, after an absence of thirty years, Three Day Sickness, a debilitating and often fatal fever carried by a tiny biting fly had affected the mob. Some sufferers on the tail were barely able to stagger past as Hardy and Bill 'counted out' the mob on delivery. Not an auspicious start.

Added to that, there was a resurgence of Dengue Fever in the human population and I became the victim of a very nasty fever whether it was Dengue or not. Fortunately, bush resourcefulness came to the rescue and our cook's sister, Mary Shephard of Musgrave, made me, at John the cook's request, a large beer-bottleful of fever mixture. It tasted vile. John assured me that it was perfectly safe. It contained gin, quinine and Epsom salts. That, from the taste, was easily believable. He also said that Mary added goanna fat and lizards' gizzards to improve and refine it. I don't think she did but it tasted as if their inclusion in the recipe were possible. All the same, as I swigged it riding along each day, I'm sure it hastened the fever's demise.

To make things easier, the worst cases were drafted into a 'hospital mob' of about sixty of the worst cattle. Of these, I became Head Nurse and Boss Drover and came along with them on my own at whatever pace they could manage. If I couldn't make it to camp by nightfall, I'd pull up and wait either for the moon or for someone to come back to help me. When daylight came it didn't take any effort to separate the two mobs. Mine were the ones left lying down after the others walked off.

Both mobs travelled slowly, but the pace my charges moved at allowed me to take in my surroundings. While at a midday camp on a chain of lagoons near Violetvale which had just been vacated by the main mob after watering there, I was intrigued by faint 'plop plop' sounds at regular intervals. There was no dip at Coen and the cattle, when we took them over, were tick-infested. As they'd watered and then camped around the lagoons some of the engorged ticks had fallen off to complete their life circle. The sounds I heard were of them falling from antbeds to the ground. Eager meat ants, spotting the fat ticks without reckoning on their size, seized them and swiftly hauled them to their homes. Unfortunately, the circumference of the ticks exceeded that of the ants' entry holes. The ticks were separated from the ants carrying them and rolled to the ground. Plop!

I was also intrigued with the messages, often defamatory, scrawled with charcoal on bleached bullock skulls lying by the side of the Telegraph Line clearing. The graffiti continued all the way to Mareeba, on water tanks or on any convenient flat surface — including bullock skulls — that was available. On one tank was scrawled in large black letters, *'A man's mind must be awful dull, to write such things on a bullock's skull.'*

I had to leave the mob at Laura, just as we were about to dip and just as the Wet decided to set in. With her adopted family, Nancy had gone down with the fever, too. The day that we dipped was the weekly railmotor day in Laura and a drover, Len, came up on it after hearing Bill was short-handed. One look at our sad mob and he booked his return seat to Cooktown. With another Len, Len Elmes, station-owner and sometime drover and myself, we three Lens comprised the entire passenger list on the trip back to Cooktown. Contrarily, after weeks of waiting for rain that didn't come, it was now coming with an unstoppable vengeance. The old railmotor had no glass in its windows, only a windscreen in front of the driver. I was dressed in riding gear, boots, leggings, cowboy hat and raincoat and was soaked to the skin when we reached Cooktown. In all this rain the cattle were forced to swim every creek between Laura and the foot of the Byerstown Range.

Back home, my domestic bliss didn't last long. A hurried horseborne message arrived from Bill. I was to catch up with the cattle. John, our cook, had been flown out by Aerial Ambulance earlier after a fall from a horse and with me gone too, and the Wet arrived, the drovers were feeling their short-handed state acutely. Nancy could stay with Johnnie. There was no time to lose. The messenger, Bill's Aboriginal foster-brother Paddy, had brought a spare saddled horse. I carried Nancy in front of me on it while Paddy slung my swag across his lap.

Going up the Range with my swag but no Nancy, I met Stan Watkin with 300 head of fat cattle from Starcke, north of Cooktown. They were all in good condition, not a bony old piker, a calving cow nor a lame stag amongst them. And, for some reason, no Three Day Sickness. Stan was pleased, however, to have an extra hand to help him up the Range. I left him at the top and rode on to catch up with Bill and my old hospital mob. In a couple of days, Stan and his healthy and happy mob passed us.

Miles Morris lived in a shed at the top of the range and I sought information from him as to where Bill intended to make camp. The answer was a little confusing. 'That little gully this side of the Palmer.' As I couldn't place the gully, I was wondering if I'd have to go on to the Palmer River and come back one, when Miles's mate, Ian, less concerned about shocking ladies with bad language, enlightened me. 'Bastard Gully.' I knew immediately. Bastard Gully lived up to its name. It was unforgettable — steep, almost vertical sides and rocky beyond belief.

I met up with Archie and our newly-elevated cook, Doug Gliddon, at Spear Creek. It wasn't a big creek but it was running fast and it looked dangerous to me, anyway. We had to 'boat' the gear and swim the horses across. Where we lived at Harvest Home was the grave of a young man drowned trying to cross this same stream early last century. My old care-taker, Arthur, would disparagingly remark, 'Fancy getting yerself drownded in a little bit of a thing like Spear Creek.' I wasn't so sure of its benignity.

I caught up with the cattle, retrieved my hospital mob and spent a night out on the northern side of a creek when I was the last to try to cross in the lowering dark and my horse refused to try the unknown. The cattle were sold, for barely enough to cover the expenses and we came home, this time with a mob of horses to augment future droving and mustering plants. As the mob contained mares and tenderfooted foals, I found myself again coming on behind the plant horses with a Hospital Mob. We left in early December to take delivery of the mob at Station Creek near Coen. It was well into March when we arrived back home.

Some Aboriginal droving hands had absconded in Mareeba from earlier mobs of cattle and we had a letter from the Superintendent of Hopevale reminding us of our obligations to return the men to Hopevale Mission at our expense. Should they 'abscond' the Police would be notified and 'labour for future droving trips will not be supplied.' We had no problems. They were a good crew. They went by railmotor from Mareeba to Cairns and from there caught the weekly launch back to Cooktown where they could hitch a ride to Hopevale in the Mission truck. Archie came back with Bill and me and the Mission later bought one of the piebald colt foals we had purchased.

Ivy Elmes from Springvale accompanied her drover husband, Sid, when needed too. On one trip she took her small children with her. Her daughter, Dennie, the eldest, was quite capable of riding on her own and helped to bring up the tail of the mob. However, Denny related, her old mare wasn't too keen on the slow pace and would spitefully bite a persistently laggard cow on the rump. This usually sent the victim at a smart trot up to the middle of the mob with the result that Dennie's Dad saw its flight and came back to reprimand his daughter.

Droving Through China Camp to Daintree

A second route was used for stock being travelled from Cooktown and properties to the north to the fattenning blocks on the Daintree River and for fat cattle destined for the Cairns Meatworks and local butchers. It was not a route suitable for large mobs although Bowie Gostelow did get down successfully with several hundred head on two occasions. The nature of the country, which was steep and heavily timbered, catered for little more than single-file transit. Purchased stock, such as bulls and horses, were taken up this way as well to their new homes on the northern stations. For some years Lakefield supplied cattle regularly to the Mossman Butchering Company and made good use of this route. It was well-used but the numbers droved and the number of mobs taken down, were much below those taken the 'long' way via the heads of the Mitchell River and Mareeba. Alec Lyall of Daintree was a drover who used both routes. For years he brought down mobs from Rokeby to Southedge between Mareeba and Mount Molloy using drovers like Mick Fittock and Andy Toomey from his home territory of Daintree and Mossman. Alec also moved cattle for butcher Fred Marsh taking stores destined for Marsh's butcher shops from the Mareeba saleyards to fattening paddocks in the Daintree area. Once fattened, he drove them back to Marsh's abattoir. Like most old-time drovers, Alec continued in the game until late in life. He didn't give his love of horses away in 'retirement'. For many years he and his horse Gold Top were popular and very successful competitors at horse sports, shows and gymkhanas in the Mossman district.

Cattle using the coastal route branched off the main drovers' road at the Laura River at Butcher's Hill. Their next camp was at the homestead where cattle had to be dipped — although without official supervision — before going on to camp. Camp was usually made at Dead Dog or Keatings before setting off again along a narrow pad through the thick timber and vines by way of Callaghan's Creek to Harlow's Ten Mile Block. Then the hill-climbing began, one step wrong and a beast, bullock or horse, would be over the steep side of the pad. Many are the packbags that had to be hauled back up the slope after a careless packhorse put its hoof wrong. Snakes weren't a problem but the rainforest stinging tree was. Should an animal — or a human — inadvertently brush against one of these big hairy leaves the pain was maddening and almost everlasting. For years, the excruciating pain would be revived whenever the affected skin came into contact with water.

After Salt Box Hill, Gold Hill and Debbil Debbil were successfully negotiated, the mob came to the Daintree River. This had to be crossed no less than five times and with Daintree's superabundant rainfall, there was always plenty of water in the river. Good leaders, cattle that automatically took the lead and which the mob happily followed, were highly regarded, but having a good leader was not a blessing that could be counted on. On one trip down with cattle my husband had in his mob a Droughtmaster bull, Wonderboy, that I had taught to lead and paraded at several shows. When all else failed at the first crossing, Wonderboy's education came to mind. A halter of sorts was fashioned from a greenhide rope and adjusted on his head. Luckily a conventional wooden boat was left at the crossing for access. With one man taking the oars and Bill taking Wonderboy's halter shank, the bull amicably swam beside the boat and coached his fellow-travellers over. This worked well for each crossing. A second, much rougher route, by way of Alexandra Creek dodged most of the Daintree crossings but was only attempted in dire situations.

Alternate Route to Daintree Through Mossman. Thylacines?

Sometimes fatteners would buy cattle at Mareeba saleyards and, if they were fortunate enough to find a drover who could handle it, would persuade him to deliver the bought cattle from Mareeba to the Daintree. There weren't many takers. For a start the cattle had to be droved along the motor road to Devi's farm between Oakey Creek and the Little Mitchell. Fortunately, there was a small yard there that could be used overnight as, in the surrounding scrub, local legend had it that the Thylacine still lurked in hiding there. Dogs, goats and baby calves had all been found terribly mauled, sometimes dis-embowelled. This could have been done by a number of wild animals but Alf Devi had two large yellow hides with blackish striped markings from animals he had shot in defence of his dogs. Bowie Gostelow of Violetvale did several trips from the saleyards to the Daintree, the last in 1963. Devi had one of the hides stuffed by a southern taxidermist and Bowie was most impressed with the result. It

Courtesy *Queensland Country Life*

Maurice de Tournoeur, Wetherby stud, with Daydawn, Daygleam and Daysprite in the 1960s

was 'half cat, half dog', he said, and about five feet six inches (roughly 168cms) from nose to tail and 'looked ferocious'.

From Devi's the cattle went to Wetherby, then owned by the De Tournoeur family who helped pioneer the introduction of *Bos Indicus* or Zebu (Brahman) blood to the northern beef herds. The next day saw the drovers down the winding old Bump Road to Jack Hyde's property south of Mossman. What followed was tricky and took a bit of skill combined with daring. The mob had to be taken quietly through the central part of Mossman township. To do this the drovers got an extremely early start, walked their cattle stealthily along the main street and, as quickly as possible, headed for Daintree. Mossman residents were sometimes amazed at finding fresh cowpats on the bitumen surface of Front Street as they came to work.

Droving Sheep from Cooktown

Cattle and horses weren't the only animals to be droved. In 1874 Henry Wheatley, seeing the market that Firth's sheep found on the Palmer, purchased 'a small mob' of sheep which arrived in Cooktown by boat, to take for sale to the miners of the Normanby River field. Wheatley and his mate, Sam, acquired the services of a Chinese shepherd to help with their enterprise. The men herded the sheep on foot with a 'small nuggety horse named Darky'[2] to carry their camp gear and rations. They slaughtered and sold a few sheep on their way through the old Oakey road but after having all sorts of problems — the Chinaman left after being assaulted by a traveller and was replaced by a 'new chum' — they missed the turn-off that would have taken them to the

Normanby. A good deal of exploration was needed to find it again but they finally reached their destination and butchered some of the stock. Tragically there were native attacks and the spearmen were mown down by rifle fire. Wheatley wrote that 'it seems something very terrible to me to be compelled to have to resort to such a fearful alternative.' The last sheep was shot and butchered as it tried to escape on the 20th December. That done, Wheatley sat down to count the proceeds. His droving/butchering enterprise grossed fifty-six pounds ten shillings.

And a Drover of Pigs

Captain Cook inadvertently released pigs during his enforced stay at what became Cooktown when a grassfire, possibly lit by the natives, set alight the pigs' enclosure and they escaped. Descendants of these pigs, crossed and re-crossed with commercial strains, were at least once participants in a droving trip. Glenville Pike, in his *Sundowner* column of the *North Queensland Register* of 19th July 1990, tells how Podge Gorton, in the first decade of the twentieth century, undertook to drove eighty pigs from Charlie Wallace's Glenrock, north of Cooktown, to the Cooktown butcher's yards. The distance travelled was 128k and the trip, with Aboriginal helpers and two packhorses to carry camp gear and two very essential bags of corn, took five days. A trickle of corn encouraged the pigs to follow the lead of the Boss drover with his corn-filled bucket, while his offsiders looked after would-be absconders and stragglers. At night, the drovers didn't engage in the time-honoured custom of riding around the herd singing suitably-pitched songs but instead lit log fires to encircle their charges' camping spot. The trip was successful and it was one of the earliest — if not the only — instance of pig droving in the Peninsula.

As the road became more trafficable, the cattle drovers often dispensed with pack-horses and carried the camping gear by four wheel drive or by truck. Ivy Elmes graduated from pack-horse droving to the mechanised approach of taking the gear from camp to camp. In time the Burton Brothers began taking cattle out by road in their single-deck semi-trailers. No one could fail to be impressed when they compared the times taken to walk the cattle over the old stock route with the time it took to get them there by truck. When the road was upgraded on the long stretch past Laura township the trucks were able to ply their trade further and further north and, in time, double-deckers were introduced.

Another innovation was the sea transport of cattle from Peninsula landings to Cairns and its meatworks. The converted landing barge, *Wewak*, was the pioneer of this new method of transport.

4

The Overland Telegraph Line and the RFDS

Cooktown connected to south by telegraph in 1876 · Telegraph Line extended from Fairview to Cape York with repeater stations en route · Connects at Cape York with submarine international cable · Morse Code gives way to voice phone · World War II brings about an upgrading of the Line by Telegraph personnel and U.S. and Australian defence forces · Cairns Aerial Ambulance instals Base Radio VKA in Cairns with communication with outlying properties · Royal Flying Doctor Service takes over from Aerial Ambulance · Rail line from Cooktown to Laura built in 1891, closes and is removed 1962

In the late 1860s there was a national move to provide for the transmission of communication signals to and from overseas. Surface mail took months to arrive. All colonists realised the vital importance of communication by telegraph with Britain and Europe. In 1846 Samuel Morse showed, in the United States of America, what could be done. A professor at the University of New York, he invented the telegraphic code of dots and dashes that bears his name. As proof of his theories, a message 'What God hath wrought' was successfully transmitted from Baltimore to Washington, an incredible distance of 400 miles or over 600 kilometres.

A telegraph cable from Europe was laid to the Dutch East Indies (Indonesia) and there was considerable rivalry among the Australian colonies to be the first to tap into this swift source of contact. South Australia, which then included the present-day Northern Territory, wanted the line to enter Australia in its own dominion, at Port Darwin. As early as 1864/5 Queensland statesmen, realising what a boon this telegraphic link-up would be in their huge, sparsely-populated colony, tried without success to raise capital through the Anglo-Australian and China Telegraph Company. They naturally preferred something closer to home than South Australia's Port Darwin and put forward a plan using the Gulf of Carpentaria as point of entry, promoting either Burketown or Normanton as the base.

Dangers of Telegraph Line repairing in North Queensland
From the *Sydney Punch*, 1870

A rather costly line from Cardwell on the east coast, to Karumba/ Normanton on the Gulf, became an 'accomplished fact in 1870'.[1] The first telegraph which arrived direct from Europe was published in the Brisbane *Telegraph* of 26th October 1872. The *Telegraph* newspaper, like its telegraph service namesake, had only recently seen the light of day. The newspaper was barely three weeks old.

A telegraph line already reached Townsville[2] and in 1869/70 it was extended north to Cardwell. Bushman/explorer Frederick Walker was sent with a party to find a suitable route to the Gulf. Starting at Dalrymple, the fore-runner to Charters Towers, on the Burdekin River, he and his party set out overland for Burketown. Fever struck the party and Walker died. He was buried at the Floraville crossing of the Leichhardt River, not far from Burketown. His second-in-charge, Young, continued on.

Telegraph Line Reaches Normanton — Branches up to Cooktown

The line reached Normanton in 1872 and was continued to its port, Karumba, on the waters of the Gulf. Junction Creek, near Mt. Surprise, one of the repeater stations set up on this line, became the starting point for another line destined to go right up to the tip of Cape York Peninsula. The Palmer gold-rush helped to accelerate this program with Mulligan's discovery of payable gold in 1873. Palmerville was the base for the first Mining Warden, Howard St. George, but his successor, Phillip Sellheim, moved the Warden's Office to Maytown. On 25th April 1876, the completed telegraph line linked the goldfield to its port, Cooktown, as well as to the south via Junction Creek. The Line followed the Old Palmer Road from Cooktown, through Laura and Palmerville. Before the sixty kilometre gap between Junction Creek and Palmerville was finalised, messages were sent from one to the other by a convenient Pony Express run by two brothers, Will and Charlie Parish[3]. They had worked on the Line since the outset and were experienced telegraphists as well as practical bushmen. The Pony Express had only a short life. On 11th July of the same year the connection was made complete and Brisbane was connected by telegraph to what was then the Colony's second largest settlement, Cooktown. Later, in 1888, the original route of the Cooktown to Laura Telegraph Line was changed to follow the then completed Cooktown to Laura rail line.

From its onset, the work on the Line met with problems. The local Aboriginals soon realised that 'well-tempered fishhooks manufactured from the line'[4] were superior to any they had yet manufactured. At one time, near Cooktown, 200 metres of the line was detached and stolen. That's a lot of fishhooks. They also used the wire to make barbs for their spears. In his *Letters from Laura*, Millais Culpin, the school teacher of that township, wrote in 1892: 'A good arrangement made for spearing fish is a four-pronged affair, made from a single shaft of hardwood quartered at the end and with each quarter fitted with a Telegraph wire barb. If I had that across my chest I could say goodbye to my best girl.' He also commented that, with overseas ships calling at the Far Northern ports, it took less time to receive a letter from England than it took to get one written at the same time from Melbourne. At times there were spearings of horses and men; the latter, fortunately, were rare occasions.

With the Jardines pioneering the route right to the Tip and establishing Somerset, people were beginning to appreciate the strategic importance of a settlement, port and international communication base at the top of Cape

York Peninsula. Robert Logan Jack followed Kennedy and the Jardines and reported back in detail on his findings. Thursday Island was eventually selected as the new settlement site under H.M.Chester, the man who, later in 1883 on Premier McIlwraith's orders, sailed from Thursday Island to New Guinea to take possession of that land for Queensland.

Bradford Surveys Route For Telegraph Line To Cape York.

The fourth expedition through the Peninsula was undertaken by J.R. Bradford. McIlwraith took a very serious view of the strategic importance of the Far North to the rest of the Colony. John R. Bradford was an Inspector of Lines and Mail Route Services. He was instructed to find a suitable route for a Telegraph Line from the 'nearest angle of the Cooktown-Palmerville line' to Cape York. Bradford had earlier supervised the building of the Cooktown to Palmerville section. His team comprised[5] William Healy, second-in-charge, James Cook, William Macnamara, John Wilson, Jimmy Sam Goon and Johnnie, an Aborigine. They were provided with thirty-six horses of which only thirteen reached Somerset. Each man was equipped with a Martini Henri rifle and a Colt revolver. Healy also carried a fowling piece. Bradford relied heavily on R.L. Jack's maps which proved to be of invaluable assistance to him.

The party left Cooktown on 6th June 1883, camped at the Laura Telegraph Station for five days from the 12th June and then moved on to 'the lagoon' as Fairview was then known. Fairview was the northernmost point of the existing Line. They left there on 18th June and headed north-west. Their CampV was at Musgrave on Saltwater Creek. On the way, Healy had a creek named after him as did the Superintendent of Telegraph, Mr. Matvieff. As with the previous overlanders, early in their mission, the horses were severely affected, often fatally, by poison plants. A roan mare purchased in Cooktown ate some of the poison bush that had caused the earlier travellers so much heartache and died on camp one night. Her memory — and it is hoped, that of her other dead mates — is perpetuated by Deadhorse Creek near Musgrave.

They pushed on with a diminishing horse-plant, marking out sites for the proposed Telegraph Line. For a few days they pulled up at Lalla Rookh, a cattle station owned by the Massey brothers on Station Creek just south of Coen. Here they 'captured, killed and cured' some beef.[6] It was Bradford who discovered that the river thought by prospectors to be the Coen of Carstenz was really a branch of the Jardines' Archer. The true Coen is short and isn't crossed by the Telegraph Line. However, Bradford was, like all mortals, fallible. He later mistook the Batavia River for the 'true' Coen. It was very confusing country for the early travellers.

After fording the Batavia came the crossing of the dreaded Wet Desert that had 'finished' Kennedy and nearly reduced the Jardine brothers to a similar predicament. It was extremely boggy even when the surface appeared to be solid and, despite the abundant moisture, there was no grass for the horses. Poison plant was also present and played havoc with the hungry animals. The bog was so treacherous that horses had to be physically dug out and hauled to their shaky feet with ropes to give them any chance at all of survival. Then it was the men's turn. Fever and ague broke out. Bradford himself suffered a particularly severe attack at their Camp XXV. Fortunately, Bradford learnt from his predecessors' mistakes and took a 'liberal supply' of rations, even enough flour to sustain his weakened horses with a daily hand-out of the milled wheat.[7] From the Wet Desert they progressed to a drier one, 'entirely destitute of grass' Bradford wrote. Horses still became bogged and streams were 'treacherous'.

On 23rd August at Camp XLIV they had moved more westerly and the waters of the Gulf of Carpentaria could be seen from 'a point near the camp.' They were approaching the end of their journey. From Peak Point, Bradford and Healy walked for two days leading their horses towards Somerset. Here they were 'hospitably received' by the Jardines. It was 29th August 1883. They returned to Brisbane by ship from Thursday Island. On the trip up the Peninsula, both Bradford and Healy took note of what timber was available locally for poles. The supply was inadequate and with the prevalence of the giant termites that call Cape York Peninsula their home, they estimated that the average life-expectancy of these poles would be only two years.

Bradford's report was quickly followed by a calling of tenders for the erection of the Line. The total construction, a distance of some 600 kilometres, was offered as two sections. The first, slightly the longer at 320 kilometres, was undertaken by Messrs Brodziak and Degen. It commenced at Fairview and continued to Mein, to the south-east of Merluna station. Steel poles were used where at all possible.[8] An 'Oppenheimer' type, sea-freighted from England, they were used in conjunction with a single galvanised wire weighing some 120 kilograms to the kilometre. The submarine cable needed to cross from the mainland to Thursday Island was double-cored and very much more heavy-duty but that didn't make it trouble-free. On one occasion it was severed by a boat anchor and its first few years of life were mainly trial, error and adaptation. The initial cable was laid by a specially equipped cable-ship, the *Recorder* and completed on the night of 17th November 1886.

The price for clearing along the Line (two chains or 45 metres in width) and erecting the poles, came out at about $90 per kilometre. Where wooden poles were found necessary they were located, cut and erected at a cost of $1.50 each. Any extra-long wooden poles attracted a further 30c per metre. 'Affixing insulators and stretching wire' was priced at about $5 per kilometre.[9]

The second section from Mein to Cape York was completed by Messrs Gordon and Moreton — Captain George Croughley Gordon and the Hon. Matthew Moreton to be exact. Frank J. Paterson, the surveyor, was a partner, too. The Post Master General after whom the far northern station was named was also a Paterson — the Hon. Thos. MacDonald Paterson. The tender for the second half allowed for slightly higher prices because of the isolation but overall both sections cost relatively the same, just over fifteen thousand pounds ($30,000) each. The second section was done from north to south to take advantage of the facilities for landing freight.

The northmost station was Paterson. Down from Paterson was McDonnell, named for the Under Secretary and Superintendent of Telegraphs for Queensland, John McDonnell. He was an uncle of John Bradford. Moreton was situated between McDonnell and Mein and was possibly named for one of the partners or for B.B. Moreton who was Postmaster General in 1885. Frank Jardine, while assisting the surveying and construction parties, rounded off his own map-making experiences by naming the Ducie River after the Earl of Ducie, 'Mr. Paterson's brother'.[10] Jardine's local knowledge allowed many of the cumbersome poles to be delivered almost on site by river transport.

Native Police Protect Workers and the Line

A detachment of Native Police was stationed with the Line party both to protect the men while their officers were off on exploratory duties and to keep a watchful eye on pilferers. Constant surveillance needed to be kept to avoid theft. Shanahan in his *Sidelights (Queenslander* 24th July 1897) tells of 'systematic pilfering' from the potato patch at McDonnell 'for several years'. While waiting for the final Moreton/Mein connection to be made, a Pony Express was used to get messages through.

Mein was named for another Post Master General, the Hon. C.S. Mein. He held this position in Queensland in 1879/80 and 1884/85. Mein was opened for service on 14th July 1887, followed by McDonnell, Paterson and Thursday Island on 25th August and Moreton on 1st September of the same year. Fairview and Musgrave came into use two days before

Courtesy Australia Post Archives

Paterson Telegraph Office. There is one gun turret clearly visible on the right

Christmas 1887 after the station at Laura was closed. Coen opened six days later.

After doing the survey work in the top section Frank Paterson, acting for Gordon and Moreton, secured the contract in 1894 for the erection of permanent buildings or 'forts' at the Telegraph Stations. Their fortlike appearance with an internal 'verandah' and heavy galvanised iron exteriors with a 'gun turret' on two diagonally opposite corners[11] were for protection of both staff and equipment. Windows were fitted with iron shutters and provision was made for siting some of the precious water tanks within the building itself. This protected at least some part of the water supply from spear damage or by pollution with poisonous substances.

Courtesy Meredith Monro

Musgrave. Once a telegraph, now a cattle station — 1965

A number of rooms opened off the internal 'verandah' and housed both the telegraph office and the staff. All 'forts' but the Mein had adequate natural water from which a supply could be pumped. Musgrave even had a hot water spring. Mein was served only by a small well and its whereabouts are now debatable. A small railed-off section is thought to mark the site of the well but some think it indicates a second suicide's grave. With its water shortages for both man and beast, plagues of brown snakes and rats, it was not a popular posting. Young Norman Dawson shot himself there in May 1947. His gravestone is still there to be seen and sorrowed over. He was twenty-one.

Mein was shut down for a time in 1929. Musgrave and McDonnell were also closed. The building at Musgrave was sold to the owners of Musgrave cattle station and became the station homestead. It is still on the same site. The Mein building was sold for removal after the station closed for a second time following Normie Dawson's suicide. Oldtime cattleman, Fred Keppel, built a house from its re-cycled timbers in Coen. It now houses the local museum. Moreton Telegraph Station was also demolished. One of the Moreton linesmen died of a heart attack when alone in a camp some 75 kilometres north of Moreton. He was W.J. Brown and died in 1945. His mates buried him there and workmen maintain his grave and headstone when in the area. There are other graves at Moreton. One is of Richard Barker, 35, who died in April 1903 of a gunshot wound. In 1914, Guy Minto Cragg, aged 40, died of malaria.

Courtesy Ron Burnet

Marked grave of linesman Sam Thompson, and unmarked grave of mailman Billy Beirnes (right), at Musgrave

The doctor at Thursday Island, Dr. Wassell, was consulted by a specially-rigged voice telephone but his assistance, sadly, was to no avail.

There are also several graves at Musgrave. Billy Beirnes, an ex-mail contractor, retired there and was buried at the homestead when he died. Sam Thompson, linesman in charge, killed in a fall from a horse, is buried near Billy under the mango tree. Sam's grave is dated 2-1-1919. Keeping them company is a small child whose death was said to have been caused by poison after drinking the electrolyte — a copper sulphate solution — used in the telegraph storage batteries.

Telephone Replaces Telegraph — Wartime Upgrade

The status quo was more or less maintained on the Line until the 1920s when telephone operations almost completely replaced the telegraph. Telephone facilities were installed at all Telegraph Stations by 1928 but there is a report that Moreton was talking to Thursday Island as early as 1914. This could have been in the instance of Guy Cragg's illness when, with no little ingenuity and know-how, the linesmen contacted Dr. Wassell. It was probably a temporary solution to a life-and-death crisis.[12]

The Telegraph circuits were 'condenser phones super-imposed over the Telegraph circuits'. The lines were very noisy and the transmission poor. The old galvanised iron wires were no longer state-of-the-art but the telegraph connection proved its worth on many occasions. Gradually the standards improved. At Thursday Island in 1941 there was still a Morse capability but there were also 137 telephone lines from the T.I. exchange. Strangely, there were no technicians either on Thursday Island or in the Peninsula but such was the dedication, ingenuity and capability of the linesmen that this wasn't then seen as a major set-back.

The big change came with the southern advance of World War 2. With the fall of Singapore this was one time when no one wished Thursday Island to be the 'Singapore of the South'. Once the United States of America came into the war, large numbers of U.S. troops arrived in the Peninsula. They built airfields there and it was imperative to update communications. Work on the Line commenced in August 1942 and all the necessary maintenance and upgrading had to be completed before the onset of the Wet season. It was necessary for cross-arms to be added to the poles to accommodate the extra three wires needed. A gargantuan task but not impossible.

Materials to be used in the upgrade were shipped to Cooktown, Portland Roads, Cape York and Thursday Island and taken overland — with great difficulty — from there to where they were required. To complete this exercise before the rain set in, a large number of men were employed. There were 1200 from the U.S. Army's Signal Corps, 600 from the Australian Signal Corps and 60 Post Master General Department supervisors.[13] Three P.M.G. engineers, Pilgrim, Frazer and Kanaley oversaw all the work. In times when miracles were rather short on the ground, these men quickly brought one about.

The work was again divided into two sections — from Townsville to the Hann River between Fairview and Musgrave, and from the Hann north to Thursday Island. The Cooktown Loop was placed in the southern section's dominion and the northern section was in turn responsible for the loop to Iron Range, an Allied army camp. The work, the placing of new arms and the running of the superior copper wires, the installation of extra poles and stay wires and other upgrades in equipment, was all completed by 23rd November 1942. They had beaten the onset of the Wet. The distance from Townsville to Cape York was 1658 kilometres. Initial testing was able to be commenced on 11th November but a few line faults bugged the system and it wasn't until December that the last of these was finally, and successfully, ironed out.

The men used Army vehicles to get around but roads were then almost non-existent except for the ones especially established by the Army for military purposes. From Fairview to Coen took two days — if all went well. From Coen to Cape York, double that time was needed. These journeys can now be accomplished in hours. Some equipment was understandably damaged in transport and delays were experienced as repairs had to be made. Even so, the short time taken to do such a gigantic job was breath-taking and can only be commended.

The new circuits were mainly for use by the armed services but each repeater station was staffed by a P.M.G. officer and two Army men. The P.M.G. man was considered to be in charge. The upgrade resulted in a three to four channel carrier system, voice frequency repeaters and power equipment — generators to top-up batteries and to keep them well-charged.

Cairns Aerial Ambulance Established — Laura Rail Closed

After the war, non-army personnel advised to evacuate during the close fighting returned and some of the Defence Forces remained to help clean up their operations. The improvement in radio-communication during the war led to a wonderful side-effect. A network had been developed in conjunction with the Royal Flying Doctor Service in the 1930s but it had not reached as far as the Peninsula. Wise heads in the Cairns Ambulance Centre saw the merit of the system and opened their own base. It began in April 1945 with five outstations; 368 outstations were connected by radio in 1968 and the initial small planes that were purchased at ex-army sales for use in casualty evacuations were replaced by larger aircraft. In 1973, the R.F.D.S. took over the Mantle of Safety in Cairns from the Aerial Ambulance which had served the Peninsula so valiantly over the years.

At one stage it was suggested that the Line from Coen to Thursday Island be abandoned because of the difficulties in servicing it but fortunately the Army intervened with good effect.

Courtesy the Aust. Railways Historical Society

A line-up of the original inhabitants on the Laura River's new rail bridge

The little Cooktown to Laura railway wasn't as fortunate. It was closed in 1961. The last official train ran the final return journey three days after Christmas in that year.[14] As could be expected — by the locals at least — as soon as the rail closed, the newly-built road went out of action due to wet weather and a special train was run on the 3rd and the 4th of March to take supplementary stores and supplies to Laura. A small modicum of good came out of the closure. Some 3800 poles were made available from the defunct railway lines. Additional wires were added and a line was put through, with railway line poles, from the main Line to Weipa. Previous to that, Weipa had only H.F. radio-telephone contact. Initially the system operated between Atherton and Weipa but that was later changed to a service between Cairns and the bauxite town. Later, additional repeaters were installed at the older stations and at the newly-established Lakeland.

The two-way radio and its service of taking in — and out — telegram traffic for transmission from the Aerial Ambulance and later the R.F.D.S. base, was used only as an emergency standby. Gradually, the convenience of telephone communication was enjoyed by most of the remote cattle stations and communities.

5

The Mail Must Go Through — 1870s

Early mails to the Palmer Goldfield, 1874 · Post Office erected in Cooktown, 1874 · Mail to Byerstown by coach service · Mail services extended to Endeavour River farms, the tinfields and to Bloomfield · The new rail line carries a mail to Laura · Packhorse mailmen operate from Laura north · Legendary mailman, Jim McDowell · Trucks and planes take over from the packhorse

While politicians were eager to obtain telegraphic communications from overseas and to be able to use the same facilities locally, more ordinary people just wanted their rights to a mail service within, at least, their own Colony. Mail services evolved in the Peninsula very soon after Cookstown or as it became known, Cooktown, opened as a port for the goldfields. The Palmer field got under way in 1873 and twelve months later, the Palmer River Goldfield had its mail service. It began in earnest just after the Wet on 5th April 1874. The first contractor, D. Lacey, felt himself unequal to the massive job and tenders were called a second time. Johnnie Hogsfleich won the contract at forty pounds ($80) per year with the mail to follow the MacMillan Track. A few months later, Mailman Powell was running the mail but by early October Hogsfleich was back. On this occasion, the mail which had been an impossible weekly service was extended to a more practical fortnightly trip, much more satisfactory to both mailman and to miners.

Cooktown Post Office, 1874

Mails were conveyed by 'various people'[1] between 'Cooktown, Palmerville and Maytown'. The distance from Cooktown to Palmerville was about 330 kilometres and from there to Maytown a further rather dangerous fifty kilometres. The new contract filled in October for the horseborne fortnightly mail was for an incredible 1,170 pounds ($2340) per annum. Cooktown Post Office wasn't much older than the ink on that selfsame mail contract. It opened unofficially on New Year's Day 1874 with W.E. Armstrong in charge. For his trouble he was paid a salary of only 24 pounds though, inexplicably, this was increased to 300 pounds when J. Allen took over from him in a permanent position in March. A Mail Order service also became available in March with 535 mail orders issued and 63 paid for the remaining months of 1874.

A Post and Telegraph office was erected in 1877 to house the two services. It was a T-shaped building with the top of the T facing the street and was divided into a Post Office and a Telegraph section with a separate room to house the batteries needed for transmission. The stem of the T was two rooms wide and provided sleeping accommodation and living space for the staff. Nine years later, the building was enlarged and upgraded. Cooktown by 1880 was part of the Torres Strait Mail Service operated by E. and A. Steamship Co..

Ancillary Post Offices and Mailmen

As the goldfield developed and expanded Post Offices were opened between 1874 and 1887 at Palmerville, Kingston, Byerstown, Gregory, Lukinville, Cannibal Creek, Ida, Earlton (Normanby Reefs) and Limestone. From 1st January 1875 the Cooktown to Maytown mail was increased to a weekly service but was still carried by horse. John Hogsfleich was a noted mailman until 1876 when he was the successful tenderer for the mail run from Port Douglas to the newly-opened Hodgkinson Goldfield. Johnnie's job was no sinecure. He had a couple of very narrow escapes involving spears, and finding forage for his horses in the Dry season could be a rather insurmountable problem with at least 250 horse teams and 200 bullock teams in 1875 competing for the same grass. The mail left Cooktown early on Monday and usually arrived at Palmerville, barring accidents and incidents, on Friday. Here the mailman spelled his horses before riding on to Maytown the next day. His schedule allowed him another 'day off' before his ride back to Cooktown. All going well, the mailman would arrive in Cooktown with the inward mail on schedule. On his day off he had to attend to his horses, treating injuries, renewing loose shoes and repairing leather gear. At that time horses were in demand and prices asked for a useful animal were high.

After 1st July 1876 the Palmer Mail Service was upgraded, though miners were by then leaving for other fields. A coach service which was dignified as Mail Service 146 some three years later, took the mail to Byerstown once weekly. From there, it was back to the packhorse mailman to distribute it further to the goldfield Post Offices. In 1884 the Cooktown to Cannibal Creek Service was extended to include Earlton at the head of the West Normanby in from Butcher's Hill near present day Lakeland. Some miners had moved from the Palmer to the Normanby which was still considered part of the Palmer

River Goldfield, rather than take their chances on the Hodgkinson which had little alluvial gold.

Farms were established on the fertile land on the northern side of the Endeavour River and a mail-service was provided in 1883 from Cooktown to McIvor. It was a weekly horse mail. Another horse mail operated to Bloomfield with mailmen risking their lives almost every week in flooded or crocodile-infested streams. Mailman Ned Feinn was drowned carrying the mail early last century. By 1885 the Palmer was in further decline and the service was shortened to Cooktown-Earlton, a mere 100 kilometres. When the Cooktown to Laura rail line was built in the late 1880s, mail was delivered by train. There were three steam trains plying the route each week. The rail line, like the Telegraph Line, was built in sections. Section 1 took it fifty kilometres just past Normanby cattle station to Palmer Road siding. By the end of 1885 Cooktown had not only a railway station with residence but also a 'carriage shade', engine shed, well, horse ramp, carriage shed, machine shop, weighbridge, goods shed, double-tier tankstand and a crane at the loop to the wharf.[2]

The second section was a further thirty kilometres towards Laura to Sandown. This stop was important enough at that time to boast its own hotel. Freight by train to Sandown was 30 shillings per ton for the eighty kilometres travelled. For the remaining 110 kilometres needed to reach Maytown, the packers charged seven times that amount — and needed to. In its first month of traffic in 1885, the line carried 576 passengers and 125 tons of freight. In the first twelve months over 11,000 people took advantage of the passenger service. The third section to Laura was opened 8th October 1888. Three trains were still operating weekly but the report for the year 1887 wasn't as optimistic as hoped. The Normanby River flooded three times during March, flowing well over the bridge and causing considerable damage. A train hit two cows and was de-railed, while a second train ran into a horse in a cutting. Fortunately there was little damage to the train. What happened to the horse wasn't recorded but another unfortunate horse fell between the transoms of one bridge and had to be killed, cut out, cut up and burnt. In the last two instances 'no delay was caused to trains.'

Courtesy Aust. Railways Historical Society

Laura rail bridge on opening day

The fourth section was from Laura to the bridge over the Laura River that was to take the train on its final stage to Maytown. The rail was extended to the river and a rather spectacular bridge built. A train ran across it to 'open' it and that was the end of the Maytown line. Things had changed and not for the better. The Palmer was no longer a booming goldfield and the recession of the Nineties had struck. There was no money. A bill was passed through Parliament for a Land Grant Railway whereby, as in the United States of America, land would be exchanged for the value of railroad constructed. Cooktown saw a glimmer of light at the end of the darkening railway tunnel and held a public meeting to support a Land Grant Railway. It was to no avail but although the three steam trains a week dwindled to one little railmotor, mail was still delivered from Cooktown to Laura by rail until the line closed after Christmas Day 1961.

Years of monsoonal floods damaged the concrete pylons of the bridge at Laura until, on the unlucky thirteenth of March 1940 over 300 millimetres of rain falling in twelve hours destroyed one of the piers and two spans were washed downstream. The remains of the bridge were sold to the Tully Sugar Mill for use on its cane train lines in 1958 and taken to its Tully owners by the new road, then called the Mulligan Highway.

The little railway served its purpose during its lifetime and helped make several mail runs faster and more efficient. The old Byerstown coach mail also declined with the lessened production of gold and the mail run was terminated at Butcher's Hill cattle station. For some time the route was run by the station owners concerned but Norman Watkin of Helenvale took on the contract using either horses or a truck depending on the weather. The mail was taken to Helenvale from Cooktown and then distributed to King's Plains, Springvale and Butcher's Hill.

Courtesy Meredith Monro

All that's left of the Laura — Maytown Bridge
July 1965

At the turn of the century there was an increasing demand for a mail service to the tin fields behind Cooktown. As the easy gold cut out, many miners made the transition to tin. Some of the heavy mining machinery was also transferred laboriously from the Palmer to the tin fields. A weekly horse mail was instituted from Cooktown to Ayton (Bloomfield) stopping at Helenvale, Mt. Amos, Mt. Leswell, Rossville and Mt. Romeo along the way. In 1904 Cooktown was described by a Postal Inspector[3]as 'a coastal township about eleven hours steam from Cairns and the district town for portion of the Peninsula and surrounding tin fields.' The population was eight hundred and the residents were given a delivery carried one day a week by the Telegraph linesman 'when he was available'. When he was otherwise engaged, letter delivery was made by casual labour at fifty cents a day plus a further fifty cents for the mail deliverer's horse.

Billy Beirnes, Mailman

The longest mail run was the one that picked up mail in Laura and delivered it to Coen. From Coen, lesser runs serviced small mining settlements. Billy Beirnes who had the contract from 1st January 1927 to 31st January 1932 told me that the distance on his contract for the mail was 182 miles (about 300k) 'out' and 165 miles (about 260k) 'in'. On the trip up from Laura mail was taken to Laura and Lakefield stations before crossing back to the Telegraph Line at Musgrave. On the trip back, mail was taken on past Musgrave to Koolburra, Fairview and Old Fairview cattle station about 3k from Fairview. When it was run as a weekly mail, two men and their horses would combine to run it, meeting halfway and thus halving the distance each had to travel.

Courtesy Reg Starcke

Packhorse delivery — Rossville

Billy himself had seventy horses and his contract was for up to seventy horses carrying loads of 150 pounds (about 67kgs). He left Laura usually with '68 bags beside parcels'. Parcels could be carried out of the mailbags as top load. Until Billy's contract ended parcels were limited to three pounds (under 2kgs) with an extra sixpence (5c) per pound (about 500gms) paid to the contractor for any exceeding the limit. The mailman, Gunter, who took over from Billy Beirnes undercut the contract price to 250 pounds a year and agreed to carry parcels up to 5kgs without charge.

According to Billy, among the earlier contractors were Martin Carey and the Corbett brothers, Fred and Peter who ran it at the end of the nineteenth century. From Post Office records, a Pat Corbett had the Cooktown to Butcher's Hill contract, M.S.154, from 1898 to 1900. The contract price paid for his weekly mail was 47 pounds per year. Fred Corbett was the Coen mailman when winds from a cyclone (Mahina) struck the Musgrave Telegraph Station in 1899. The building was blown 'clear off its piles and split in two halves'. It blew the telegraph wires into the forest country in a fifty kilometre strip and according to Billy 'killed all the birds from Laura to Coen.' Billy didn't meet with any major cyclones while he was mailman but, at Dead Horse Creek (named for that dead roan mare) a lightning strike knocked him off his horse and burnt his trousers. When Fred Corbett was asked by a reporter if tribal members had mail delivered, Fred was able to say 'yes'. On several occasions he had taken carved message sticks from one tribal representative to another.

Billy Beirnes recalled a mob of 400 naked Aborigines camped at the Morehead Crossing early in the century. There was 'no harm in them'. In 1901, at the new Ebagoolah goldrush a man named Louis Mock strayed away from his camp. A party of miners and Police went looking for him without finding anything but boot tracks in a dry gully about 25k from his camp. Everyone assumed that the 'wild blacks' had got him. After seventeen days, a mob of 'fifty or sixty' aborigines turned up at Ebagoolah with Louis. They had found him about sixty kilometres away, given him food and water, looked after him and brought him back safely. The Police took up a collection of flour, calico, tobacco, matches and knives plus 'a lot more' and gave them to Louis' rescuers. Louis said that if it weren't for the Aborigines, he'd have been 'done for'.

Some of the tribes from the Gulf side would come inland during the Wet season and drive away any horses that they could find. They'd take them down the Lukin and Coleman Rivers and eat them, Billy recalled.

In his retirement Billy lived at the old Musgrave homestead, died there and is buried under the old mango tree near another mailman Matt Carroll. Matt had been a sandalwood cutter working inland from Cooktown at the head of the Laura River, near the present-day Lakeland. A deep hole on the Laura River, above the crossing, Carroll's Hole, and the twin camel-humped peaks, Carroll's Peaks, bear his name. Matt had the Laura to Coen contract at the turn of the century. He had a urinary condition that entailed the use of a catheter. When he did not turn up at Musgrave as expected, a party went looking for him and found him dead in his camp on the south bank of the Morehead. Apparently he'd either lost the catheter or was unable to insert it.

Quite a few mailmen died on the job. A young Cooktown 'lad', Billy told me, was running the mail to Coen, possibly from the Rocky Creek Goldfield. He camped at the foot of the range on the Coen to Port Stewart road but though the mail and his horses were at the camp, there was no sign of him. They 'only found one boot' and the opinion was that he'd gone looking for a horse and hit Breakfast Creek which was 'full of alligators'. His name was Bannon and he was working for Matt Carroll. Billy thought it happened before 1900.

Another mailman, lost and fearing he would die an agonising death from thirst, shot himself on Lakefield. He didn't know that a search party was close enough to hear the fatal shot and galloped up, thinking he'd fired it to alert them to his whereabouts. Calder's Lake perpetuates his memory.

Packhorse Mailman, Jim McDowell

The most famous of the packhorse mailmen and one who also died on the job was Jim McDowell. Before taking on the packhorse mail from Laura to Coen, Jim was in charge of Lakefield cattle station, one of the best runs in the Peninsula. He was there from 1926-1935. Jim was an excellent horseman and sometimes could be persuaded to show his talent by cutting-out a beast from the mob without using a bridle on his horse. His best camphorses were well known, Boodgerie (good) and Pinchgut. A hard rider, very few, if any, cattle ever got away from him, yet he never had a sore-backed horse and few could equal him in his day as a bull-tosser. Jim had a few anxious moments one day in the company of Brian Grogan of Laura Station and a visiting cattle buyer. He was riding Pinchgut when a wild boar charged him. It slashed out at Pinchgut cutting four joints from the unfortunate horse's tail. A good bush vet., Jim stopped the bleeding and Pinchgut's only worry was when the flies were bad. Its tail was far too short to reach them.

Jim was multi-skilled even more than most bushmen. He repaired his own saddlery gear, tanning the leather used and making superb plaited bridles, whips and breastplates. Whittling was another of his occupations and he and his mates were never short of handmade pipes and cigarette holders. Entertainment-wise he was an excellent teller of tall tales. It was hard to tell when the truth ended. His stories were so exciting yet believable, both at the same time. Another talent was for playing the gumleaf. To those who have never had the pleasure of hearing a leaf 'played', it is well worth listening to. It is also an excellent way to alert someone of your approach. The sound travels for miles on a still night and the player could always be sure that the billy would be boiling when the leaf-player rode in to the alerted camp.

For a period[4] Jim ran the shorter Coen to Moreton mail. After leaving Lakefield in the mid-1930s he took on the big one — Laura to Coen. Someone good at maths calculated that, in the fifteen years that Jim ran the Laura to Coen mail he rode 144,300 miles with the mails — or an even more impressive 232,323k. This worked out at nearly 10,000 miles or 16,000k each year by horse

Courtesy H. Macquarrie

Packhorse mailman, Jim McDowell

and with packhorse mail-carriers. Jim carried corn for his pet horses in dry times, a fruit-tinful each at night. In emergencies he sometimes had to airfreight corn to Coen but usually laid by a generous supply brought up by coastal boat.

As a rule Jim would leave Laura with fourteen loaded packhorses. The 185 miles (300k) took seven daylight-to-dark days with the horses. He would arrive in Coen on Tuesday night, stay over on Wednesday checking gear, washing clothes and doing his routine chores, before commencing the return journey which took another six very long days. At this time, it was a fortnightly mail service run by the one mailman. Jim took one day 'off' in fourteen. He had a base of about a hundred from which to select his work-horses. Some were left at Laura, another mob roughly halfway at the Morehead and some in Coen. In emergencies, the Gostelow family and other cattlemen would lend him a spare horse or two.

The year 1951 was a bad year for Jim and a very sad one for the people of the Peninsula. Passing through Violetvale, Bowie Gostelow[5] gave Jim a gelding to ride. Bowie had not long bought it in Mareeba and it had a rather rudimentary education but Jim was experiencing one of his rare horse shortages. Fred Gostelow also gave him a mare to pack. The mare had a foal and it was left behind in the Violetvale stockyards to be weaned. It was a Sunday and only two or three hours after Jim and his team left, the Gostelow packmare came galloping back to her foal in the yards. Realising something had gone wrong — the mare still carried the packbags — Fred, his brother Matt and an Aboriginal stockman they called Oscar or The Jap hurried out to see what had gone wrong.

They found Jim lying on the ground, unconscious, in the middle of his scattered horses close to the Eight Mile Creek near the Telegraph Line on the Coen side of Violetvale. Bowie's horse, still saddled was feeding about with the others. Fred tried to make Jim comfortable without moving him much and, leaving Matt and The Jap to watch over Jim, Fred immediately rode off to Musgrave where he was able to contact the Aerial Ambulance by phone. Fortunately, Ian Pratt was there with his truck and with John Barry and Maurice

Shephard to help road-build, they set off to reach the injured man. Though they became bogged twice and had to negotiate what looked like impassable patches they got through to the injured mailman. He was still unconscious. They transferred him with the utmost care to a mattress laid in the tray back of the truck and proceeded carefully back to Musgrave. From there the valiant little Aerial Ambulance plane flew him quickly to the Cairns Base Hospital. Tragically, Jim never regained consciousness but died in hospital about a week later. His death signalled the end of an era.

The Violetvale men mustered the scattered horses and Ian Pratt took the mailbags straight on to Coen using the old Port Stewart road. Fred Gostelow ran the mail for three years after Jim's death. His brother Bowie and Christie Steensen did a few trips for him when Fred was too busy with station work but the days of the packhorse mailman were numbered. Firstly, trucks and four-wheel-drives took over when traffic became possible on the new road from Laura north, an extension of the Mulligan Highway. Finally, the mail came by air. Bush Pilots Airways took on most of the more remote mail services and proved themselves to be excellent mailmen.

Shorter Mailruns ex Cooktown

The smaller mail runs operating out from Cooktown continued on with a combination of horse and vehicle mail depending on the weather. Trucks were used when road surfaces allowed. Often repairs had to be done as the vehicles progressed, especially after the Wet when the rain caused so much damage. So much more could be carried on a truck than with a team of packhorses that the drivers persevered. When the road was completely untrafficable, the mail reverted to four-legged transport or the stations went without mail and emergency supplies.

Charlie Wallace took his turn at running the mail from Helenvale to his property Butcher's Hill, delivering and collecting mail at King's Plains and Springvale on the way. Vehicles could usually make their way from Helenvale to Cooktown and vice versa. When Charlie was mailman it was a good idea not to order that new Akubra hat from R.M.Williams. Bulky cardboard hatboxes were anathema to him and to most packhorse mailmen. The chosen hat looked so entrancing in the Bushman's Catalogue with its high crown with an aesthetic dent either side of the front and its wide curling brim upswept elegantly at the sides with a slight droop fore and aft, but it usually ended up pork pie shape as Charlie re-modelled the box and its contents to fit his packbags. The message was crystal clear. Order your new hat for The Races only when Norman carried the mail on his truck.

6

The Sandalwood Trade and Pearl Diving

Sandalwood, its excellent quality and the harvesting of it · Hughenden wood for Gandhi's funeral pyre · Trials and tribulations of pearl and trochus shell · Burns Philp's part in the action · Ion Idriess' vision of commercial sandalwood plantations and a future for the healing and other qualities of native flora and fauna · Trepang collection and export · Mrs. Watson of Lizard Island, 1881 · The Bathurst Bay cyclone, 'Mahina', 1899

Sandalwood or *Santalum* was as precious to the Chinese and other Orientals as their tea leaves were to become to Europeans. There are many varieties. *Santalum Album,* which grows in India, the Sandwich Islands and Polynesia, was perhaps the largest producer of oil and incense wood. *Santalum Austro Caledonicum,* a very good 'producer of highly scented oil'[1]came, as the name suggests from New Caledonia. At first, Sydney was the closest base for trading with the cutters of New Caledonia and Fiji and as early as the first decade of the nineteenth century American, British and Australian traders worked from this port to export to the East. When natural supplies of this tree became low it was cultivated both in India and in New Caledonia. The North Australian tree to be harvested was usually *Santalum Preissanum* of the same family as the Quandong or Native Peach. The sandalwood oil was obtained by a slow distillation process and yielded about two and a half per cent oil.

Want's Will O' The Wisp

During the surveys of the Far Northern Coast undertaken by the *Rattlesnake, Bramble* and the *Asp,* with Captain Owen Stanley and naturalists John MacGillivray and Thomas Huxley on board in 1846-50, they met up with the *Will O' the Wisp,* a 25 ton cutter owned by an eccentric Sydney businessman named Want. The survey vessels were anchored off Fitzroy Island and the yacht was sailing from the south. Want customarily sent the cutter north in a great deal of secrecy to search for sandalwood on the north eastern coast of Cape York Peninsula. When a commercially viable amount of the scented wood was cut, the *Will O' the Wisp* returned to Moreton Bay and Want commissioned a larger vessel to take the sandalwood on to China. This was in June 1848, well before Queensland became a separate Colony. The previous year almost a thousand tons of sandalwood were exported to China at thirty pounds ($60) a ton from New Caledonia, the New Hebrides and other island bases.

When Huxley boarded the *Will O' the Wisp* off Fitzroy Island[2] for an unofficial call, he found that the services of a surgeon were required. The *Will O' the Wisp* had been attacked off Palm Island. Roach, the Captain, had made contact with the natives 'giving them presents and allowing some on board'. Unfortunately this only whetted their appetite for more of the white man's treasures. They attacked in the early hours of the morning, throwing lighted bark into the cabin to smoke the sailors out. Roach, the skipper, and Sam, a Kanaka, received serious head injuries and became Huxley's patients. Roach's skull was fractured. Using a sword, the sailors eventually managed to clear the decks during the attack and escaped further assaults for the time. However they were again attacked at Goold Island and returned from there to Moreton Bay.

Matt Carroll

Matt Carroll, the mailman who died a painful death on the bank of the Morehead River, was one of the cutters who worked the slopes of the Byerstown Range near the head of the Laura River. The tree did not grow to a great size and the trunk rarely exceeded six inches (15cm) diameter. Roots were also used for oil extraction and the best timber was reserved for use in carving and in making fancy boxes. Like camphorwood it contained a natural insect repellent. The Laura River sandalwood-getters packed their sandalwood to Cooktown in four to five feet lengths (120-150cms) each weighing today's 13 to 18 kgs. It was estimated that ten packhorses could comfortably carry a ton of wood a distance of 25k in a day. Most wood was slung in straps from the hooks of the packsaddle but a few cutters sent their wood attached vertically. They considered that the ends of the lengths at times became damaged as they protruded and hit trees. The latter method wasn't common usage but Sam Elliott, the last of the Maytown miners, in his posthumous autobiography, *The Lone Wolf*, tells of carting it in this vertical mode. To clinch the argument he wrote, 'I have done years of work with packhorses so I know what I'm talking about.'[3]By 1900 and for the next two decades, sandalwood whose price had risen to just under $300 per ton, was an export of considerable importance.

Coastal Landings For Sandalwood Trade

Lockhart River, named by Robert Logan Jack for a boyhood Scottish friend, was one of the waterways used by the sandalwood cutters on the north eastern coast of the Peninsula. Gold prospectors working the adjacent goldfields took advantage of Giblet's Landing, 12k from the mouth of the Lockhart River also. From Giblet's Landing the sandalwood was usually taken to Thursday Island. Burns Philp's[4] small ships often picked up the scented wood direct from landings on the mainland and on the coast of New Guinea. From Thursday Island it was transhipped by the larger E. and A. steamers for sale in the East. Hong Kong was a favoured trading port. The trade wasn't without risk for Burns Philp as the price of sandalwood on a free world market was apt to drop suddenly without warning. Money advanced by Burns Philp to small traders to cover their costs, at times could not be recovered from the sales. Attempts were made to establish a combine to regulate the overseas marketing of both sandalwood and pearlshell but this did not necessarily result in a better price for the sandalwood cutters or for the divers. Burns Philp seemed to have moderate success in manipulating the risk-prone sandalwood market but as the supply in New Guinea lessened so did the desire of the cutters to supply the commodity. In 1907, in a worldwide recession, the Hong Kong sandalwood market virtually collapsed.

Hugh Giblet and Harry Edmundson were the more successful among the earliest cutters. Giblet handled the business and marketing side while Edmundson was responsible for the cutting and packing. It was a good combination. The partnership commenced operations in the hills inland from Cooktown, moving up through the Princess Charlotte Bay area to the Nesbit, Hays Creek, Lockhart River and Portland Roads area. A 'slab hut' [5] was built as a receiving depot. Aborigines, paid in tea, sugar, tobacco and clothes, did most of the cutting. Women and often children helped with the salvage of the sandalwood's roots. George Craig and Billy Partridge were in charge of the cutting and packed the timber to the landing places using horses bought from departing prospectors. As many as two hundred Aborigines would be employed in cutting and stacking the wood together with their women and juvenile assistants. Tomahawks were the preferred implements used. Axes were considered to be too heavy to swing and considering the size of the sandalwood they weren't really necessary.

Sandalwood was cut from the slopes of the McIlwraith, Macrossan and Janet Ranges, all sites too for gold prospectors. As that area became cut out, the cutters moved further north to as far as Kennedy's Escape River. For a while, when the industry was at a high, veteran Peninsula prospector Willy Lakeland and his West Australian counterpart Peter White, forsook the search for the more elusive mineral gold to cut the readily available sandalwood for Craig and Partridge then sub-contracting for Giblet and Edmundson. According to M.W. Sheehan, Partridge must have done some prospecting on his day off from his sandalwood duties. Sheehan reported[6] that Partridge's party obtained 30 ounces of gold on the Batavia, as a result of which Partridge 'made quite a figure in London society'.

Another sandalwood base camp was at Mackunga Creek on the west coast near where Arukun was later established. Morey and Co., Townsville, were agents for most of the three hundred tons shipped from there. Tommy Ah Kum and Hip Wah and Co. also bought the scented wood in Coen. Cutters worked the hills around the McIlwraith Range for many years. Frequent references are made of the activity in the reports made by James Dick, John Dickie and Arthur Sheffield in mid-1910 when they were on a Government-sponsored expedition to the McIlwraith and Macrossan Ranges on a mineral survey. They often met the cutters and their packhorse teams. On July 8th they made camp with Ned James who was packing for Giblet. Ned had twenty-five horses fully loaded with the precious timber and had three Aboriginal helpers to assist with the packing and unpacking. They encountered Ned again in early October in a 'party of blacks',[7] the latter generously provided the explorers with a feast of poultry, 'an emu, a turkey and a hen which they had shot.' It was very welcome.

The best quality sandalwood came from the arid country around Hughenden. It was said to be equal to the best Mysore (India) wood. This reputation for high quality was borne out when Mahatma Gandhi was assassinated in 1948. The wood used in his cremation pyre came from Hughenden. Santalum from the Gulf was almost as high in quality and the Peninsula wood a little below that. The native sandalwood in Western Australia was slightly inferior to these three but the cutters there were much more business-orientated. They vertically integrated into a plant to extract the oil and exported a large proportion as oil rather than as just the raw material for someone else to reap the profits.

'Bob Bloodwood' (Bob Pearce) of Hughenden in his old *Sundowner* column in the *North Queensland Register* told the tale of the Hughenden sandalwood cutter who tried to put one over the State Government — and lost out. Once the Government realised that there was money to be made from sandalwood growing on their Crown Lands they imposed a heavy Royalty payment, far above that on the more ordinary timbers. This cutter, when shipping a load of sandalwood to his buyer in Townsville, decided to send it as rosewood which attracted only a fraction of the sandalwood's Royalty. The astute buyer paid rosewood prices for the wood and as it was described as just that in the accompanying paperwork, there was nothing the cutter could do about it. Bob Pearce, a sandalwood cutter himself, must have felt deeply for him.

Ion Idriess Recommends Growing Sandalwood Commercially in 1945

Sandalwood harvesting had a renaissance in the late 1980s and 1990s when phenomenal prices were offered for the aromatic wood. Sandalwood is now being grown commercially. Western Australia and the Northern Territory are the leaders in this enterprise. Ion Idriess, Light Horseman,[8] miner and author of dozens of books about the bush and his W.W.I experiences, was also a sandalwood cutter. With his mate Dick Welch he first cut the fragrant wood in the Cooktown area. Dick previously worked for the Sandalwood King, Hughie Giblet, and often told Jack stories of harvesting the wood in the Far North. In 1926 when Ion re-visited the top country with 'Bootles' Jardine in the twenty-seven foot (nine metres) cutter *Somerset* they landed at Giblet's old camp at Lloyds Bay, 320k north of Cooktown. After hearing Dick's tales, Idriess was sadly disappointed to find that even after diligent searching, very little of the old settlement remained. Giblet had a fleet of small boats in which he took tons of sandalwood to Thursday Island, returning loaded with stores and other necessities for the Lloyds Bay settlement.

Idriess's trip was sponsored by the Queensland Government Mines Department but it turned out to be, according to Idriess 'the silliest wild goose chase'. He and Jardine were to prospect for gold deposits. However Idriess thought that the idea of finding gold there was based on the legendary story of Deadman's Gold in which fabulous gold is found, rich beyond the wildest dreams. The discoverer dies after telling the secret on his deathbed to another man who re-discovers the gold and himself dies after bequeathing the gold's whereabouts to another. And so the story goes on — and on and on — but the gold has not yet been located. Idriess was a man with many passionate interests. As well as recording the days of a long-gone era he had a practical, if visionary, insight into the future. In a book published in the *Battle for Australia* series in 1945 he gives evidence of his forward-thinking by suggesting that sandalwood could well be grown commercially. He also advocated using today's value-adding principles as Western Australia did so that the precious oil could be exported from local extraction plants.[9] As well he recommended the extraction of oil from a range of suitable indigenous trees.

In the days of the Palmer goldrush, oil was extracted from the Lemon-scented Iron Bark native to that area and sold to local miners for medicinal use. Possibly the idea came from some of the thousands of Chinese miners on the field. The traces of the oil stills would be easy to miss as the stills were merely domed ovens made of antbed, dirt and rock. The leaves were arranged on a rack over a metal tray to collect the escaping oil and heat was applied from small fires within the dome to extract the oil from the leaves. Tannin from the bark of suitable trees was another of Idriess's ideas. In 1906 Australia exported

189,699 pounds worth (not much short of $400,000) of tannin bark for leather tanning. It also exported seeds from the trees used. South Africa wasn't about to miss this opportunity and with the Australian seed started its own tannin industry so that, forty years later, this country was importing the product from the more technically-minded and astute South Africans.

Idriess wrote in *Onward Australia* of the elation experienced by the sandalwood hunters on finding a good stand of the timber. It equaled 'the thrill of a prospector striking the yellow metal' and he makes the point that the trees 'were gold; they were good money.' Eventually most of the prolific stands were cut out. Idriess suggested that young trees could be planted out 'in places not so liable to fires' as their oil content made them very fire-prone. As the sandalwood grew on poor country, often along the banks of creeks and gullies, he considered that an added bonus would be a 'protection against creek bank erosion'. While the trees were reaching maturity and profitability, cattle could still be run on the property thus providing a supplementary income.

Experiments With Local 'Chicle'

He was also impressed with the Aborigines' 'first class knowledge of botany' and predicted a successful future not only for the commercial production of what is now fashionably called 'bush tucker' but also for the medicinal products inherent in their 'bush' remedies both plant and insect. One product Idriess was interested in went a step further. With 'old Joseph Campbell, the parson, chemist and metallurgist' he gathered a quantity of native gum like the chicle used in chewing gum. The locals called its source 'milkwood'. The Cook Shire Chamber of Commerce had faith in the experiment and put a room at the Council Chambers at the enthusiast's disposal. Using it as a lab., Campbell purified the gum to the required standard and sent samples to chewing-gum manufacturers in the United States of America. The chicle 'passed with flying colours' but no orders resulted. Chicle gum from neighbouring South America could be imported more cheaply and once again the Peninsula missed out.

Idriess's vision extended to making the inland blossom by the use of Dr. Bradfield's irrigation scheme which would divert eastern coastal rivers over the range to water the west. He supported plans for hydro-electricity from 'tidal rivers and waterways', for cultivating pearl shell for nacre and gems and also for farming sharks for their vitamin-rich liver oil. Americans experimenting with shark liver after the Germans captured the Norwegian cod fisheries in WW2, found that the substitute shark oil was even superior to the original cod liver oil. Other propositions Idriess put forward were to manufacture paper from the ubiquitous, but otherwise useless, Blady Grass and, one dear to cattlemen, to establish abattoirs in the cattle-producing areas rather than at the ports. When it is realised that these ideas were promulgated in the 1940s, it makes Idriess a true visionary.

Cabinet Timbers and Logging

There was a ready market for the rich cabinet timbers growing in the far northern rain forests. Cedar and silky oak, maple and black bean were avidly sought after and led to the logging and milling of stands of timber in the higher rainfall areas. While much timber was lost in the clearing of farmland, trees felled for timber were subject to stringent Forestry Department regulations. When milling was stopped in the Ravenshoe area of the Atherton Tableland local residents were more than a little cynical when the then Senator Richardson expounded on the beauties of the pristine rainforest before him. The section he referred to had been logged three times, each time with the harvest restricted to large trees and with heavy penalties for any possible damage done to younger growth in the process.

Cooktown had its own sawmill and many neighbourhood homes were furnished with household goods made from the local product. The handiwork of local cabinetmakers like Albion Seagren was eagerly sought after in Cooktown and in towns to the south. Mission stations set up around the Peninsula coastline usually erected their own sawmill to prepare timber for the Mission homes and other buildings. Bloomfield went one step further and established a plymill.

Captain Banner Starts Pearling 1869

The resources searched for were not confined to those on the land. The sea provided the opportunity to make a living from its denizens. Luggers sought out not only the highly prized pearl and pearl shell but also trochus shell and trepang or beche de mer. Turtles and fish were also caught for local consumption. A Captain Dawson was the first Australian-based mariner to report the presence of pearlshell[10]. He was on his way from Sydney to Western Australia and did not attempt to acquire any of the shell. That honour goes to Captain Banner who obtained a 'sample' of five tons of superior shell from Woppa Reef in the Torres Strait in 1869. His financer, a Mr. Merryman from Sydney, was so impressed with the quality that he sent Banner back to Woppa the following year. The schooner returned to Sydney with seventy-five tons of shell which were sold on arrival for fifty pounds ($100, then a very substantial sum) a ton. The following year, Banner made another trip but on the return voyage the schooner was wrecked. Fortunately, the astute Mr. Merryman had

Trochus boats on the Endeavour River

insured the vessel and its cargo and he was paid for the ship and fifty tons of shell.

Banner, a 'black bearded giant'[11], found pearls by chance. With Kebisu of Tutu (Warrior Island), another giant of a man, he was watching a corroboree and a war dance. Supper was barbecued pearl mussels. The pearl shells were thrown onto a cooking fire regardless of the beauty of the shell until the 'agonised oyster within' popped open the shell to 'stew in its own juice'. Then followed the feasting. From time to time Banner noticed that the Islanders would spit out or throw something annoying them into the sand. This attracted the Captain's attention and he followed the path of these throw-aways. 'Roasted pearls!'Apart from wearing the odd huge pearl as decoration, the lustrous gems had no value to the Islanders.

Kebisu, although concerned about the effect European customs and behaviour would have on his people, continued his friendship with Banner that lasted until the latter's death. With the coming of 'civilisation', diseases hitherto unknown in the Straits wiped-out great numbers of the island people.

Captain Banner revisited Woppa Reef in 1872 but died there and was buried on Tutu (Warrior Island). As well as Thursday Island, known initially as Port Kennedy, pearling stations were scattered throughout the islands of the Torres Strait. On Nagheer (Mt. Ernst) Island, a Samoan, James Mills, operated a fleet of three pearling boats.

In the early days, there was no need to dive for shell. Islanders and New Guineans would merely wade or swim over the reefs to obtain the nacreous shell for their beautiful pearlshell ornaments. Somerset, and later Thursday Island, became the base for the pearlers and their native crews. Two types of shell were found, the larger *Meleagrina Margaritifera* and the slightly smaller Blacklip. When diving dress and airpumps were introduced, shell could be obtained from greater depths and the 'swimming' boats gave way to 'diving' boats. Expert swimmers could work in depths of up to six fathoms (12 metres). 'Dress' divers could operate at depths almost four times as great and deep-sea divers could dive to depths of sixty metres.

Swimmers and divers were at first paid at a fixed rate per hundred shells. Later it was set at a percentage of the weight of the cleaned shell. Pearls were a welcome bonus at any time but the pearl shell was also very much in demand for inlay, jewellery and buttons. It was very marketable. Once the industry got under way it attracted Japanese interest and Japanese divers were employed.

The Reverend White [12]quoted figures from the years 1909 to 1913 to show the numbers of divers engaged and the fatalities incurred. The number of divers ranged between 149 in 1909 and 198 in 1912. Thirteen, on average, died each year from divers' paralysis with another one or two divers succumbing to 'accidental' fatal injuries.

Very large, 'irregular and imperfect' pearls found a ready market in India and the Orient but the higher quality, more uniform pearls were reserved for the European market and sold through outlets in London and Paris. Trochus shell was also a valuable resource. Both Thursday Island and Cooktown served as bases for the luggers. In the mid-twentieth century, the Anglican Mission at Lockhart River also had its own fleet of three trochus boats. The superintendent, John Warby, had considerable experience with shell before he came to Lockhart and guided the Lockhart River people in their enterprise. The Mission did well out of this operation financing some of the improvements at Lockhart but unfortunately, plastic buttons came upon the scene and the trochus market plummeted.

Courtesy Reg Starcke

Trochus and pearl luggers at Thursday Island

Japanese, Papuan, Philippine and Local Divers

Burns Philp established themselves at Thursday Island and extended to branches in New Guinea. By the late 1880s the company had a large stake in the industry with a considerable financial interest. They were, according to C.A.W. Monckton, a 'good old Scottish firm of trade grabbers ..... sending their ships, in spite of any risk, wherever a possible bawbee could be made and took their hundred per cent of profit with the same dour front they took their frequently trebled loss.'[13]By 1895 the fleet in which Burns Philp had a financial interest had grown to thirty-four boats valued at some 40,000 pounds ($80,000).[14] Japanese divers and often Papuan crew were used. After 1895, the profitability of pearling at Thursday Island decreased. Part of this was due to the numbers of boats trying to cash in on the market, from 204 in 1895 to 341 in 1900. This brought the average catch down as the number of boats went up making it unprofitable for some boat-owners. Manilla-men and Papuans were also used as divers but Japanese were preferred because, a Burns Philp manager reported to a Royal Commission, of their fatalistic attitude. If one were paralysed with the divers' 'bends', his mates kept on diving. It was his 'fate' and his fate was not necessarily the same as that of his compatriots. With the Manilla-men and Papuans, the reverse was true. If one man were affected 'the whole lot knocked off.'

Burns Philp attempted to 'regulate' the overseas marketing of both sandalwood and shell as the profits fell off at the beginning of the twentieth century. With the falling market individual shippers were undercutting each other's prices to get what contracts were on offer. Pearlshell was sold to merchants in London who were very astute in dealing with disorganised producers. As John Steinbeck wrote in his book *The Pearl*, 'The best and the happiest pearl buyer was he who bought for the lowest prices.' By 1905 Burns Philp's Wyben Pearling Fleet was producing one-third of the shell from the Torres Strait. The world production was of 3,000 tons valued at a million dollars. Of this the northern Western Australian pearl luggers produced a third and the boats from the Torres Strait a fifth. As is usual in Australia, the problem was that the shell had to be exported to find a market. There was none existent in Australia. The shell's main use was for button making, jewellery and decorative inlay. Pearls found were a welcome extra. With the outbreak of W.W.1 pearlshell became almost unsaleable at any price. Other commodities were considered to be more necessary.

Beche De Mer , Mary Watson And Cyclone Mahina

In earlier days beche de mer, sea-cucumbers or trepang met a ready market in China and many boats up and down the coast of the Peninsula were engaged in supplying the demand. As well as the local boats, schooners, cutters and luggers came in from Asia to join the quest for trepang and shell. Joining the local men, other divers came from the East, the South Sea Islands and the Malay Archipelago. As the fleets plying the trade increased, a small Government vessel, the *Albatross*, was used to patrol the shell and beche de mer fisheries of the Peninsula and Gulf. Fleets of proas from the islands of Indonesia frequented the northern coasts also looking for trepang. At low tide, the sea slugs were easily harvested. They were boiled, dried in the heat of the sun and smoked. The finished product was highly regarded in China as a base for soup, but only the wealthy were able to afford this luxury.

Captain Robert Watson, husband of the tragic Mary who died of thirst while trying to escape with her baby and Chinese helper from an Aboriginal attack on their Lizard Island home, was a beche de mer man. He and his partner had made the decision to move their base on Lizard to the more northerly Night Island. Mary asked that she and the baby stay on Lizard Island until a home was ready for them on Night. It was before the men returned to pick up the family and their Chinese helpers that the Aborigines attacked killing one of the Chinese, Ah Leong. Mary made her escape with the three months old Ferrier and the other Chinese servant, Ah Sam, who was wounded. She left the island in the metal ship's tank used for boiling the trepang. The *Kate Kearney* found their remains on one of the islands of the Howick Group. Mrs. Watson's skeleton was embracing the skeletal remains of her baby, her hand clasping the tiny finger bones. She was found on 16th January 1882 on the day before what should have been her twenty-second birthday.[15]

Another tragedy struck in 1899 when over a hundred schooners and their attendant cutters were sunk in Bathurst Bay by the savage winds of Cyclone Mahina. Over three hundred lives were lost. Included in the death toll were some Aborigines who lost their lives trying to rescue people from the stricken boats. The catastrophe decimated the pearling fleet and it never regained its strength.

7

From Gold to Tin Mining and the Nascent Cattle Industry

Palmer alluvial cuts out · Miners leave for Hodgkinson Goldfield, 1876 · Harry Harbord and his Anglo-Saxon mine · Miners on the Normanby, part of the Palmer field · Far northern goldfields discovered and working from 1878 · Kitty Pluto, an Aboriginal woman, discovers gold at Lower Camp, 1915 · Miners find profitable tin in the watercourses behind Cooktown · Farmers diversify into traditional crops while others value-add with dried banana flour and medal-winning cigars

While the Palmer was an exceedingly rich goldfield, it could not continue producing large amounts of gold indefinitely. It was predominantly an alluvial field though some very good reefs were worked. It did not take long for its speciality, the small nuggets that lodged in the crevices of the rocky bars and could be picked up 'like hens pecking corn' by eager miners, to disappear. Alluvial workings made good money for years and tens of thousands of Chinese worked hard to harvest the golden gullies that were their province. How much gold left illegally from coastal landings to the north of Cooktown can only be guessed at. In 1876, the Hodgkinson, also discovered by Mulligan, attracted a swathe of miners from the Palmer to work what proved to be mainly reef gold.

R.L. Jack reported that 90% of the gold produced from the Palmer, which totalled by 1896 to a value of some five and a half million pounds sterling, was of alluvial origin but the reefs also produced well. The prospect of a railway line from the port to the field caused more interest in reef mining and additional operations were initiated but, of course, the rail line didn't eventuate. Lack of capital for the ever-increasing need for water pumping and winding machinery limited the progress of the reefing sector. Many mines were abandoned when water could not be handled simply by windlass and bucket. Suitable timber for reinforcing the shafts was in short supply locally also. It was hoped that rail transport direct from port to field could alleviate this problem. Some of the mines, despite the 'heavy water', were excellent producers. Both the Ida and the

Louisa consistently returned two ounces of first grade gold to the ton of ore crushed. They were not alone in this average but were consistent producers. The names of some of the mines reflected their owners' sentiments colourfully — the Just in Time, Best Friend, Better Luck, Hit or Miss, Happy Go Lucky, Jeweller's Shop, Keep it Dark, Good Hopes and Happy Thoughts were some of the up-beat names. On the other hand there were also mines with the names Disappointment, Last Chance and Passed By.

Harbord, Groganville, Quartzborough and Normanby Fields

Some of the miners leaving the Palmer pulled up on the headwaters of the Mitchell at what was to become Harbord, Groganville and Quartzborough. Harry Harbord with his mate Owen Foley did well on the Palmer, obtaining an incredible 24kgs[1] — not ounces — in six weeks. In a report of the Palmer Field by Robert Logan Jack in 1899 he quotes the Anglo Saxon P.C. as producing 22,683 ounces of gold from crushings of 14,178 tons since 1887. Anglo Saxon West No 1 produced a further 6,488 ounces. Harbord left the main Palmer field to check out the Hodgkinson and found on his return that Chinese had appropriated his claim there. The Anglo Saxon reef at Groganville was, as Robert Logan Jack recorded, 'a considerable producer of gold.' It was situated over sixty kilometres from Maytown, a long day's ride but well worth the effort. Paddy Grogan, publican, backed Harbord in his gold search. Harbord's working partner was a Hans Kummer from Saxony. Harry Harbord was an 'Anglo'. They put the two places of origin together to get the name for their claim and obtained an exceptional result. In the early 1880s prospecting had been undertaken along Limestone Creek, the Mitchell tributary on which Groganville, Harbord and Quartzborough took their places. Fortunately for Harbord, Grogan and Kummer the early prospectors missed finding their rich Anglo Saxon Reef.

Other miners crossed the Dividing Range to the Normanby River which was still on the Palmer Goldfield despite the waters of the Palmer River flowing west while the Normanby River entered Princess Charlotte Bay on the eastern coast. The Normanby sustained mining for quite a few years but as early as the late 1870s, a group called the Cooktown Prospecting Association arranged with miner Donald Laing to take a party further north seeking gold. Laing left Cooktown just before the Wet on 13th November 1879 and with the monsoonal rain and lack of geographical knowledge of the area to which he was going, the expedition was not a success. The party returned safely after the Wet in 1880. They reached the headwaters of the Archer River and Laing named Sefton Creek after that worthy pioneer prospector of the far north, Robert Sefton. They did find some gold but it was not, they considered, in payable quantities.

The shortage of both feed and water for themselves and their horses added to their problems.

Some miners had been so disturbed by the influx of Chinese goldseekers to the Palmer that they left early to seek their fortunes further north. Even before Laing made his trip, Robert Sefton and Sam Verge rode northward with a party of disgruntled Palmer men. The fifteen prospectors split into three parties to search for gold but it was Verge, Sefton and their three mates who struck it lucky. They found payable gold, alluvial, on the Llankelly and Coen Rivers and Shanty Creek.[2] Their first prospecting trip saw them return with 60 ounces of gold. Buoyed with their prospects they returned after the Wet and in December 1877, just before the Wet set in again, they rode in to Cooktown with over 140 ounces of the precious metal. When the mines opened in Western Australia at Coolgardie and Kalgoorlie in 1898, Sam went over there to try his luck.

Ebagoolah, Starcke and Coen Gold Strikes

Jack Hamilton, M.L.A. for Cook, an ex-miner on fields including Gympie and the Palmer, managed to obtain a small grant for prospecting in the far north. John Dickie was his man in the field and he was soon able to report the discovery of gold at Ebagoolah. The field was named the Hamilton Goldfield after 'Dr'. Jack Hamilton and was, for a time, noted for the nuggets found there. A miner named Byrnes found one weighing ninety ounces (about 2 kg), while another miner and his mate picked up one that topped the scales at seventy-two ounces. Later Nichols and his mate outweighed the Byrnes nugget with one of 128 ounces but the big nuggets didn't stop there. Andy Stewart's golden lump weighed 216 ounces. He received a thousand pounds ($2000) for it. A small fortune.

In Cooktown, schoolboy Arthur White met up with some of the Ebagoolah miners. The stories they told inspired him to try his luck as soon as he was able. He worked at whatever job he could find to buy packhorses and mining gear. At last he made it to Ebagoolah. His carefully purchased gold scales weren't big enough to weigh his first nugget but it balanced a seven pound (over 3kgs) tin of dried potatoes on the storekeeper's scales. That wasn't the end of it. With his mate, Palmer River born Alf Gostelow, he went one better again. This nugget was twelve inches (30cms) long and five inches (about 13cms) wide. It was called the Gold Brick of Ebagoolah and was put on display at the Bank of N.S.W. (Westpac. Now closed as a bank but the home of the Cooktown Historical Society.) in Cooktown. The mates received today's $1200 for it and thought that their fortunes were made. Its find started another rush to Ebagoolah.

As the Hamilton Field cut out, Arthur and Alf moved further north through the Rocky and Hays Creek area to the Pascoe. They found good gold 'in almost every creek'. Rocky Creek is linked to that almost legendary miner Willy Lakeland who worked gold there successfully from 1893. He built a battery powered by a waterwheel to process the ore and lived at the mine with his wife and two children. Lakeland was an inspiration to many miners including latter-day mining magnate Clive Foyster so that, coupled to Clive's dream of lakelike irrigation dams, he called his farming enterprise at Butcher's Hill, 'Lakeland' in Will's honour. In the good times Ebagoolah and its mines had an estimated population of 350 men and ten women. Arthur and Alf were interested in anything 'mineral' and found a good patch of wolfram inland from Lloyd Bay which they sold to a buyer in Thursday Island. After packing it to the beach they flagged down a returning lugger that came in to pick it up. Unfortunately, the heavy bags of wolfram caused the shuttle dinghy to swamp, roll over and sink. Utterly dismayed and shocked, the Manilaman skipper immediately sent his two Island divers down to try to remedy the disaster. They retrieved all ten bags of wolfram and then re-floated the dinghy.

Troughing wash dirt at Batavia River
— *The Queenslander* 28th January 1932

Later, both these intrepid miners, still in their twenties, took jobs as patrolmen on the Overland Telegraph Line. Sadly, Alf was one of the first from the Peninsula to enlist when World War 1 broke out and was killed in France.

The gold at Ebagoolah was discovered in 1900 at the start of a State-wide drought. There was very little surface water and dirt had to be carried on packhorses for several kilometres to procure enough water to wash it so that the gold content could be revealed. A small town sprang up at Ebagoolah but although the 'main street' served for a while in later years as an airstrip, little now remains apart from the ubiquitous mango trees and a few date palms.

Closer to Cooktown, gold was mined at Starcke and Cocoa Creek since Bill Bowden discovered the yellow metal, often in nugget form, at Starcke in 1889. Billy and Jesse Webb with Harry Asmus were the ones who found the Cocoa Creek gold three years after Bowden's initial strike. The gold went deep and was mined on and off for thirty years.[3]

Prospectors worked the northern part of the Peninsula well but maybe that bonanza of Deadman's Gold still awaits discovery.

Gold continued to attract prospectors to the north. A battery, the Great Northern, was erected just outside Coen township to handle ore. At Wenlock the Empire mill took care of local crushings. William Baird whose loyal Aboriginal helper Romeo gave his name to the tinfields of Mt. Romeo southwest of Cooktown, worked gold at Bairdsville from his discovery of gold on the Batavia River in October 1892 until his death in 1896.[4] Baird was fatally speared when, with two other miners, he was engaged in digging a trench. Experienced prospectors Dick, Dickie and Sheffield also worked the Bairdsville field in the early 1900s.

When in late 1910, the Aboriginal Pluto found a big nugget along the Mein to Bowden Wolfram Field pack track near the mouth of the Batavia River, he started another rush. The field was called Plutoville in his honour and miners left Coen and Ebagoolah to try their luck there. By 1911, 2500 ounces were recovered including one nugget found by partners Foley and White. It weighed 74 ounces.(over 2 kgs). Five years after Pluto's discovery, his wife Kitty found a second source of gold at what became known as the Lower Camp, a sandy river flat not far downstream from Plutoville. Pluto was encouraged and backed financially by a 'white' mate, Wade Robinson from the nearby Mein telegraph Station. Robinson was reputed to be a descendant of the one the *Bounty* mutineers.

Courtesy Reg Starckey

Kitty Pluto, discoverer of Gold at Lower Camp, Batavia River Goldfield — *The Queenslander* 28th January 1932

Later, Duke Delaney became the acknowledged uncrowned king of Batavia, when, after overlanding by buckboard from Croydon, he found what he considered to be the richest lode of them all. To celebrate his find, Duke shouted for the bar at the Coen pub. His generous act was said to have cost him 300 pounds.($600 then but now greatly inflated.) In the early

1930s Jack Forsayth, also from Croydon, brought a Huntingdon crushing mill to Wenlock. He railed it to Normanton and then shipped it to Weipa Mission. After many months of back-breaking work spent making a road to Batavia, with the help of a team of Aborigines from the Mission, Jack delivered the mill by motor truck to its goldfield site. Wenlock continued as a gold-mining centre until machinery was shut down and people evacuated in the invasion scare of World War 2.

Reef gold was also found on Possession Island by Surveyor Embley in the early 1890s. Nearby Prince of Wales Island introduced a then novel method — open cut — to retrieve some 5000 ounces of gold up to 1901. Alluvial was also recovered, a further 900 ounces. A forty-stamper mill was erected by the discoverers Smyth and party, to handle the ore.

Tin at Rossville, Mt. Romeo and Trevethan

While gold was the most magical of minerals, tin was mined with financial success for many years at the mines in the Mt. Romeo, Rossville and Trevethan area along the Annan River catchment. Early discoveries were made by Charlie Ross, his brother and William Baird who had earlier with Leslie, Jack and Harry Edwards, Hackett and Duff prospected the heads of the Tate, Walsh and Lynd in the 1870s before Mulligan made his great gold discovery on the Palmer. They, too, were seeking gold, but it was on the banks of the Annan that Baird and Ross made their name with their tin discoveries. With Hackett, Ross prospected the hills around Herberton before its tin was 'officially discovered',[5] so he had some knowledge of the mineral. When the Annan tinfields opened in 1885, it is most likely that the settlement of Rossville was named in Charlie Ross's honour.

As the Palmer was entering into its death throes at that time, a number of the gold miners turned their interest to tin and some of the heavy machinery was transported — with great difficulty — from the Palmer to the new tin field. Tin mining wasn't the only form of diversification undertaken by those who wished to remain in the north.

Farming Comes into its Own

Cattle-raising was one alternative. Farming was another. The rich, red soils north of Cooktown attracted farmers to the Endeavour and the McIvor Rivers while others went further south to the Bloomfield. As early as 1882 Frederick Bauer and his two sons took up high rainfall, forested country to experiment in sugar-cane growing. He formed the Bloomfield River Sugar Co. and became both its manager and its promoter. Bauer had prior experience with sugarcane having been in the industry further south. Land was cleared and Bauer brought in Malays from Singapore to work the farms. This caused no little trouble with the resident Chinese who had come to Bloomfield looking for a future there when the Palmer closed down. Within two years 400 acres had been cleared and half of it planted with cane. A new innovation, the steam plough, was used to cultivate the newly-cleared land and a steam tramway ran from the mill to the wharf at Ayton.[6] Wildflower hunter and artist, Ellis Rowan, visited Bloomfield on her botanical trip north in the late 1890s. She spent a week with the Bauer family at Cooktown before setting sail in the coastal vessel *Lizard* for the Bloomfield. Mrs. Bauer kept a diary which was a great help in preparing Ellis Rowan for her trip. After some problems she was able to visit the Halletts' 'pretty bungalow house'[7] at Wyalla Plains, a cattle station then but previously a cane farm. Ellis Rowan refers to the tobacco grown around the Bloomfield which 'took a first prize at the last Melbourne Exhibition.' Rice, tea, coffee and 'all kinds' of tropical fruit grew there. Mrs. Rowan especially mentioned the coconuts, mangoes and 'grenadillas'.

She visited the Bloomfield Sugar Mill which was in the process of being dismantled after being sold. The steam train must have gone, too, as they visited the Moravian Mission by taking the 'horse tramway' from the mill to the river and proceeding from there by boat. When dismantled, the mill was shipped to Bundaberg. Despite producing first grade sugar, the enterprise failed badly. Isolation from markets played no small part in its demise but the *Cooktown Courier* complained that the management was 'recklessly expensive' and that the labour was both 'inefficient and disorderly'. It took a work force of 272 men to produce 525 tons of sugar. At that time too, the sugar prices on the worldwide market were unusually depressed. The company was wound-up with the investors bearing heavy losses. Louis George Bauer began a mission for the local Aborigines which was later transferred into the care of the Lutheran Church in 1887. Now known by its Aboriginal name of Wujal Wujal, it still flourishes as a community.

The engineer of the sugarmill, Cochran, began an enterprise of his own. From his farm on the northern outskirts of Bloomfield he manufactured not only powdered milk but also an excellent flour derived from bananas. His powdered milk was well in advance of the large milk-processing factories that came later.

In 1894 a cyclone which missed Cooktown did considerable damage to both Bloomfield's port, Ayton, and Port Douglas, the coastal outlet established to serve the Hodgkinson goldfield. The tin mines and the tin miners contributed to Ayton both economically and socially. There was a school and a police station and two hotels erected in about 1885. As a port, Ayton boasted a clientele of visitors from the sea lanes. One of the hoteliers was Jack Thompson who later became a noted identity in both Ebagoolah and Coen. The other hotel was run by Granaghan who subsequently took over the Criterion Hotel in Cooktown. As well as the miners from closer in, tinscratchers from China Camp also made Ayton their base.

Sawmills on the Bloomfield

In the 1890s a man named Chapman was cutting red cedar on the Bloomfield. He used horse teams to get the logs to a chute on the riverbank from which they were rafted downstream to be picked up by boat and taken to Townsville. A sawmill was built by another entrepreneur called McCredie. Unfortunately, isolation again made it difficult to meet expenses and McCredie was forced to sell. The new owners, Johnson and Shaw, managed to run it at a profit. The logs were brought in by bullock wagon and the sawn timber delivered to the Cooktown wharf by the small coastal steamers. From here it was transhipped to the larger Burns Philp boats and taken to Townsville. Most of it went on to Charters Towers which was experiencing a building boom after its own golden beginning. Houses with walls of cedar or silky oak and floors of black bean were not unusual in that era. The small steamers sailed almost daily carrying their precious load to make up the lading for the bigger vessels.

Cedar was a valuable product of the Far North but often logs were lost at sea or in flooded rivers. On his second expedition in 1879/80, R.L.Jack and his party were near Temple Bay when they moved closer to the coast to make contact from the 'Remarkable red cliffs'[8] north of the Carron Range with the 'keeper of the Piper Island lightship'. On the way, they came upon some Aboriginal huts of bark and saplings. One of them also had a copper-sheeting roof. Three kilometres further along the beach the copper roofing mystery was partly solved. They saw cedar logs 'strewn along the beach' and the wreck of a 'copper- sheathed brig'. It was the *Kate Connolly* which left Cairns, over 500 kilometres to the south, for Sydney with a crew of seven or eight aboard in March 1878. Neither the ship nor the crew was 'heard of again' until Jack's party came across the wreckage. Most of the logs were branded, either L or DH. Weather records showed that a 'memorable storm' on 8th March that year 'partly destroyed Cairns'. Jack attributed the wreck to that unfortunate aberration of the weather.

One of the first farmers on the Bloomfield was Captain Asmundsen[9] who settled there at the end of the 1870s. He grew coffee and tobacco which he sold both in Cooktown and in Port Douglas during the 'eighties and nineties'. He also grew good quality cotton. The tobacco was specially cured and made into cigars which were marketed to the south in boxes made of Bloomfield cedar.

These cigars won a blue ribbon at the Melbourne Exposition. Unfortunately the enterprise's success could not be sustained.

Other successful farmers were Frank and Tom Pierce (or Pearce), Wilson and the Scandinavians, Svendsen, Jonssen and Olufsen. Philip Jonssen was given his Bloomfield land in appreciation of a good deed he perpetrated. He was the man who searched for and found, the bodies of Mary and Ferrier Watson and Ah Sam. The Olufsens were probably the most successful farmers longterm. Mrs. Olufsen was an Asmundsen before her marriage so totally understood the vicissitudes of living at Bloomfield and Ayton. The Olufsens were almost self-sufficient growing tropical fruits, rice, coffee, potatoes, maize and tobacco. If that wasn't enough to keep them occupied, they produced honey for sale at four pence (4c) a pound (500gms). Olufsen also ran cattle and held a slaughterhouse licence. He delivered beef on horseback to miners and others at tuppence (2c) per pound. One problem that he had with him continuously was the local crocodile population. He often lost stock to the saurians and had an unusually high proportion of tail-less cattle in his herd — the crocodile's near-misses. Even into the 1950s the Olufsens were still farming and supplying the market by way of the weekly Cairns-Cooktown launch the *Merinda.* Oscar would meet the launch in his small boat at the river mouth and tranship his produce. Mrs. Olufsen was Postmistress and the family also ran the general store.

Cooktown's Population Shrinks to a Thousand

By 1915 Cooktown's booming population had shrunk to about a thousand with another two thousand odd scattered through the district.[10] However, Saint Smith, the Assistant Government Geologist, did comment in his report that the 'number of business places and hotels, particularly the latter, appears out of all proportion to its requirements'. Individual miners, the Annan River Company at Rossville and the Big Tableland Tin Company produced rich tin at lucrative prices. No doubt the tin miners contributed generously to Cooktown's well-being as did the men in the marine industries, fishing, trepang and shell.

8

Exotic Cooktown 1871 - 1901

Cooktown becomes an important port with communication to the Colony's capital, New Guinea and the islands · Burns Philp's part in commerce and shipping · Newspapers and newspapermen — The Cooktown Herald and the Cooktown Courier · Bailey, Spencer Browne, Hodel, Louis Becke · A visit from Louis de Rougement, the 'Greatest Liar on Earth' · Cooktown social life, balls, travelling entertainers, rowing and horse racing

It did not take long for more permanent structures to take the place of Cooktown's original tent city. As the population increased and stabilised, amenities were introduced to cater for the township's needs. At the height of the goldrush, Cooktown was the largest population centre and the most important port except for the Colony's capital. For many years in the 1870s Cooktown's trade far exceeded that of its older and closest coastal rival, Townsville, but as the gold dwindled and the Hodgkinson attracted miners away, Cairns as the port for the latter, came into its own.

Burns Philp, Shipping and Trading

Though Burns Philp didn't establish its official branch in Cooktown until 1887[1], they were active in previous years in shipping between the south and Cooktown, as well as in operating a service from Cooktown to the New Guinean ports. At first, Burns Philp chartered ships as needed but soon purchased a small wooden vessel, a steamer named the *Banshee*, to carry goods and passengers between Townsville and Cooktown. Unfortunately, the *Banshee's* reign was short. She was wrecked on her first voyage in 1876 with the tragic loss of twenty lives. Burns Philp continued their interest in shipping and the trade that accompanied it and at one time exported red cedar to as far away as New

Zealand. During the 1880s, though the Palmer had declined, B.P.'s business grew rapidly with the burgeoning mining, pastoral and sugar industries in the near north. An impressive two-storeyed building was erected on the river side of Charlotte Street and, for a time, the Cooktown branch also had the sole agency for the German New Guinea Co. at Finschafen.

In addition, Burns Philp won the tender for a mail service to New Guinea operating from Cooktown to Samurai and Port Moresby. The ship used, the *Lucy and Adelaide*, was a schooner, a sailing vessel. B.P.'s tender was the lowest because of the very competitive cost of sail against steam but after Federation in 1901, mail services became the responsibility of the new Commonwealth Government and they decided on Sydney rather than Cooktown as the terminal for New Guinea services. The much larger steamships, powered by coal from nearby Newcastle, won the day. The gold finds at Woodlark Island and the Mambare River sparked off a lively traffic of miners seeking their fortunes in New Guinea. Hundreds of diggers travelled on the *Ivanhoe* and the *Ysabel* from Cooktown to try their luck. B.P.'s emerging losses turned into a profit. In 1902, the Queensland Government belatedly part-subsidised B.P.'s 106 ton steamer, *Parua*, to service between Cooktown and the New Guinea ports with passengers and freight but the venture did not prove profitable given the uncertainty of gold mining.

As well as the shipping business and agencies for trading in copra, pearl shell, trepang, sandalwood and so on, B.P's also operated a retail business at their Cooktown branch. They offered a wide range of goods, 'Ceylon shirts, soap, notepaper, ginger, potatoes, shot and powder, and a bottle of eye lotion'.[2] G.R. Hepburn, the Cooktown manager in the early 1900s, reported that the *Moresby* frequently called at Cooktown to load bullocks for the Solomon Islands. Usually twenty head of live cattle made up the shipment but on at least one occasion some mules accompanied them. Unfortunately, the beautiful Burns Philp building and some of its neighbours were destroyed by fire.

Cooktown's Newspapers and Newsmen

In 1881 Cooktown had a population of 2,300 and two newspapers, the *Cooktown Herald* and the *Cooktown Courier* whose chief reason for existence 'seemed to be in vituperating each other'.[3] Maytown, despite being on the wane, still produced its own *Palmer Chronicle*. The *Herald's* first editor, W.H.L. Bailey, was also on the paper's imprint, the Printer and Publisher. He came to Cooktown in 1874 from another outpost town, Rockhampton, where he was reporter on the *Northern Argus* during the previous year. A Philip Hardy, objecting to something Bailey had written, assaulted him with a horsewhip for which expression of bad behaviour he was given a stiff ten day sentence.

Horse whipping was not a rare occurrence in Rockhampton. Earlier, George Elphinstone Dalrymple, taking umbrage at what he considered were Magistrate John Jardine's (father of Frank and Alec) 'slanderous charges', also attacked that gent with a horse whip. This assault took place almost at the local police station's front door. Libel actions and horse whippings were not unusual in those days among the people engaged in journalism. Spencer Browne, who later served as editor of the *Cooktown Herald* was taken to court over a libellous statement it was claimed that he made. The magistrate found him guilty and fined him a farthing (a quarter of a penny. At the time of metric conversion, twelve pennies equalled ten cents). When he left the courtroom he was beset by well-wishers all offering to 'lend' him the farthing.

Editor Bailey was an Englishman with a background as both a soldier and a sailor. Somewhere along the line he realised that his future lay in words and not in wars. In his first leader in the *Cooktown Herald*[4] he voiced the opinion that the first thing Spanish or Portuguese colonisers did, was to build a church. The French were 'in equal haste to get up a theatre' but the Englishman 'forthwith sets to make a road.' Bailey thought it would be wiser to 'give preference to a newspaper'. Cooktown already had two churches, Roman Catholic and Church of England, and worshipping arrangements for Jews and Chinese. Bailey was tempted to return to his early belligerent stance when he was burnt in effigy in Cooktown[5] over his stand on a petition to exclude Chinese miners from 'newly discovered' goldfields. Politically, Bailey supported McIwraith who was not wholly against Asian labour.

Reginald Spencer Browne, later Major General Browne, and author of *A Journalist's Memories*, was one of Bailey's journalists in Cooktown. Spencer Browne, with Charles James, bought the *Herald* from Bailey. The town was on the decline and the deal was a profitable one for neither the buyer nor the vendor. Bailey left the north to work in Sydney on *The Evening News*.

Charlie Wallace, Butchers Hill, gives riding instruction to son Bill — Cooktown 1950

Joseph Hodel's father, Francois, acquired the *Cooktown Herald* from J.G. Smith in 1876 and became mayor of Cooktown six years later. Francois, later anglicised to Francis, emigrated to Australia from the Channel Islands and worked as a building contractor for Robert Towns in Townsville before moving north to

Cooktown in 1873. Joseph's working life began as a baker but he always had a very lively interest in horses. He was a friend and associate of J.S. Love and Cruikshank who operated the Newmarket Horse Bazaar in Townsville. Hodel later sent two consignments of remount horses to India on his own account. In 1887 he financed his two brothers Francis and Frederick into a Townsville newspaper, *The Northern Standard.* It was anything but a financial success and was sold. The brothers Francis and Frederick were newspapermen at heart and Fred went to Cooktown in the early 1870s to work with his father, firstly on the *Courier* and then on Maytown's *The Palmer Chronicle.* Joseph is more remembered for his interests in hotel proprietorship and his undying support for horses, horse-racing and in promoting Agricultural Shows in the North. When Hodel senior owned the *Cooktown Courier* one of his editors was a young Fenian, John Flood, who, as Spencer Browne put it, 'left his country for his country's good' after campaigning rigorously for Home Rule for Ireland.

Spencer Browne, New South Wales born, worked his way in newspapers to Townsville — the *Townsville Herald* — and then, when he was only twenty-two, to the *Cooktown Herald* then owned by Bailey and where he was working when he was fined the farthing 'costs'. He returned south and gained a commission as Lieutenant in the Queensland Mounted Division in December 1887. He commanded a 'flying column'[6]during the Shearers' Strike in 1891 and later served in the Boer War where he participated in the relief of Kimberly. Invalided home as a result of a severe bout of malaria in 1900 he recovered and joined the 5th Light Horse as an officer. At the age of fifty-eight he sailed for Egypt with the 4th Light Horse in World War 1. On his return he again took up journalism and died in November, 1943.

Louis, Arthur And Cecil Becke — Blackbirder And Bankers

One of his friends in Cooktown and later in Townsville was Louis Becke. Becke's early years are difficult to trace. From Becke's point of view, deliberately so. He was with the notorious black-birder Bully Hayes and was himself charged at one time with piracy but was acquitted. He returned to the South Seas and took a native wife. His brothers, Arthur and Cecil, were more conservative. They were both engaged in banking. Cecil was manager of the Australian Joint Bank firstly in Maytown and then in Cooktown. He wrote to his adventurous brother suggesting that Louis join him. Louis spent two years, possibly from 1875 to 1876, on the Palmer or working on nearby cattle stations. During this time he gained a wealth of experience but no monetary fortune. He was popular and was a noted rifle shot at a time when there was a proliferation of excellent marksmen. A photo of him taken with Spencer Browne in 1878 shows him still with his rifle. Louis left the North and was later heard of when a namesake, Louis de Rougemont, hit the world's headlines as an adventurer *extraordinaire.*

Louis De Rougemont, 'The Greatest Liar on Earth'

Louis de Rougemont was a man both of many parts and of many names. At his burial at age 74 years in the Roman Catholic cemetery, Kensal Green, England, he was Louis Redman. He was also known as Louis Redmond and Henry Louis Grin or Grien and was French/Swiss, born in 1847. Before his death he was reduced to abject poverty and the selling of matches in London streets but before his fall he lived in a blaze of glory. At one stage between 1878 and 1879, Louis Grien, as he was then known, was in Cooktown where he had a photography business and in Port Douglas where he plied a similar trade. Two years earlier he had sailed on an 11 ton cutter, the *Ada* with 'at least four companions'[7] from Fremantle. The *Ada* was never seen again 'in that port'. She was officially declared 'missing' early the following year, 1877. Later in that same year, the *Ada* was found by the Cooktown pilot vessel near Cape Bedford, fifty kilometres from Cooktown but 5000 kilometres from Fremantle. Henri Louis Grien was the only person on board. He claimed that he and his companions had been pearl-fishing, attacked by natives and his shipmates killed. By locking down the hatches and sheltering inside the ship, he fortunately escaped their fate.

A Thomas Williams wrote to a West Australian newspaper saying how he had been in Cooktown in 1877 or 1878 when several strangers walked into town saying that they had walked overland from the Gulf of Carpentaria. Their boots were in too good order to bear this out and their stories were discredited. Shortly afterwards, the pilot rescued Grien. The general opinion was that Grien had sailed from Western Australia and put the other men ashore just north of Cooktown and that they had walked in from there. No one knew why there was all this secrecy, but assumed it was so that they could change their identities. The *Ada* sailed for New Guinea with a new crew. Williams was urged to join it but declined. Grien also remained. He stayed in Cooktown initially before going to the Palmer goldfields. Tiring of the hard work mining entailed, he set up practice as a doctor, but without any 'notable successes or failures'. From there he left and went to Port Douglas. Here, Spencer Browne says he knew of him as a photographer but Grien later left on a pearling boat as cook and in May 1880 arrived in Sydney.

Here he married and seven children, of whom only four survived, were born in fifteen years. Henri tried various con jobs to make money. They proved unsuccessful and when his long-suffering wife lodged a maintenance order against him, he left for New Zealand. With him he took the diary of Central

Australian explorer Harry Stockdale, an experienced bushman. Henri left for London taking Stockdale's book and an extensive repertoire of Stockdale's reminiscences with him. These he used as a base for his 'most amazing' stories that created a sensation internationally when published in *Worldwide Magazine.* His stories were mindblowing to say the least. He was pearling (rare black pearls, naturally) when a tidal wave swamped and sunk the ship. He and a dog, Bruno, were left on the sinking vessel. The ship was caught on a reef and took fifteen days to sink. Grien and the dog set out in wild seas for the shore. The dog kept swimming just in front of him as he floundered along in the waves. Finally, he realised why. Grasping the dog's tail with his teeth, it towed him safely ashore. Then his real adventures began. He rode turtles to get about, steering them by thrusting a foot in their 'optic' to make them turn. Using this unusual form of transport he salvaged what he needed from the wreck and built a house of pearlshell in which he sheltered.

At the time the book came out, Louis Becke was also in London. As he was in Cooktown at the same time as Grien it is possible that he may have known him. Becke had also had the same sort of dodgy past, but was now one of the 'more respected critics' who wrote letters to editors concerning Grien's claimed exploits. Using the pen-name, An Australian, Becke wrote that he'd seen and handled thousands of turtles and yet 'had never seen one which when afloat and when touched anywhere on its body, did not sink almost vertically. Furthermore, if a turtle's eye is touched, even when he is on land, he contracts his neck and turns his head downwards and won't go for a spin even if you use spurs…'

Grien answered this by giving demonstrations riding turtles in the zoo to try to deflect criticism. Criticism and cynicism abounded, but Grien's book sold 50,000 copies in two editions. *Worldwide* published a little jingle to promote it, which went:

'Truth is stranger than Fiction
But De Rougemont is stranger than both.'

'Louis de Rougemont' returned for a lecture tour of Australia to promote his book. He was almost seventy. For a while he was again a star. He promised to pilot a turtle across the English Channel and to perform other outlandish feats but on his return to England his public deserted him. He was reduced to selling matches in the streets, destitute and old. 'An eccentric member of the great line of inventive impostors who have astonished and amused the world' was the epitaph provided by London's *Daily Chronicle.*[8]

As Warden E. Cecil Saint Smith reported, Cooktown had a surfeit of hotels and shanties but it is difficult to find any record of commercial brothels. There was enough entertainment available to keep the locals in good spirits. The very siting of Cooktown provided a variety of leisuretime activities. Finch's Bay, named for a bank manager, was a popular picnic spot although two small girls were tragically drowned there. Grassy Hill and Mount Cook attracted the hikers and the river provided a venue for oarsmen as well as sailors. Teams of rowers competed in regattas and shooters found a range of targets for their guns. The migratory Torres Strait pigeon was a popular choice when it came south and shooting competitions in which young men tried to outdo each other were regularly held. Dr. Korteum especially loved a day's roo-shooting.

Entertainments — Balls, Music, Rowing and Racing

While Cooktown was visited by travelling musical companies, it was an era when singing and/or playing a musical instrument was a favourite personal

Preparing for the Blackboys' Race, Old Racetrack, Coen — 1950

past-time. Dances and the more formal balls were well-attended and roller-skating was available for afficionados of that sport in the Town Hall. Boxing was also popular and very competitive among the young bloods.

At a time when the horse was king, horse racing was perhaps the most eagerly contested activity, especially in the 1870s and 1880s. Some keen horsemen and equestriennes rode in from as far as Maytown to participate in the annual race meeting. A bar served refreshment to the men and Mrs. Trotter's tea stall refreshed the ladies. It really was a race carnival with wheels of fortune, shooting galleries and a tote, 'all the means of making or losing money'.[9] As well as being an enthusiastic roo-shooter, Dr. Korteum was also a successful racehorse owner. In 1880, his Vandyke beat Wallace's Never Can

Tell by two lengths but Never Can Tell might have been running a bye. He won the Packers and Carriers Race easily later in the day. There was provision made too for the Chinese population. Much in the same way as Cooktown, Laura and Coen later had a well-contested Blackboys' Race each day of their programs for horses ridden by Aboriginal jockeys. For the Chinese owners race, the horses had to be ridden by Chinese jockeys with 'their pigtails down'. Chick Tong, the manager of Sun Ye Lee and Co., was a very keen racehorse owner according to the *Cooktown Herald's* Spencer Browne. Chick Tong was an above average rider and had a smart performer in his skewbald horse, Faugh a Ballagh, a name that his owner had problems pronouncing. Chick Tong also nominated Faugh a Ballagh, with his Chinese groom up, in 'ordinary events'. At the skewbald's first start, the money was on a horse called Starlight. It was a close finish until Starlight's jockey subtly edged the skewbald off the course at the turn and won the race. Faugh a Ballagh still came second despite this manoeuvre and won another event — without any interference — later in the program.

Novel Ways of Customs Evasion

While there were thousands of Chinese on the goldfields, others took up agricultural pursuits providing food both for men and their horses. Several were prominent businessmen while some worked in town as cooks, gardeners and houseboys. Others were engaged in less overt operations which worried the Collector of Customs, Mr. Fahey. Spencer Browne wrote 'there was an Egg Pool in Cooktown in 1878 or 1879'. The local production of eggs was small so the Chinese imported them. 'Encased in well-salted clay' they were preserved. The Second in Charge at Customs, J.W. Knight, decided to try a couple for breakfast. Once broken, there was neither yolk nor egg-white, just a 'thick treaclish substance'. Opium. Opium smoking and gambling were favorite Chinese past-times in Cooktown. Fan Tan, played with circular coinlike counters with a small central square cut-out, was very popular. These brass or bronze counters could be found in large numbers after the Chinese left the district. When the Chinese departed for the Next World, it was an honourable practice to return the bones in burial urns for interment in their home country. It was suggested that often gold was smuggled out with the bones. Bartley Fahey, filling his Customs' export files out in triplicate, couldn't find any heading to cover 'human bones'. His sub-ordinate, Knight, proved 'equal to the occasion' and created a new category. 'Specimens of Natural History'. Under that heading, the relics were returned safely to sorrowing relatives.

9

Aborigines, Missionaries and Cattle Stations

Early Aboriginal tribal life · Establishment of the Missions · Bloomfield River (Wujal Wujal) and Cape Bedford (Hopevale) established by the Lutherans in the 1880s · Yarrabah, Mitchell River (Kowanyama) and Aurukun founded in the 1890s · All Missions aimed for self-sufficiency · Lockhart River, on the east coast, established Australia's first registered Aboriginal Co-operative in 1954 · Other Aborigines perform valuable work on the cattle stations · Freeing of Aborigines from the rigors of the Protection Act in 1965/6

Before the white settlers moved in to mine or to seek pasture for their stock, the present-day Aborigines led a relatively peaceful life. There was some inter-tribal fighting over boundaries or clashes of interest but these were not overwhelming. Fighting did break out then, as it does now in all cultures, and for a variety of reasons. It was manners, and certainly the wisest decision, to seek permission before entering other tribal land. This was a golden rule of which many early settlers and explorers were unaware. Once authorisation was given, a message stick guaranteed the visitor's safety as he passed through on his own business.

Although New Guinean visitors to the northern part of the Peninsula brought with them their bows and arrows, the locals failed to be impressed and used, by choice, their spears, throwing sticks called woomeras and clubs. It was a nomadic hunter-gatherer society with the women usually contributing the fruit and vegetable section of the diet, 'sugar bag' honey of the native bee and some of the seafood and produce from the freshwater sources. Traditionally, men provided the main item on the menu — meat. It could be the larger animals, wallabies or possums or the feral pigs which were added in the post-Cook period. Anything that required an accurately thrown spear or deft club attack, birds, turtles and the larger type of seafood fell into the category of men's business. Fruit bats were a delicacy captured by both sexes and their seasonal return was heralded with pleasure. Roasted on the coals they made a tasty meal.

Seeds gathered by the women were ground by way of their version of stone-age mortars and pestles to provide a grainy substance to be used as flour or as a basis for something not unlike gruel. Women were adept fisherfolk and caught fresh and saltwater fish on handwoven lines with hooks innovatively fashioned from bone. Fish could also be stupefied to a degree that they were easily caught by hand by spreading crushed freshwater mangrove leaves on the surface of a still pool. The chemical compound in the leaf withdrew oxygen from the water and rendered the fish incapable of movement. As the white man came with his metal products, they were eagerly appropriated when beachcombing after shipwrecks or 'borrowing' from isolated camps. Wire, and porcelain insulators from the Telegraph Line, other useful metal items and glass bottles were eagerly sought and incorporated into the traditional implements. Fire was another tool used by the Aborigines both in hunting and in smoking out the cattlemen.

Native Women's Pharmaceutical Knowledge

The women in general possessed a great knowledge of herbal remedies and the use of insects in their natural pharmacy. Green ants, usually thought of as a dreadful menace, were a source of many cures. Their formic acid worked wonders on almost every complaint from arthritis right through the whole alphabet of afflictions. I was also let into a secret that a poultice of squashed green ants would encourage virgin breasts to lactate and was given instances of Aborigines in my acquaintance who had been successfully reared as a result of this treatment.

Languages varied from tribe to tribe but they usually carried enough in common to be understood, at least partly, by neighbours. There was no alphabet or written word but such stories as had to be told were handed down orally or depicted in artwork. The rocky overhangs and cave walls usually used by the tribes were commendable sites for the drawings that told of tribal emblems, traditions and historical happenings such as the advent of the white men, the horses of the Native Mounted Police with the troopers' strange headwear and Snider rifles. Isolated sites, well hidden from prying eyes, were used for sorcery drawings done with intent to cause harm to a particular person.

Polygamy was practised, with young girls often 'promised' to a mature man at a very early age, but there was also an elaborate system of laws to ensure that the marriage was for the future benefit of the tribe. One law that appealed to some of the young white men of my youth was the one that forbade speech between the husband and his mother-in-law.

There had been intermittent association with Europeans and Asians over the years. Some of these meetings were amicable and others were not. Even in the mid-nineteenth century, explorers and shipwrecked sailors told of being helped generously by some Aborigines and of being pursued relentlessly with obvious evil intent by others. Similarly some shipwreck survivors were treated kindly and supported by the tribe, while other of their ex-shipmates were slaughtered. The cattle and horses brought in by the Europeans must have seemed preposterous monsters to people accustomed to land animals no bigger than kangaroos. The sight of a man mounted on his horse was even more mystifying, especially when the giant animal divided into two parts when its rider dismounted.

Among the white settlers, most adopted the live-and-let-live attitude and while running stock on erstwhile tribal lands they also provided the necessities of life to the many relations of the aboriginal stockmen they employed. With a depletion of their traditional hunting grounds, hunger was often the trigger for feats of Aboriginal daring against their better-armed opponents. However, in all races, there are always people who do not value the lives of those who appear to threaten their own well-being. The Native Police were usually enlisted from distant tribes which had no ties of friendship with the local groups and they often became the butt of condemnation when blame was apportioned after 'dispersals'.

Alcohol Use Abused. Exotic Diseases Introduced

Perhaps the worst practice introduced by other races was the use of alcohol. The indigenous people quickly gained a thirst for it and it became a more than useful tool to attract both the males and the females to work on the luggers and at other occupations. When their employment ceased they were rarely returned back to their own land, a very important factor in their lives. Alcohol is still the major problem affecting the communities and cause of much of the indolence and violent behaviour there. Another deadly result of contact with the new arrivals was the disease that they brought with them. The indigenous people usually had no prior experience with these diseases and hence had no resistance. Venereal diseases proved fatal to many and rendered others barren. A friend of mine was one of only two people left of a tribe to the north of Cooktown that was wiped out with syphilis. The disease she contracted at birth left her sterile, no little tragedy to someone who wanted a child as passionately as she did. She died in her forties of an enlarged heart, a side-effect of the disease. The influenza epidemic after World War 1 also decimated the tribes in numbers out of all proportion to the already high fatalities in the white population.

Churches Establish Missions for the Indigenous

The London Missionary Society was interested in the early days of the Colony in establishing missions outside the Brisbane district. Soon after Barbara Thompson's rescue in late 1848, attempts were made to establish a mission settlement in the furthest north but none of these plans met with any lasting success. The Church of England established mission settlements at Yarrabah, near Cairns and at the Mitchell River on the lower western coast of the Peninsula in 1892[1]. A similar mission was established at Edward River some decades later. Schools were opened for the children and nursing facilities established for the sick. Farming practices were introduced, mainly to produce fresh food for the community but other more ambitious projects were set up. One concerned the production of peanuts. The growing and harvesting of them was a success but, at that time, the Queensland Peanut Board insisted that the nuts be forwarded to Brisbane for sale through the Board itself. Individual sales which could upset the price structure were frowned upon. The cost of freight involved in the transportation south made the otherwise flourishing enterprise uneconomical. Cattle raising became the income-earner for the west coast missions for many decades.

Lockhart River, near Portlands Roads and Iron Range on the eastern coastline was also set up by the Church of England Diocese in 1924.[2] It was established at Lloyds Bay at a place called Waterhole. It received that name from a small freshwater spring, but the soil there was very sandy and unsuited to agriculture. Later in the same year it was moved to Bare Hill (named by Captain Cook). Only the eastern slope was 'bare'. Behind it, the lush rainforest was growing in fertile red soil, excellent for farming. Once the land was cleared and prepared, the vegetables 'grew like mad'. Water was obtained from the nearby creek. As an aftermath of World War1, the new Lockhart River flood plain was suggested as the location for 600 acre blocks to be offered for Soldier Settlement. The project didn't proceed.

Lockhart River Aboriginal Co-op

The Australian Board of Missions appointed the Rev. Alf Clint as Director of Native Co-operatives and he considered Lockhart to be the ideal place for him to try out his[3] 'Christian Socialist' ideals. Clint argued that, in his natural state the Aborigine was a born 'co-operator' who hunted for his group, not for himself. His portion was allocated by tribal law and if the meal caught happened to be his clan totem, he was forbidden to eat any of it. The good of the community was more important than the well-being of the individual.

In 1954 Lockhart River Mission was the site of the first Aboriginal co-operative registered in Australia. The shareholders were the members of the five tribes that made up the indigenous population of the area. They elected a Board of Directors and proudly nailed 'a shingle to the door of a bark and corrugated iron structure. It said The Lockhart River Aboriginal Christian Co-operative Society Limited.'

As well as making plans for farming, they had three trochus boats and the services of a rather extraordinary man who had previously owned one of the boats, operating it as a pearler from a base at Thursday Island. He was John Warby. John was born in Sydney but spent most of his life in the very far north including New Guinea where he served in World War 2. Like many Australian 'diggers' he was an ingenious innovator with a strong practical streak. He could make something useful out of the proverbial nothing. John, his wife Bunty and their three children arrived at Lockhart on their boat *The Seabird.*

Like the Rev. Flint, John's aim was to develop the new Lockhart into a self-supporting community. He encouraged experienced divers to come back to work on their own mission luggers, gathering mainly trochus shell from the reefs. Trochus was the shell from which the very popular 'pearl' buttons were made. The community at Lockhart consisted of about 300 Aborigines and ten Europeans. The co-op trochus venture went exceedingly well until plastic buttons were invented. The more durable but much more expensive shell buttons became redundant and the bottom fell out of the trochus industry.

While they were operating, the boats supplied Lockhart with a reliable income. Forty per cent of the takings went into maintenance, another forty into wages and the remaining twenty per cent was put back into amenities for the community. One of the first purchases was an ex-Army blitz truck to be used in bringing loading from the coastal wharf up-river to the community. Unfortunately, it was one of the very rare blitzes that didn't have four-wheel drive and was forever getting into trouble on 'roads' and in unbridged creek crossings. Fortunately, the good-natured caretaker at the airstrip at nearby Iron Range, George Nankervis, had a big heart, a Fergie tractor and a mechanic's training. George rescued them from most of their predicaments without undue delay and a lifelong friendship was formed.

A successful night school for adults was opened as a result of the Co-op and, for a while, author Kylie Tennant gave her time without stint to assist in its establishment and progress. All manner of fruit and vegetables were cultivated. Timber was cut and milled for the settlement's buildings. Cotton was successfully grown and harvested by hand by both adults and children. Everyone was jubilant about their future as farmers. The rainfall at Lockhart was reliable and fell at about 1200mm per year. With that, it was expected that two cotton crops could be produced each year on the rich flats that had previously grown only blady grass. The cotton would be sent by sea to Cairns and from there by rail to the ginnery at Rockhampton. The price for cotton was good and it was expected that a profitable industry would be set up. After growing cotton for a couple of seasons, the paddock would be used for improved pasture to fatten the Mission's cattle, with cotton and pasture crops rotated over the years. Trial plots, each containing one acre, of seven different varieties were planted and 'flourished'. Unfortunately, although they had favourable reports on the progress of their venture from the Director of Tropical Agriculture, finance could not be found to continue with the project.

Cowpea, also grown at Mitchell River, was produced as a legume favoured by canegrowers spelling their cane paddocks. Unfortunately as freights rose, profitability declined until production of both the cotton and the cowpea was unrealistic. Another project which looked like being a success, also failed because of the problems brought about by isolation. A ready market was found in Thursday Island for refrigerated beef from cattle killed from the Mission's herd but costs again proved to be too great for the project to survive. Isolation and lack of outside interest prevailed over the Lockhart people's enthusiasm. On 29th March 1963 the Co-op was officially declared bankrupt and voluntarily wound-up. It was sad day for Lockhart, its hopes and its dreams.

West Coast Missions

Always ardent settlers, the Presbyterian Church, with a working agreement with the Lutheran Moravians since 1863, looked to establishing farming settlements for the protection of Aborigines on the western coast of the Peninsula. Nicholas Hey, a Bavarian born in 1862, was one of the Moravian missionaries. Hey was no stranger to hard work and adversity and his spirit never failed to inspire him. On the death of his father when Nicholas was thirteen,[4] he assumed the care of the family farm and ran it successfully for the next eleven years. He then volunteered for missionary work with the Moravians and was sent first to Jamaica, then to Ireland and finally to Australia. With his friend, the American James Ward who was the son of a Moravian missionary in Jamaica, he arrived in the Peninsula at the end of 1891 at a time when ex-Premier Douglas was still exerting considerable influence. Douglas was passionately endeavouring to establish missions for the care of Aborigines in an attempt to keep them out of the hands of black-birders and the abductors of young girls.

Land was granted by the Government near Cullen Point at the mouths of the Ducie, Batavia and Dalhunty Rivers, at a point on the west coast of Cape York Peninsula equidistant from both McDonnell and Moreton Telegraph Stations. Hey and Ward[5] with a 'white police constable and two native troopers, four carpenters and the material' to build a modest shelter, sailed for the proposed site. John Douglas visited the infant settlement regularly and he and Ward, not entirely happy with the choice of the original location, found an even better and more fertile site. Unfortunately, on one of these forays, Ward contracted a fever that later caused his death. Hey married Ward's sister and she worked with him at the new mission. When Ward died, his widow left to live for a while with family in Brisbane but the call of the north and the Missionary work drew her back. She returned to take charge of the school at what was later called Mapoon.

The missionaries encountered a reverse in public opinion when, in 1893, two white pearlers were killed on the *Schearden River* and Mapoon and Batavia River tribesmen were blamed for the double murder. Douglas was able to stall a punitive expedition, but much of the public sympathy for the plight of the Aborigines was lost. Backing up the saying that there is both good and bad in all people, the missionaries and their people were redeemed when, in January 1894, the *Kanabook*[6] was wrecked near Normanton. Immediately, the missionaries went to the rescue with their more-than-willing helpers. The heroism freely exhibited in risking their own lives to save the survivors 'restored the mission to popular esteem.'

Aurukun was selected in October 1891 at the mouth of the Watson River. It was to be administered by missioners the Rev. and Mrs. Richter and Harry Louis, a Samoan. It wasn't until September 1895 that the missionaries found the place for a more permanent, second location on Surveyor Embley's York Downs Station. The river beside which it was founded was the Embley and the mission was called Weipa. By 1904 the State Government created a Native Reserve to protect the two mission sites. It extended from the Batavia River to the Archer River. Four years later it was expanded to take in 1345 square miles (over 2000 square kilometres). The Mission Superintendent was officially deemed its administrator and the recruiting of lugger crews was prohibited within the reserve. Nicholas Hey gave it its new name. Like Cook with his 'kangaroo', he got it a little wrong. The Aboriginal name for the area was Ol-nul-pru-koon, meaning 'big water sits down' but, hearing it indistinctly and without a knowledge of the language, Hey translated it as 'Aurukun'.[7]

Aurukun followed the policy of self-sufficiency as soon as it was possible. Fruit trees, coconut palms and vegetables were planted immediately gardens could be tilled. The fibre from the coconut was also found to be useful for stuffing pillows. Once the more practical plants were doing well, others were planted for their beauty and colour. Poinciana trees were very popular and soon created shady playgrounds for the children.

Bill and Gerrie MacKenzie went to Aurukun as missionaries in 1925 and worked there with their Aboriginal friends for forty years. The community brought together 'clan groups' from 2,500 square miles of country (4000 sq kilometres) on the west coast of the Peninsula. As with other communities there were tragic fatalities from diseases like whooping cough and measles that are easily avoided in these days with vaccination. Having no immunity, the death rate was high in the Aboriginal children. Hookworm and diptheria also took their toll. Mitchell River to the south had a strip used by the Flying Doctor and in 1935 they even had a visit from a female Flying Doctor, Dr. Jean White of Melbourne, who flew in to carry out hookworm treatment.[8] With much effort Aurukun built a small airstrip. At first, only pilots as daring as Cairns' Tom MacDonald chose to land there, but as its reputation grew a Flying Doctor plane came in from the base at Cloncurry to carry out monthly clinics and emergency evacuations. Financed by the Rockefeller Foundation Trust, Alec McLeod, later to be Superintendent at Mitchell River, rode 'with a string of pack-horses from bush camp to bush camp' giving treatment for the dreaded hookworm.

Aurukun also had its cattle herd. The first cattle, with 'four or five' horses were sent as a gift from Mapoon. By 1923 the herd had grown to about a hundred and the horses extended by seven geldings. Additional mares were gained by swapping bullocks in a horse-trading deal with some sandalwood cutters and a 'good stallion' was purchased from Rokeby cattle station. The resulting foals were greeted with wild enthusiasm. Mackenzie noticed that the horses were particularly attracted to a 'great high grass', a native. By taking roots from the existing patch they established a fenced-off plot near the swamp at the Mission. The horses did very well on it, eating it right to ground level. When Townsville lucerne made its way into the Peninsula pastures, seeds were obtained and the legume introduced into the native pasture. Hay, cut and heaped in large stacks, was a very welcome standby in the dry season. Seed was also collected for sale.

Mitchell River gave Aurukun the gift of a sizeable mob of cattle from their herd, plus a 'clumper' (heavily built and hairy-legged) half-bred Suffolk Punch stallion. Bill MacKenzie was boss drover on the trip back to Aurukun and inappropriately the cattle rushed one night during his watch. 'Being Anglican cattle, they could have objected to the Presbyterian psalm' he was singing to them as he rode around. He also sang 'rag time' so maybe they were just opera lovers.[9] Later the Government financed a further purchase from the Mitchell River herd and following his generous tradition, Alec McLeod of Mitchell River again added an extra '7 heifers, 3 'killers' and 3 brood mares'. It took about two weeks to walk the cattle back to Aurukun. By 1938 the herd had grown to over 600 head and the following year over a hundred were walked down to Mitchell River to be sold with the local turn-off from there to a visiting cattle-buyer.

From then on the sale of cattle was an annual occurrence and, at four pounds ($8) a head, returned a very welcome 500 pounds ($1000). By 1945, 161 head sold for five pounds five shillings per head, ten dollars fifty in today-speak. Two years later, the turn-off reached three hundred head. When cattleboats were introduced, the cattle were sent direct to Cairns. The voyage took three to four days and, on at least one occasion, the boat returned with Droughtmaster bulls for the growing herd. Aboriginal stockmen, Willie and Jerry Hudson, father and son, were responsible for the cattle enterprise. With the help of the Presbyterian Women's Missionary Union, cattle sales funded the purchase of a small Cessna plane which was used 'for a few brief years'. It was lost, with its pilot, in an unexpected and powerful storm. Aurukun also had its own dairy herd bought from Thursday Island in the mid 1920s. The lives of many babies and small children were saved by the milk these cows provided.

Bamaga, closer to Cape York, was peopled largely by Saibai Islanders. Cowal Creek, a little further inland, was home to the mainlanders. Here the Presbyterian missionaries again concentrated on making the settlement self-supporting. Travel writers, the adventurous Coralie and Leslie Rees,[10] visited Bamaga and Cowal Creek in the late 1950s to find to their pleasant surprise, two native women tractor-drivers working on the Mission's fruit and vegetable farm. Pineapples, peanuts, bananas, pawpaws, melons and numerous varieties of vegetables — plus sugarcane — were grown. Pigs and cattle were reared and large numbers of poultry were in evidence. As a reverse of today's trend, each week the Mission sent to Thursday Island on the Mission's launch, fresh fruit, fresh veges, meat and eggs. The growing cycle was extended to almost the full year by the judicious use of sprinkler irrigation with water from a large dam in the dry weather. Timber was also cut, milled and sold to buyers in T.I., Weipa and other Torres Strait islands.

The Wealth of Weipa

Weipa, the bauxite town, sat on its wealth for many years. It was reputed to be the world's largest bauxite mine. The mineral takes its name from the concretinary granules of alumina, mica and water, first found at Les Baux near Arles in France. Flinders commented on the striking 'red cliffs' on his voyage in the *Investigator* in 1802 and a hundred years later, geologist C.F.W. Jackson made the first report of a vast bauxite field. Its full potential wasn't realised until July 1955 when another geologist, Harry Evans, wrote, 'As the journey down the coast revealed miles of bauxite cliffs, I kept thinking that, if all this was bauxite, then there must be something wrong with it; otherwise it would have been discovered and appreciated long ago.' Fortuitously, it was as good as it seemed.

Itinerant ministers of religion found means of transport other than launches to visit families in the Peninsula. In 1938 the Rev. P.J.Thomas and his wife spent three months in the saddle riding 700 miles (over 1100k) to bring friendship and what help they could offer to households there. They estimated that, in the 40,000 square mile shire of Cook, there were at the time of their visit, 230 white men, 33 women and 33 children living there. Australian Inland Mission Padre Colin Ford and his wife Margaret took over after the road was pushed through and regularly visited homesteads and outposts delivering a helping hand and stacks of donated books and magazines. It was mostly due to their representations that the small cottage hospital/hostel was opened in Coen to care for the sick and to provide accommodation for bush children which enabled them to attend the Coen primary school and also to enjoy the company of their peers.

Closer to Cooktown, in 1881, the Government made over 50,000 acres (about 20,000 hectares) of land near Cape Bedford for use as a Mission. George Schwarz, who was fluent in native dialects, was an early superintendent. Like Bloomfield, the Mission was run by Lutherans. The Bloomfield Mission, begun by Louis Bauer in the mid-1880s, was administered by the Lutheran Church from 1887. Pastor Schwarz who was a young missionary of German birth, was assisted by an indigenous convert from South Australia, Johannes Pingilina. Johannes and his wife came to Hopevale, as the Pastor named his Mission, and both he and Pastor Schwarz quickly set about learning the local Gugu Yimidhirr and Gugu Yulandji languages. Together they translated the Old Testament stories, the Lord's Prayer and the Ten Commandments into the native dialects. Being able to converse with their parishioners made their calling less onerous and created a strong mutual trust.

Johannes and Rosina Pingilina who came from South Australia to help at Hopevale

Children were taught to read and write elementary English, to understand simple arithmetic and to master handicrafts. Schwarz hoped to make Hopevale, eventually shifted further inland from the coast, self-sufficient. By 1894 the Mission had four hundred head of cattle which provided them with both meat and milk but the entry of the dreaded tick fever decimated the herd. At the turn of the century a school was built, followed by a church. Schwarz married Mary Allen, the daughter of the Cooktown Post Master and when they grew up, the Schwarz's two daughters helped out, Marie as a teacher and Grace as a nurse. Besides attending school, boys were given experience in farming. Girls, while also helping on the farm and garden, were taught domestic skills.

People were brought to Hopevale from as far away as Proserpine when the local Lutheran Mission there was forced to close. As was customary then, half-caste children were brought in from out-lying areas as well as other full-blood Aboriginal children whom the Police Protector — rightly or wrongly — thought were at risk. Hopevale, too, lost funding when, unlike the Yarrabah administration near Cairns, Schwarz decided against using Hopevale as a Government Reform School. With the onset of World War 1, funding from the German Lutheran Church ceased and self-sufficiency became even more imperative.

Hopevale Evacuated During War — Missionaries Interned

When World War 2 broke out and civilians were evacuated to the south, Mrs. Schwarz and her daughter Grace, now Mrs. Behrendorff, also left the Mission. Shortly afterwards, because of nothing more than their German ancestry, both Schwarz and Behrendorff were arrested and sent to an internment camp interstate. The Mission itself was re-located with its nearly three hundred men, women and children to Woorabinda in Central Queensland. The people of Cooktown organised a petition in support of the two missionaries. Schwarz was then in his seventies. Fortunately, the authorities saw the light of reason and released him. He immediately rejoined his 'people' at Woorabinda and tried to have them returned to Hopevale. Nearly a fifth of the Hopevale transferees died at Woorabinda, mainly of a fever but it is thought that homesickness also contributed. Eventually, they returned to their old home and set about enlarging the farmlands and building new homes with timber cut and milled on Hopevale.

A large proportion of the Aboriginal population in the Peninsula in the days of the Protector and before full citizenship rights were granted, lived on cattle stations. The cattlemen needed stockmen and the Aborigines soon found an affinity with the once fearsome monsters — the horses and cattle. Their skills as horsemen and cattle musterers quickly became apparent and they took a great pride in their competency. Their traditional prowess as trackers was in demand when wandering animals needed to be located. Conditions on the cattle properties up until at least the middle of the last century were rather primitive. A visiting American scathingly remarked that the Peninsula was still 'in the longhorn days'. There was, of course, no electricity — even generators need fuel and without roads, that was accorded a low priority when goods were brought in — no refrigeration or radio reception. Running water was a luxury and the only hot water available was that heated on the wood stove. Houses were, for the most part, made of galvanised iron sheeting with concrete or antbed floors.

Aboriginal families were usually employed and lived in their own camp a little apart from the house. The older man usually acted as gardener and handyman, with his wife helping both the missus in the house and her man in the garden. The young adults revelled in stockwork and the mustering camp. With limited mail services and no radio, education was very difficult for the white kids as well as for the Aboriginal children. Mothers usually had to adapt to being teachers and when correspondence lessons became possible, some of the dedicated ones included school age Aboriginal children in their classes as well. Book-learning wasn't the most popular kind of lesson but opportunities to acquire the expertise of the stockman were often available and weren't passed up. There were always willing hands to help out with the cattle and to do small jobs on killing day. That was a great occasion which ensured fresh beef on the menu for a day or two instead of the usual salt meat, and the chance to learn the art of plaiting stockwhips and greenhide ropes from the late-lamented killer's hide.

Aborigines weren't paid direct, as their knowledge of money was rather neglible. The same could be said about many of the white 'ringers' or stockmen who were regularly taken-down when paying for purchases and taxi fares on their rare visits to town. Part of the Aboriginal wage included a tobacco ration. This was usually their favourite 'plug' tobacco, Sunlight by name, which came in a solid cake and was shredded with a pocket-knife before it could be smoked in a pipe. It wasn't as successful in roll-your-own cigarettes but some persevered, rolling them in newspaper. Meals were cooked in the homestead and for the most part, eaten on the kitchen verandah. The exception was usually on Sundays when, important things like the bullock muster permitting, 'dinners' were cut and taken on the day's walkabout to supplement any bush tucker gathered.

'Protection' System

Wages were small but the wage paid to white stockman was comparable and the station owners didn't appear to be doing much more financially than to make ends meet. In 1950, the Aboriginal wage was seven pounds ($14) per week, plus keep and tobacco. Two pounds ($4) of this was able to be taken as pocketmoney and the remainder paid to the worker's account under the supervision of the Protector. When in town, a visit to the Protector, the Police Sergeant, would furnish money from the stockman's funds for clothing and other necessities. Extra money was usually available at celebrations such as the annual race meetings for 'entertainment'.

At the race meetings, there was the opportunity to compete in the final race each day staged for Aboriginal jockeys. It was one race where you could be absolutely sure every horse was a 'goer'. Competition was very single-minded, as winning the race brought great prestige in addition to prize money. As the road opened, travelling boxing shows like the famous Jimmy Sharman's, made the trip up at race time. There was no shortage of volunteers to take on the travelling pugilists.

A wind-up gramophone to play the old 78 rpm hillybilly records was a goal well worth saving for. These were greatly valued possessions and were spun, at exactly the right speed, by hand when the main spring broke and the instrument would have been unusable until a replacement could be found. Similarly, lemon tree prickles made passable substitutes for the steel needles when that supply wore out.

"The Aboriginals Protection and Restriction of the Sale of Opium Act, 1897 to 1934."

The Aboriginal Protection Regulations—Schedule No.

Permit for Casual Employment. No 19754

"Hopevale" LUTHERAN MISSION

I, V.F.H. Wenke, Protector of Aboriginals for the District of COOKTOWN, hereby approve of the employment of the aboriginal ~~half-caste~~, named hereunder, by Bill Wallace for the period specified and in accordance with the following conditions:—

Employee's Name Oulo Gordon. Identification No.

Period of Employment 19 days. Commencing 26th June, 1953

Nature of Employment Casual Farm Work.

Rate of pay payable weekly as follows:—

To the Employee as Pocket-money 7/6 per week.

To the Protector 132/6 per week.

Total 140/- per week.

V.F.H. Wenke.
Protector.

Date 8/9/53

I, Bill Wallace, of Harvest Home, Cooktown agree to employ the abovenamed employee on the conditions set forth and to comply with the Regulations made under *"The Aboriginal Protection and Restriction of the Sale of Opium Acts, 1897 to 1934."*

Bill Wallace
Signature of Employer.

Date / /

Government Printer, Brisbane.

Permit to employ an Aboriginal station worker

At the time that the Aboriginal stockmen was paid seven pounds a week, I was paid four as a female stationhand. I thought that was fair enough. I couldn't throw a wild cleanskin bull and at my previous job as a trainee nurse I was paid one pound sixteen shillings and sixpence ($3.66) a fortnight in my first year. I did get free board and uniforms as well at the hospital. Even that was an improvement on my aunts' day. Their father had to pay the hospital to have them trained.

Many of the Aboriginal stockmen adopted the surname of the family for whom they worked. Sometimes they used the station's name as a second name. It was not at all a rarity when an Aboriginal mother died or found caring for her children too onerous, that the children were brought up by the station missus. There must also have been procedures within the Protection Act which allowed Aborigines to 'get out from under the Act' and thus be permitted to handle their own affairs. Often the people who befriended individuals and families managed to have their charges removed from under the Protector's jurisdiction. To do this they had to learn some rudimentary literacy and numeracy skills and to be able to handle money. Aboriginal women 'under the Act' had to get permission from the local Protector before they could marry a man who was not in the same category. The marriage would automatically give the bride her husband's status. A Police Sergeant in Laura who acted as Protector as part of his duties, told me that he had never refused permission for a woman to marry this way but would have if he had thought that the man 'would abuse her.'

Seasonal workers, such as drovers or additional hands for a big muster, could be obtained from the Missions. They had to be collected and delivered safely back at the employer's expense. The remuneration was the same except that the wage, less pocketmoney, was paid to the worker's account at the Mission where the Superintendent acted as Protector. These workers didn't accumulate the funds of the permanently employed station men as, when they were not in work, expenses incurred by themselves and their family (if any) were taken from their limited earnings. If they had only worked for a small part of the year, the funds usually ran out by the end of the year.

When the Award Wage became mandatory and accomodation had to meet much higher standards, many station owners reluctantly found that they could no longer afford the permanent labour the Aboriginal workforce provided. Without jobs, the Aborigines moved back into towns or to the Missions. At best, short periods of temporary employment was all that became available for them.

10

Labor vs The Pastoral Industry — 1915

Labor Party in Government in Queensland with a policy of the nationalisation of wealth · Government purchases coal mines, fisheries, sawmills, butcheries, a hotel and cattle stations · Merluna and York Downs, Silver Plains and Maitland Downs bought by the State in the Peninsula · Enterprise not a success — Most enterprises were later sold · Some of the cattle properties have been re-purchased by the Government in recent years as National Parks

⁂

As a result of the Shearers' Strike of the early 1890s, the Australian Labor Federation of Queensland, later to become the Labor Party, was formed. Electoral reform was the first plank of its platform but another less immediate one was for the 'nationalisation of wealth'.[1] The Federation wanted its members to share in both the natural and the commercial wealth of the State. Just before the turn of the century, the then Labor Party had formulated a list of proposed State Enterprises. They were as diverse as railways and rolling stock, a State bank, a sugar refinery, abattoirs and Fire and Life Insurance. As the State Government Insurance Office, the latter was one of its lasting successes and thrived until recent years. The lottery, The Golden Casket, begun to provide funds for the Queensland War Council in WW1, continued its good works by funding hospitals and welfare from 1920. By 1958, it had contributed eighteen million pounds ($36M) to hospitals and funded dental clinics, the University Medical School and projects for the unemployed.[2]

Labor Party Endorses Policy of State Enterprise

The Party hoped to reduce prices to consumers by competing effectively against commercial cartels. It was not merely a desire to overthrow the Capitalist System, they argued, but an attempt to make that system work for the benefit of all. Kidston had earlier retained Government with Labor support. T. J. Ryan and Red Ted Theodore were ardent supporters of the grand plan and in 1915 the Labor Party won the election in its own right. They promised to reduce prices and to stop non-competitive trading. The list of State Enterprises was extended to encompass coal mines, a shipping line and sawmills but there was no mention of State-owned butcher shops and cattle stations until October of that year when it was decided to open a State-owned butcher shop in Brisbane. This operation would give the Government sound and practical experience and a knowledge of the costs involved. Some butchers complained that they would be forced to close should they attempt to sell their meat at the retail prices suggested by the Government.

The Labor men were confident. Under the wartime Meat Supply for Imperial Uses Act, they were empowered to negotiate to purchase beef from the meat companies. The export market was then for 100,000 tons per year and the meat companies were paid 4.5 pence per pound (a little over 10c per kilo) f.o.b. (free on board) ship. Ten thousand tons were reserved for the domestic market with the new State shops purchasing in bulk for the equivalent of seven or eight cents per kilogram. Fillet steak retailed for about 30c/kg in Victoria but was half that price in Queensland's State shops. Unlike privately-owned butcher shops, the State shops did not deliver meat. A Mr. Hunter writing in the *Daily Standard* of 28th September 1915 pointed out that, when a customer had to pay fourpence (4c) tram fare to get to a shop to buy meat for seven pence (7c), he or she was, in reality, paying eleven pence (11c) for the purchase, 'to say nothing of the waste of time'. Ironically, although the workers in the State shops received an extra five shillings (50c) a week above the Award, they complained of poor working conditions.

To protect themselves from any future shortages of supply, the Government decided to buy its own cattle stations. By 1917 the State owned not only ten new shops including one at Rumula near Julatten, but also thirteen cattle stations of varying sizes and carrying capacities. In the next twelve months both the shops and the stations made a profit. Almost 700,000 pounds ($1.4M) had been outlaid in purchasing the properties, a third in cash and the other two-thirds in debentures, and the venture returned a profit in excess of 100,000 pounds ($200,000)[3]. None of the other enterprises, the sawmill, the fishery, the Chillagoe mines and smelter, the coal mine at Warra or even the pub at Babinda scored an entry on the credit side of the ledger. The idea behind the State hotel was to do away with the prevalence of sly grog in the district. Often consumption of these deadly brews led to severe sickness, often with fatalities, among the sugar plantation workers.[4] In 1915 Queensland's Labor Party took a prohibitionist stand and hoped for total prohibition in the State but some Parliamentary wag commented that the state of the Babinda hotel's finances drove them all to drink and they gave up on their crusade.

As with National Parks and Aboriginal land today, State-owned stations paid neither local rates nor rentals. This did not endear them to the councils of shires struggling to make ends meet, nor to other Queensland rate-payers.[5]

By the time 1920 came around, the Government was faced with a serious fall in beef prices and a lessening in the quantity of cattle available for slaughter. The War ended, and with it the crucial need for bully beef to feed the soldiers. The Queensland Government was, quite understandably, unskilled in the art of cattle station management. The multi-skilled and very practical Robert Logan Jack wrote, 'I cannot imagine any trade less adapted for communistic management than that of the grazier or squatter. Hitherto the runs have been held by pioneers or their successors, with a limited staff of stockmen, some of whom are of pure Aboriginal blood, although the majority are white….. I can see no end to the State Stock-raising experiment but fiasco and *reductio ad absurdium.*'[6]

Neighbours and travellers, as fellow shareholders in the enterprises, wanted a return on their investment and the outback art of 'poddy dodging' — rustling, in America's Wild West — was rife. With little money spent on amenities, the stockmen became less enamoured of their work. Seeing the spartan conditions as a lack of consideration for their needs, they responded uncooperatively with the better-treated management. A story is told of the mustering camp at Maitland Downs at the top on the Byerstown Range, the headwaters of the Palmer River. Due to the isolation, supplies were only brought in by wagon or packhorse every few months. In the Wet, when flooded rivers and creeks barred the way, stores were brought in before Christmas and were expected to last until the country dried out again in April or May. The men weren't at all happy. They ate separately to the manager and they considered, with jam ordered by the 'mixed' case, that they were getting all the plum jam while the management dined on strawberry, apricot and the like. A spokesman delivered an ultimatum to the manager. 'No more plum jam or we walk off the job.' Consequently, the bookkeeper carefully ordered the two dozen cases of mixed jam with the added underlined note, 'any bar plum.' Everyone gathered when the packer arrived with the new supplies. The cook hurriedly opened a case of the 'mixed' jam. It contained Dark Plum, Light Plum and Angelina Plum plus a note of apology saying, 'Sorry. No Bar Plum.'

State-owned Cattle-stations Unsuccessful. Sold Off

By the mid-1920s the properties were up for sale. The losses had accumulated to 1.5 million pounds ($3M). The Moore Government decided to get rid of them as soon as they could, and a time-frame for their sale was set up from 1st

July 1929 to 31st December 1930. The Depression was just around the corner and the omens were not good.

In the Far North, in the electorates of North Kennedy and Cook, there were ten stations involved. Four of them, Merluna and York Downs, Silver Plains and Maitland Downs were in the Peninsula. The total area of the State-owned leases was 13,985 square miles or about 26,000 sq. k. They were thought to be running approximately 160,000 head of cattle. Unfortunately for the Government, most of the properties had been bought on 'book numbers' and not on the number of cattle actually mustered in a 'bangtail' muster where each beast mustered was identified by 'banging' or cutting off the brush of the tail. These 'tails' could be counted as proof of the cattle actually mustered (and the hair was used by station saddlers to re-stuff saddle linings.) In most cases, there was a considerable discrepancy in what the Government paid for, and what they actually received for their money.

For the Peninsula properties there was very little choice of market. Either their fat cattle were sent north to supply the limited Thursday Island market or were walked down the long route to Biboohra meatworks outside Mareeba. Biboohra probably supplied bodies of beef for the Rumula butcher shop as well.

An auction of the properties was set for 2p.m. at the Wool Exchange, Brisbane, on 17th September 1929. J.A. Armstrong of Sturmfels Ltd. was the auctioneer selected by the combined agents, Dalgety, A.M.L&F, Australian Estates and Sturmfels. Merluna, York Downs and Maitland Downs were to be offered among the stations listed for sale that day. Most of the properties were passed in but Frederick Henry Keppel was the successful bidder for the 5400 square mile aggregation of Merluna and York Downs. The Pastoral Lease rental was set at five shillings (50c) per square mile, 1350 pounds a year or metrically, $2700. The first rental period was for thirty years.

Communication-wise, Merluna was up-to-date. It was connected by telephone to the nearby Telegraph Station at Mein. It was watered by 'rivers, creeks, lagoons, swamps and billabongs,'[7]and 'many of the swamps and lagoons are permanent'. It had a four bedroom homestead, a meat house, men's quarters, Aboriginal quarters, 'hide house' (for storage of salted and dried cattle hides which had some commercial value) and a 'dray shed and saddle room'. There was an abundance of mango trees, bananas and other tropical fruit both at Merluna homestead and its outstation, York Downs. Merluna had an excellent vegetable garden as well — 'all kinds of vegetables are grown'. There was a cattle dip at the head station and at Picanninny Plains 20 miles (32 k) south-east of the homestead, 15 tailing yards and 29 miles (46k) of fencing in 'good repair'. The average rainfall was 45 inches (1125mm).

In the 'remarks' section, it was stated that 'under the State Station method' station supplies were landed at Thursday Island by the *Kallatina*, and taken by the Mission boat, *J.G.Ward,* to Weipa Mission on the Embley River, then only 14 miles (20k) from York Downs. The freight per ton from Brisbane to Thursday Island was two pounds twelve shillings and sixpence ($5.25) and from Thursday Island to Weipa, a further six pounds ten shillings. ($13). Surprisingly, for its isolation, this wasn't the dearest freight rate. Keeroongooloo, another State station 140 miles (224k) north west of Quilpie, had its rates listed as nine pounds three shillings and sixpence ($18.36) per ton from Quilpie and the freight charge to Wandovale from the rail at Pentland west of Charters Towers was the equivalent of $15/ton.

There were 350 head 'more or less' of mixed shorthorn cattle and '700 horses' offered with the sale of Merluna and York Downs. The State had bought it, 'walk-in, walk-out' with 12,960 head of cattle and 335 horses for 228,00 pounds ($456,000), 50,000 pounds ($100,000) in cash and the rest in debentures.[8] The brands were XNO and YDO with the 'D' on its side. These have been used there for decades since. Conditions of the sale were 'Half cash, the balance of purchase money to be payable in seven equal annual installments, bearing interest at the rate of 6% per annum, such balance of purchase money and interest to be calculated from date of delivery.' A property mortgage and a mortgage over the stock were also taken out and the deals were W.I.W.O. (Walk in .Walk out.)

Maitland Downs had been run in conjunction with Brooklyn, another State property 15 miles (24k) from 'Mt. Molloy railway station' and 42 miles (66k) from the meatworks at Biboohra. Brooklyn, too, had a telephone from the Mt. Molloy Exchange and Telegraph Office. On the old Palmer River Goldfield, Maitland Downs, 80 miles (130k) further north from Brooklyn was more isolated. It was situated at the top of the Byerstown Range which was the divide for the Palmer River which eventually ran into the Gulf, and the Laura River, a tributary of the Normanby which entered the sea in Princess Charlotte Bay. The 1088 sq miles (1760 sq. k) Maitland Downs listed a 'galvanised house with a verandah back and front on the bank of the Palmer River'. There was a separate kitchen and a shed. It had no boundary fencing but boasted 'two branding and sixteen tailing yards' and a horse paddock. No stock went with the deal and the rent was seven shillings and six pence per square mile annually for the first ten years of a thirty year lease dated from 1st January 1927. Its average rainfall was 30inches (750mm).

No Bids for Maitland Downs

There was very little interest in an unimproved run in the middle of nowhere and, in the case of Maitland Downs, no sale eventuated. It reverted to unoccupied Crown Land. It wasn't altogether a write-off to pastoralism. Pioneer Maytown cattleman, George Ahlers, carried out the occasional muster there and kept the cleanskin (unbranded) numbers down for a couple of decades until his death. Later, as the road from Mareeba to Cooktown was being pushed through along Mulligan's old wagon track, Ian Pratt and the Morris brothers, Hank and Miles, took it up and again made a station out of it.

American Archbold Expedition Studies Fauna and Flora

Silver Plains was acquired at the auction by an old Coen family, the Thompsons and it was held by them for a couple of generations before being sold in 1971[9]to an American, Richard Rand. In 1948 an American expedition from the Archbold Biological Station at Lake Placid in Florida gathered information on the natural history of Cape York Peninsula, spending some time in the area around Silver Plains. An A.L. Rand was a member of the Archbold organisation and with L.J. Brass who headed this expedition, had carried out similar botanical and zoological studies in New Guinea. The expedition had a busy time. Mr. Vernon of the Queensland Museum estimated that they collected 'Mammals. 1504 specimens. Reptiles and Amphibians. 477 specimens. Fresh-water fishes. 118 specimens. Larger insects and spiders. 5400 specimens. Plants. 2215 numbers.'[10] The expedition co-operated with the Queensland Museum and also with Australian Council for Scientific and Industrial Research for which they collected over a hundred plants 'for pharmacological testing'. On the Thompson side, Dr. Wassell, married to Eileen Thompson, was an Australian entomologist of note.

Richard Rand, Senior, died not long after the property was purchased and his son Richard carried on. The Rands surrendered 70,000 hectares of the unique rainforest, the home of the beautiful black palm cockatoo, on the McIlwraith Range in return for a deal with the Government which permitted them to freehold a portion of the remainder after improvements to the value of almost $1M were carried out on it. The country that they surrendered was said to be the largest stand of rainforest in the far north. The Rands timing was not good. They bought Silver Plains at a time when the price for cattle plummeted to less than cost of production while, with galloping inflation, input costs kept rising.

History repeated itself in 1994 when another Labor Government decided to buy the cattle station, Silver Plains. Premier Wayne Goss purchased the property on behalf of the Government for $4.5M. It followed the Government's earlier 'purchase' of the nearby Starcke holdings. But the Government wasn't going to try its hand again at cattle-raising. Both properties were destined to become National Parks.

One of the State's better stations, Wandovale, in the basalt north of Charters Towers, did sell but became the basis for an inquiry into the sale. A Royal Commission was convened in October 1917 under Judge O'Sullivan. A cattleman, who was not at that time employed by the Government, inspected the 1280 square mile property on their behalf over a period of ten days. At the end of his inspection, he agreed on account of the Government to purchase the property for 82,000 pounds ($164,000). His report to the Secretary for Public Lands was verbal, but the sale went through on his recommendation and he was given the position of manager of the Government station, Dotswood, near Wandovale, at a salary of 300 pounds ($600) per annum. What sparked the inquiry was that the vendor, Mr. Barnes, was reported to have said and was 'not prepared to deny', that he had put a price of 65,000 pounds ($130,000) on the property only months before it was bought by the Government. The Minister for Lands was cross-examined and asked, 'You will admit if it (Wando Vale) was in Suter's hands for 65,000 pounds, it was bad business to buy it for 82,000 pounds ($164,000)?'

The Minister's answer was a simple but emphatic, 'No.'[11] Nothing further developed from the inquiry.

In the twenty-first century, while live cattle exports, particularly from the port at Weipa, have opened up opportunities for far northern cattlemen, the state of the industry is in doubt. The current trend is for the non-renewal of Pastoral Leases in the Peninsula. When the cattlemen and their herds are disposed of, the area will most likely revert to Native Title, National Park and Wilderness.

11

The Clouds of War 1939 - 1945

Invasion by Imperial Japanese Army threatening · Airfield at Horn Island repeatedly bombed · New site for aerodrome selected near today's Bamaga, 'Higginsfield' · Another airstrip constructed at Iron Range · People evacuated from Wenlock, vehicles and movable machinery commandeered by the Army and the rest rendered inoperable · Wenlock airstrip upgraded to take heavy air traffic and Coen strip used in emergencies · Signs along the coast of enemy landings and radio messages in Japanese intercepted · Additional landing facilities provided at Cooktown · Mareeba aerodrome chosen ahead of Cairns for a Defence Force base

Even before Pearl Harbor, when Australia entered the war against Japan, reports were not uncommon of sightings of people other than the local population along the coastline and further inland on the Peninsula. Prospectors fossicking besides the creeks that flowed into the sea north of Coen often told of temporary camps they had discovered and could not logically explain. More sightings were made closer to Cooktown at Cape Bedford where people were seen coming and going in small boats. The Japanese, with their interest in the pearl, shell and trepang industries, were quite familiar with the seas washing the Peninsula coasts and soon became suspect.

After the attack on Pearl Harbor on 7th December 1941, when Japanese bombers surprised and sank a large part of the American fleet anchored there, Australia joined Britain and the U.S. in declaring war on Japan on the following day. The Prime Minister, John Curtin, immediately ordered R.A.A.F. planes based in Malaya to attack Japanese land troops invading that country from the north. On the same day, Australia also declared war on Finland, Hungary and Romania. On 11th December, under the State of Emergency that existed, the 'call-up' for military duties was extended to all Australian single men aged from 18 to 45 and for all married ones in the 18 to 35 year age group. Leave that had been granted to Defence Force personnel was cancelled until further notice.

John Barry and Sam Elliott

Many young men from the Peninsula hurried to Cairns to enlist. Most succeeded but others failed. John Barry, returning from Coen races was intending to head for Cairns to enlist when he and his mate spotted a dingo following them. With the adrenalin of the Coen race meeting still flowing, John gave chase. As he removed his stirrup iron and its leather strap preparatory to smashing it on the fleeing dingo's skull, his horse stumbled and fell. John's neck was broken. It takes more than a broken neck to keep down a man like John and after years of treatment from the Tableland wonder-healer Kjelberg, John calmly continued his life as a ringer. By this time 'protected' industries were declared and anyone engaged in these vital activites wasn't eligible for service in the armed forces. Agriculture and pastoralism were two industries that had to be 'protected'. The Army, Navy and Air Force needed to be fed.

Sam Elliott, the last of the Palmer River's 'hard rock' miners was another who missed out. He rushed to 'join up' but was knocked back because of a lung complaint, miners' phthisis, dust on the lungs. That didn't hamper Sam either. He joined Colonel Murray's Volunteer Defence Corps based at Cooktown. They were rough and tough and were often referred to as Murray's 'Gorillas'. Often on his own, the wily Sam, with years of living off the land behind him, acted as a one-man coastguard observation unit. Unnoticed, he patrolled the coastline and Sam, too, had tales to tell of deserted camps and refuse left behind that was easily identified as having Japanese origins.

Courtesy R.A.N.

One of the Japanese midget submarines which raided Sydney Harbour in WWII

American forces hastened to form bases in Australia. Darwin was bombed on 19th February 1942. This was followed by an attack on Sydney Harbour by three midget submarines in May of the same year. One little sub was sunk, another trapped in Navy nets and scuttled by its crew and the third escaped. The ex ferry *Kuttabul* was a victim of the raid and nineteen people were killed in its sinking.[1] Townsville was bombed by four flying-boats on 24th July 1942 and a bomb dropped near Miallo, north of Mossman, injured a young girl and killed a cow.

Horn Island had an airstrip and it, too, was a frequent target for enemy attack. However, the existing strip wasn't considered suitable for use by heavy bombers even though it was quickly upgraded. Drainage was a problem after heavy rain and conditions became more than difficult for the heavier aircraft, the bombers that would use it. Horn Island was only eight kilometres from side to side and a lot of that was hills. The U.S.A.F. and the R.A.A.F. looked south to the mainland for a more acceptable location. Pilot Officer 'Jim' Trench, R.A.A.F.[2] and Lieut. Colonel Mills representing the U.S. Engineers, were sent out to find a new site for an airfield.

Need for Airstrip on Mainland Australia

They flew to Horn Island and from there crossed to Thursday Island, from where they left by motorboat with an Army skipper for Red Island Point on the mainland. Here, the local butcher, Capt. Cadenza, pastured his cattle herd. He kindly lent them, very novice riders though they were, two of his saddle-horses as transport. They set off early the next day and soon came to an Aboriginal settlement and a C.M.F. (Citizen's Military Forces) camp. Riding along the Overland Telegraph Line and counting the posts which were five chains (about 100m) apart, they were able to calculate that 'the horses walked at almost exactly 3 miles per hour' (5k). They determined that if they rode 'on a compass-guided straight line for half an hour' they would have sufficient length for a 'possible airstrip'. It wasn't that easy. Some of the sites selected looked good but 'petered out' after only twenty minutes of riding. On the second day they found a site that they were sure would be suitable. They knew where it was but the only maps available, except for the Japanese ones, were the old style four-mile maps on which it was hard to pinpoint the position accurately.

Invasion money printed by the Japanese for use in New Guinea and Australia — WWII

Feeling rather jubilant, they returned to Horn Island and an American battalion was dispatched to the selected location. When Jim Trench re-visited the area some weeks later with Lieut. Colonel Mills, construction was 'in full swing — the only trouble was, it was about 5 miles (8k) away from the site we had selected!'[3] The port facilities were shifted from Red Island Point to Muttee Head, a safer anchorage.

For some time Horn Island remained the main supply point for the new Jackey Jackey strip, later known as Higginsfield. Supplies destined for the new airfield were transferred onto smaller craft for delivery. With the intensity of the war increasing, additional men were sent up from the south to make ready the Higginsfield strip for use in all weathers and to repair and upgrade the Horn Island one. In such isolated situations any communication facilities were of vital importance. All wireless transmitting stations and walkie-talkie units 'were camouflaged as thoroughly as possible.' In the middle of these frenzied attempts to improve the facilities and to construct the flying fields, some civilian workers from the C.C.C. (Civil Construction Corps) staged an eight-day strike over conditions. It was the day of the Red (Communist) Peril. Eventually Horn Island was 'phased down in favour of Higgins.'

Jackey Jackey perpetuated the name of Kennedy's faithful Galmarra and Higginsfield took its name from another, more modern, hero. By the orders of Lt. Gen. Kenney, the aerodrome was re-named to honour Flight Lieut. Brian Hartley Higgins — 400620 — of the R.A.A.F. who was killed during operations on 25th May 1943.

The onset of the 1942 Wet season halted construction temporarily and the U.S. Engineers returned to a job in progress in New Guinea. The A.W.C. (Allied Works Council) took over immediately after the Wet of 1943 eased. Progress was retarded by a shortage of manpower and equipment and an irregular shipping service to the site's port but by August 1943, the 7000 feet runway was serviceable. The Repair and Salvage Unit was based at Higginsfield from March 1943 and No 7 Squadron moved down from Horn Island.

Higginsfield wasn't without casualties. In May 1945 a DC3 Courier, VH-CXD, crashed as it came in to land at 5.20 a.m. The crew of four and the two U.S. passengers were all fatally injured. The plane was carrying a cargo of frozen meat for the troops in New Guinea. The meat was splattered everywhere making identification difficult. Today Bamaga is thought to be situated on Trench and Mills' original airfield site and Red Island Point is better known as Seisia.

New Strip at Iron Range

While Jackey Jackey/Higginsfield was being constructed, the Engineers were not only working on the upgrading of Horn Island but were also engaged in constructing a new strip at Iron Range to the north of the Lockhart River and north east of the small mining settlement of Wenlock. Iron Range wasn't the G.I.'s favourite posting. It was set in tropical rainforest, the weather was hot, wet and steamy and all manner of scary snakes and 'wild life critters' flourished in the area. A rudimentary road — later sealed — was constructed to the jetty at Portland Roads but road conditions were such that it was not always trafficable. Fortunately, the jetty, constructed in 1939, was in fair order and only minor upgrading was needed. The R.A.A.F were extremely relieved that the Army hadn't blown it up as was proposed during the mercurial Japanese advance through New Guinea.

Jim Trench and Colonel Mills with another U.S. Colonel, Cox, did the preliminary inspection of this area also. There was a radio at Iron Range owned by the 'State of Queensland'.[4] It was of great assistance when several U.S. aircraft were forced down 'some 40 miles (60k) to the north' of Portland Roads. The heavy rainfall prevalent in the area necessitated the urgent sealing of the strips and every attempt was made to keep them serviceable at all times.

On a map of Iron Range, 2nd November 1942, two runways are shown and '3 campsites each for 400 men'. Bridges were constructed on the improved roadways and attempts were made by Operational Base Units to provide off-duty recreation for the men. The thrill of chasing snakes and wild life critters soon palled. Stories were told of the extraordinarily large proportions of the mosquitoes stationed there. They were much bigger than any found elsewhere in the world. One of the ground crew is supposed to have admitted he re-fuelled one before he realised it was not a B25 bomber. A rest camp was established at Larradeenya River and facilities for tennis, badminton and basketball set up. There was also a small swimming pool. In August 1944, Operational Base Units recorded that 'twenty mango trees were planted.......also pawpaw and lime seeds were sown in boxes........ a piggery

Courtesy US National Archives

The Liberty ship *Payne Wingate* loading at the Portland Roads Jetty. This was a period of embarkation for various Army and Aircorps Ground Echelon elements. Visible in this photograph on the right are three shallow draught landing barges moored to a floating pontoon. They were likely the most favoured form of quick supply transfer from ship to shore. Although not very clear, just beyond the right hand six-wheeler truck, there appears to be the top of a US staff car. It must have been brought ashore from shipping and doubtless taken out by ship as it would have had difficulty making it by road to Portland Roads in those days. That's so even today! After the war the jetty was little used. It was demolished in the 1970s.

was started after some escapes and re-captures…..eight Jap prisoners passed through; they all seemed quite happy.'

A coded message from North East Area Base to Brisbane in mid-August 1942 tells of the success of the building operations. The mess hall, showers and latrines were all completed. A water reticulation service was successfully installed. The bakery staff were in business and the butcher shop personnel had everything in readiness for the supply herd that had started on its way to them. The pier at Portland Roads was of single-track pile trestles, sixteen ton capacity and there was still sixteen feet (5m) of water available at low tide. Gasoline was available in quantity and was stored for the time in drums near the strip. Things were looking up.

Homebrew

Mention of gasoline in drums being available, recalls a story of later years after the Defence Forces had pulled out. It was rumoured that there was still gasoline in the drums abandoned there and an enterprising cattleman decided to rescue it. He loaded some drums onto his small truck and left for home. The road had suffered somewhat during the Wet seasons since the War and the surface was not at all smooth. None-the-less the driver and his helpers were dumbfounded to hear a terrific explosion behind the cab after they had travelled but a short distance. Brakes were immediately applied and a quick inspection showed that one drum had been shattered and debris from it scattered on both sides of the track. Among the wreckage were yellow beady-looking things which proved to be grains of corn.

The only explanation was that, by mistake, they had loaded a drum of the G.I's 'moonshine', an illegal but satisfying and highly potent liquor. Very little was said but the best-kept secrets still seem, if not always with explosive effects, to leak out. Tales had been circulating about the production of 'moonshine' and 'dried fruits as part of the mess rations are said to have rarely seen the mess table'. On 16th November 1942 a Board was appointed to investigate the death of seven of the Defence Forces and the illness of seven others. The cause of death was found to be ptomaine poisoning. It gave the mythical moonshine a bad, if libellous, reputation.

Joe Fisher, writing in his book *Battlers in the Bush*, his reminiscences of life on the Batavia Goldfield, tells of how, after removing the machinery from Wenlock, the army left the 'galvanised iron riveted cyanide tanks in place'. Fisher knew of the distilling of corn whiskey and puts forward an argument in favour of the later removal of the tanks for use in the distillation process. Residual cyanide could have remained in the seams in minute but deadly amounts. He mentions 'some went blind' in describing the Iron Range casualties.

The original jetty at Portland Roads was built by the Queensland Mines Department in 1937 as an outlet for the Iron Range goldfield discovered by Jack Gordon some years previously. Ships also delivered goods and supplies there for stations and settlements in the region. When the Defence Forces first moved in, three shallow-draught landing barges were used at Portland Roads to off-load supplies and personnel from the large Liberty ships lying off the jetty. Six-wheeler trucks, command cars and jeeps could be brought in this way from the 'south'. Land access from the south would have been highly impracticable if not impossible.

Iron Range was virtually the same distance from Horn Island as that strip was from Port Moresby so, once Iron Range became operational, it often became the departure point for aircraft proceeeding from Australia to Port Moresby. As the Japanese Airforce were easily able to bomb Port Moresby, it was not a favourable place to stage Allied bombers. The war had come to a very serious pass especially for the Defence Forces who thoroughly understood the gravity of the situation. One of the U.S. maintenance men, Dale Kruger, could not understand the laid-back attitude of the locals who were left. Most of the women and children had been evacuated under Government orders. Dale wrote. 'One time out of the blue came two Aussies and three of the natives driving several ranch cattle through the jungle. We couldn't believe our eyes. Here we were in a war area and these guys didn't seem to care.'

Nor did the rest of Australia. They were content merely to draw a line from Brisbane to Adelaide on the map and to make sure they protected that part of Australia to the south of the line. The infamous Brisbane Line of General MacArthur.

A New 'Island' in the Nassau River

In the 'war area' there was more than a suspicion that the enemy were closer to the mainland than those in charge admitted. Peninsula residents often told of landings of presumably Japanese people prior to the outbreak of war and, less seldom, after war was declared. In this very sparsely-populated region it was not at all impossible. Radio conversations were also intercepted in 'what was thought to be Japanese language'. At Aurukun, near the Nassau River, Aborigines reported a tiny 'island' floating on the tide, 'athwart the current'. It had two 'masts'. These were later interpreted as a periscope and an extended radio antenna after live Japanese grenades were found in the river near the sighting.[5] Aurukun's powerful new radio transmitter was placed under restrictions in case useful signals were picked up by the wrong people. Ironically, radio reception at the mission was not good and the 'clearest and loudest' station that they could pick up was Zeisin, Radio Germany. It transmitted in German so was not of

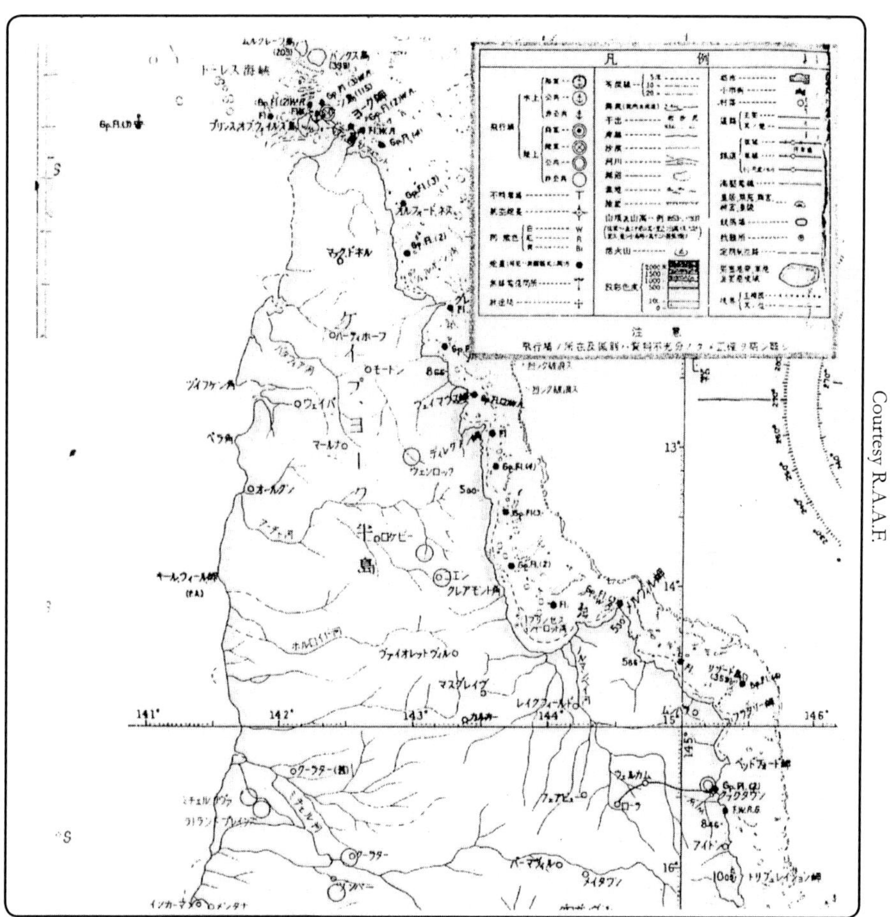

Map of Peninsula captured from Japanese submarine — September 1942

Courtesy R.A.A.F.

any use to the Mission people. Two Americans from the Combined Intelligence Centre in Canberra were sent up to Iron Range to investigate the Japanese radio conversations. The investigators also looked into 'objects washed ashore'. These exhibits included two mines, 'presumably our own' and an 'unidentified object' which turned out to be a belly tank from a fighter plane

Security was of the highest importance. All mail from the Services and for a period, all that from members of the Civil Construction Corps, was censored. The relations between the Australians and the U.S. servicemen were on a 'good footing' and cooperation was the order of the day. Even in June 1943 reports about Japanese transmissions kept recurring. There was also a report of a Japanese landing on the Staaten River in the Gulf. All reports were investigated and the two-way conversations were thought to be transmissions between Japanese submarines or between an agent on land and a sub. on reconnaissance.

As Japanese divers had spent considerable time in the area in the days of the pearl and trepang industries, these reports were taken seriously, locally at least.

A Civil Construction Corps worker found drums containing rice (12 tons) and dried fish (1 ton) on the coast just to the north of Iron Range. At first it was thought that it was wreckage from the Bismarck Sea Battle but then, with stories of secret agents rampant, it was suggested that the Japanese had landed it for future use under the cover of darkness. The drums were labelled 'Burma' which country was then in enemy hands. A Wenlock miner, Ted Densley, reported on 15th June 1943, having seen 40-50 drums of rice and dried fish, sealed cases of 'semi rimless rifle' ammunition — approximately .303. Two other oldtimers on their way from the Cape to the hospital at Iron Range, told of finding a Japanese boat 'in the Olive River' near Iron Range. It had 'about 40 tons of rice on it, some tea, candles, powdered milk and salted meat.' The informants considered it was a storehouse for visiting submarines.

Civilians Evacuated from Wenlock

Wenlock Goldfield was 90 miles (145k) from Portland Roads. During the fever of threatened invasion, miners' families and finally miners were evacuated, machinery removed and some of the improvements destroyed as part of the Defence Force's Scorched Earth Policy. Even underground pumps were taken away.[6] The menace of invasion was ever-present and steps to foil the enemy advance were taken seriously.

The Officer in Charge listed all the equipment and assured the Fishers and other miners at Wenlock that compensation would 'eventually be paid'. It proved to be rather inadequate. Motor vehicles, tractors and fuel were also commandeered. Like others, the Fishers were prepared to stay, to keep their .303s and to take their chances while exercising the opportunity to protect their assets. Wenlock's small airstrip had regularly been used by intrepid Cairns aviator Tom MacDonald who serviced the area in his tiny plane. When the army arrived, the existing strip was upgraded and some of the Wenlock miners were employed in the

Viewed from the north, the GORDON strip (runway 120°) is pictured with loop taxi runway 'E' in the foreground. In the background can be seen the OLD CLAUDIE strip in the middle and parallel and away to the east (left) is the NEW CLAUDIE strip.

operation. The little strip at Aurukun, built after three years of back-breaking work with picks, shovels, saws, axes and crowbars, was also used by planes from Jacky Jacky (Higginsfield). One one occasion three planes made use of it, two Kittyhawks and a Rapide. Mrs. MacKenzie of Aurukun wrote that such was the jubilation of the visit, the fowl house was raided and the visitors left with twenty-seven roosters, two sacksful, 'each with a hole cut in the sack for his head so that the sacks bristled with most indignant looking heads'. There was to be a 'feast' at the R.A.A.F. camp that night.

Iron Range was constantly on the alert. Their radio service worked three shifts to cover the full twenty-four hours. Cypher de-coders were also on the job and ready for anything. The Overland Telegraph Line could be used at times to speak with Townsville if necessary. This voice contact was greatly appreciated and was more than a step or two ahead of Morse.

For recreation the servicemen could also watch U.S. films, very patriotic and with, as one soldier complained, 'no sex and very little violence'. On free days they could also go fishing. The catch was sometimes accelerated by the use of hand grenades. The fish were cooked on fires carefully lit on the beach, and eaten with relish. Snakes were still a problem and, accompanied by scorpions, often crept into the sleeping tents and bedding. By 1944, the tide of war had turned and Iron Range was 'no longer required as an operational base'. By 11th August 1945, just before the end of the war, only one airstrip, Gordon, was being used. The other three strips were in varying states of decay but Gordon was still in 'excellent condition'. Similarly, the road from Iron Range to Portland Roads was deteriorating. The monsoon rains played havoc with culverts and bridges and the road was 'broken up and corrugated'. No funds were available to repair it. Plant and personnel were finally withdrawn at the end of August.

Coen Airstrip

Coen, in the centre of the Peninsula, south of Iron Range and just a little to the south of Weipa, was another emergency wartime airfield. There was an old landing ground there, but the citizens' patriotic fervour had tried to render it useless to enemy planes by placing obstacles in the form of 44 gallon (200litre) drums part-filled with dirt or cement at strategic points along the strip. Coen airstrip, with a ring of hills around it, was a tricky place to land, but the B25s used it quite successfully when needed. Allied planes in trouble often landed there, with the locals swiftly removing the obstacle drums and just as speedily replacing them when the plane took off successfully. Other planes in trouble landed on beaches. Some were able to get airborne again. Some weren't.

AMERICA'S latest beach-head! They're showing us how to develop the North.

Courtesy *Queensland Country Life* — 17/3/1966

U.S. and Australian Bases at Cooktown

Cooktown was also used as a wartime airbase. Jim Trench was once more deputised to find a suitable site. A short distance further inland, Laura was also considered and its strategic value studied. The little railway line was still there but there was no road. Trench decided against Laura and one of the staff on the little railmotor suggested that he look at a locality used by the Mission (Hopevale, which had by then been evacuated) and which might prove to suit the Allied Forces' needs. Trench inspected the site suggested and decided that it would be a better proposition than the existing Cooktown Civil Aerodrome. Work on the Four Mile or Mission Strip soon commenced. A light plane flew low over the 'Bloomfield River timber milling settlement' dropping a message, 'Bulldozer to be taken to Cooktown post haste.' The dozer was immediately shipped to Cooktown with two tractors 'freighted by land and sea' from Coen. Rollo Gallup, later to become more famous as the man in charge of the Mulligan Highway connecting Cooktown with Mareeba and later again as Cook Shire's Administrator, began work on the airstrip. Working with him was Reg Jennings, the man who dropped the request for the 'dozer over Bloomfield. He was a Main Roads engineer.

They met with an unexpected problem at first. From the air, the taxi-way stood out a glaring white from the other ground. The Camouflage Section of the Department for Home Security in Townsville swiftly fixed most of the camouflage troubles. Paint was rushed up to disguise buildings at Horn Island, Coen and Cooktown but there is no record of painting the taxi-ways. There must have been some alternative to paint. The runways were bitumen sealed.

Both Cooktown strips continued in use. The Mission strip was used mostly by the U.S.A.F. to refuel. The R.A.A.F. and U.S.A.F. also continued to use the somewhat inferior Civil strip to avoid congestion. Water was piped from the Endeavour River to supply the airstrips and later this was incorporated into a much improved town water supply.

Suspected Espionage

Towards the end of the war, in April 1944, the Commonwealth Security Services sent Major K.L. Murray to Cooktown to report on continuing stories of suspected espionage in Cooktown. Tales were still many and not too varied about 'someone' being in radio contact with the enemy. He spent sixteen days investigating and produced a document twenty pages long, but found no spies. Though, according to him, 'communistic tendencies' were rife. Russia was on the same side as the Allies but anything 'Red' was considered extremely dangerous. At the time the civilian population of Cooktown was less than 300. There was an R.A.A.F. unit of, according to a report of 23rd November 1943, 116 personnel at the Mission Strip and a smaller group of U.S. weathermen and signallers. A Field Survey Unit of the Army occupied a Hotel and a unit from the U.S. Navy was housed in the Convent. Radio communication was provided by an A.W.A. coastal station and the Civil Air Radio, as well as some secret operators (on our side) who worked with the Defence Forces.

Entry and egress to Cooktown was controlled, and permission to leave or to enter had to be granted by the local Police Sergeant before any movement could be made. Further south, Mareeba was a very important airfield. That site was preferred to one on the coast at Cairns because of better weather — less rain and fewer fogs. Again the ubiquitous Jim Trench was active in getting the construction under way. It was a busy airfield and planes based there certainly played their part in turning the tides of war.

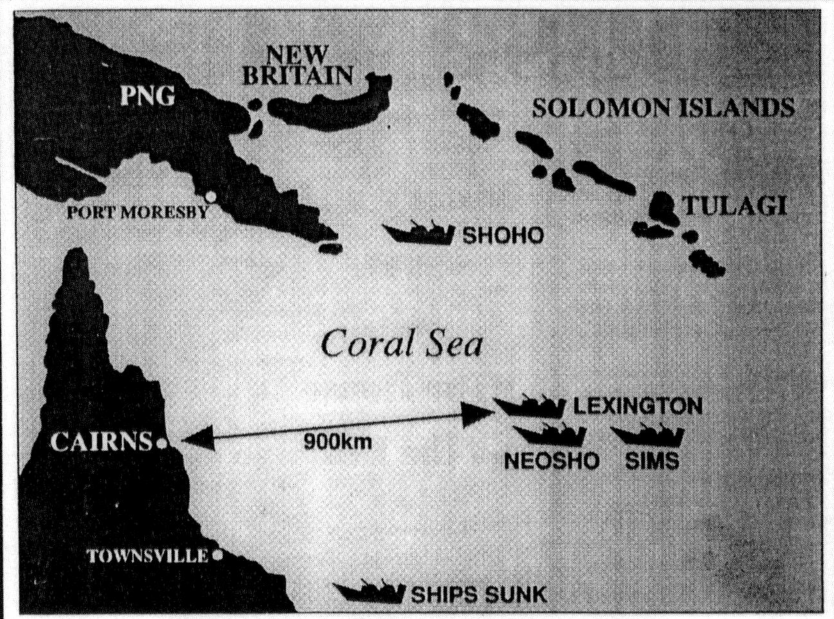

THE area where the Battle of the Coral Sea was fought.

No winners in naval onslaught

WORLD War 2 historians differ when it comes to summing up the Battle of the Coral Sea.

One school claims that there were errors by the commanders on both sides, but they agree that the US learned by their mistakes and put thoses lessons to good use in future naval actions.

Others maintained that although the Japanese could claim a victory by destroying three US ships to their one, the Allies won the day be preventing the invasion of Port Moresby.

However, other historians classified the outcome as a draw, even though Japan's most modern carriers were put out of action for months to come.

The end result of the Battle of the Coral Sea saw:

American losses

- The USS Lexington (aircraft carrier)
- The USS Sims (destroyer)
- The USS Neosho (oil tanker)
- 66 aircraft
- 564 US airmen and sailors killed.

Japanese losses

- The Shoho (light aircraft carrier)
- 77 aircraft
- 1074 men killed
- The Shokaku and Zuikaku (aircraft carriers) badly damaged.

Courtesy *Cairns Post*

12

Crocodiles Galore!

Increase in crocodile numbers — Fish population in rivers noticeably decreased · Growing markets overseas for the skins at attractive prices · Fresh and saltwater varieties taken · Intrepid shooters, both men and women, involved · Closure of the industry when crocodiles became protected, 1972

The crocodiles in the Peninsula have been there a very long time. They could possibly tell us a tale or two about the dinosaurs. For years the Aborigines speared and ate them. In turn, the crocodiles sometimes ate the Aborigines and, more often, their dogs. If the crocodile happened to be the totem of a particular clan, killing the saurian and eating the flesh was prohibited, as was the eating of the eggs. For those with no totemic connection the croc provided very tasty meals. The eggs were a popular dish when gathered by the women.

When Hann and his party travelled up the Kennedy River towards Princess Charlotte Bay he came across 'numerous alligator heads'[1] suspended from a sapling. He wondered if they were 'trophies of the chase' or part of a ritual. Every last skerrick of meat had been removed from the freshly-killed bones and hide. Even in recent years, especially in these days of crocodile farming, crocodile steaks are looked upon as a first class meal for the connoisseurs of cuisine as well as by Aborigines.

Crocs — A Problem to Man and Beast

The crocodiles had a field day when the cattlemen came with their herds and their horses. Beef was so much preferable to wallaby and there was much more of it obtained from the one kill. The big saurians, four metres in length and even bigger, had no difficulty in killing stock as they came in to water. Occasionally a stockman, too, joined the croc's menu. Naturally, the cattlemen retaliated and shot as many of the marauders as they could, though they mostly lacked the finely-tuned skills of the professional shooters who came later.

Crocs were also a problem on the settlements closer in. At the Barron River crossing near Smithfield, which is now a suburb of Cairns but was once a town in its own right pre-dating Cairns, crocodiles menaced travellers. One was shot and its gut found to contain 'a Chinaman's pigtail' and a 'Temperance medal'.[2] A Captain Innis who was engaged in delivering bread to Smithfield always carried extra loaves to 'heave at the crocodiles'[3] when he darted swiftly to the other side of the crossing. He managed to evade their crushing jaws but his dog didn't. Several people lost their lives to the crocs at the Barron River crossing.

Where the crocodiles were extremely active, on the rivers that ran into Princess Charlotte Bay and the Coral Sea, the depredations made by them made cattle-rearing exceedingly difficult, if not impossible. One property to the north of Cooktown at Wakooka, was abandoned by its owner after the crocodile population proved uncontrollable. At neighbouring Starcke Station, the head stockman, Bill Rootsey, estimated that, by the late 1920s, the big lizards had claimed half of the cattle there and killed or maimed many of the station's saddle-horses.

After World War 2 in the mid-1940s, the interest in professional croc-shooting took hold. There were men keen enough to pit their wits against the dangerous creatures and a market had opened up for the skins. Prior to that, some of the innovative local stockmen, like Jim McDowell, had experimented successfully with tanning the hides and converting them to more readily saleable items like belts, watchstraps, hatbands and the pouches that stockmen used to wear on their belts to carry pocket knives, matches and watches. Most of these were sold in Cairns and while none of the bushmen made a fortune from the enterprise, it provided them with an interesting occupation plus a bit of drinking money on their time off.

Pioneer Shooters — Male and Female

Guido Juneo was one of the earliest of the professional shooters. He usually camped, with two Aboriginal helpers, on the Annie River which enters Princess Charlotte Bay to the north of the larger Kennedy and Normanby Rivers. With his team he worked the country bordering the bay. The skins, after being cleaned, salted, dried in the sun and painted with a preservative arsenic-based product, were rolled into convenient bundles and taken to Cairns by one of the small boats that serviced the northern coastal settlements each month. Skins were bought by the 'inch' (about 2.5cms) and the measurement was taken across the width of the belly — not along the length of the creature. In the 1940s, the going price was a princely one shilling and sixpence (15c) per inch. Cooktown butcher, Norman Palmer, was one of the local buyers in the early days.

Courtesy Tom Braes

The Braes family's croc-shooting rig

For a period in the late forties, Juneo had a willing apprentice as well as his usual offsiders. He was Frenchborn Rene Henri from Melbourne. Rene would leave his society friends in the southern metropolis to spend some time each year chasing crocs (and often vice versa) in the Peninsula. He later teamed up with veteran Vince Vlasoff of the *Tropic Seas*. The *Tropic Seas* was rather unusual among the small boats of that era. Vince was tired of the depredation caused in wooden boats by the teredo worm and made his boat of steel. Together the enthusiasts organised an adventure holiday, flying Southerners north for a fortnight's croc-shooting and fishing, with visits to other places of interest, like the Atherton Tablelands and the Chillagoe Caves, sandwiched in between sea trips.[4] It proved very popular. Rene's marketing flair also resulted in a greater demand for the skins and a subsequent rise in the price paid for skins. A mighty two shillings and sixpence (25c) an inch.

Vince's wife, Olive, was the caterer for the holiday tours though Olive also performed well with the shooter's rifle. There were several women who did at least as well as the men as shooters. Grace Braes and Krys Pawlowski are two memorable examples. A replica of a gigantic, almost nine metre-long (28 feet 4 inches) crocodile shot by Krys in the Norman River is on display outside the Shire Office in Normanton. Vince and Olive Vlasoff gave the crocs away as a fulltime occupation in the 1950s and established the Underwater Observatory near Cairns to highlight the incredible wonders of the Great Barrier Reef. Vince later dived successfully to retrieve the cannon jettisoned by Captain Cook when the *Endeavour* ran aground. Not content with that feat, he later rescued the *Endeavour's* anchor.

As well as the wives, children also helped with the various chores associated with croc shooting, skinning, salting and preparing the skins for sale. When it was considered they had gained sufficient responsibility, they were allowed to use the gun under supervision. Mareeba solicitor, Tom Braes, has fond memories of his childhood days in the croc-shooting camps of the north.

Henry Hanush grew up in Cooktown and was one who really made good in the crocodile-shooting industry in the Peninsula. Mention Henry's name to the oldtimers and they immediately think crocodiles. His early days were spent as a 'ringer' (stockman) on the Peninsula cattle stations bordering Princess Charlotte Bay. Henry was not only a superlative marksman but seemed also to be absolutely without fear in his dealings with the ferocious monsters. He served a short apprenticeship with Palmer miner, Sam Elliott a.k.a. The Lone Wolf. Sam successfully worked his mines on the Palmer for many years but sometimes took time off to do a bit of croc-shooting. Sam's prowess with a firearm was mind-boggling. During his stint with Murray's 'Gorillas' (Volunteer Defence Corps) in WW 2 he often rode along the coast from Cooktown to Princess Charlotte Bay checking for any trace of enemy infiltration. In his travels, superb bushman that he was, he soon learned the whereabouts of all the waterholes and swamps along the way and gained an expert knowledge of the creatures that made their homes there. Sam found a very eager and able pupil in Henry. The younger man quickly absorbed much of his mentor's skills as a bushman and a wily hunter. He was the first to be called when a 'rogue' croc was known to be lurking at a river crossing or a waterhole waiting for unsuspecting stock to approach.

Henry Hanush

From there, Henry drifted away from stockwork and became a full time crocodile shooter, selling his skins at first to Jack Fearnley in Cooktown, who bought for a Sydney firm, George Johnson and Sons. In his dealings with crocs, Henry appeared to be fearless, diving out of his small boat to attach a rope to a recently-shot croc so that it could be hauled to the bank for skinning. At times, the crocodile wasn't quite dead and quite a lively struggle eventuated but Henry always won. Over the years he shot thousands of crocs but but always regretted he didn't get a twenty foot (6 metre) monster like Krys's. He did catch one huge one that looked as if it must pass that twenty-feet mark. Unfortunately when Henry hauled it to the bank, he and his mate, Jim Rollinson from Lakefield, were horribly disappointed to see that the croc had lost over a metre's length of his tail in an earlier mishap. Henry's dream of a record catch was once again shattered. He was the accepted champion of shooters and the whole community was desolated when, on 6th November 1973, just over a year after croc shooting was placed off-limits, Henry was found dead in his boat in the Endeavour River. His gun was beside him. He was forty six.

Olive Vlasoff also had a tragic end, though at a greater age, when the car in which she travelling hit a large rock that children had thoughtlessly rolled onto the highway for a prank.

The Raymond Family

Some graziers embarked upon croc shooting to gain extra income. The Raymond family who took up the virgin block, Kimba, in the early 1960s diversified into croc shooting to make ends meet while their small cattle herd was growing. Gordon, with his son Bill, worked mainly the fresh water or Johnstone River crocodiles. Gordon's wife Belle and the girls branched out as taxidermists and preserved the baby crocs they found, the 'stuffers'. These were eagerly bought as souvenirs by tourists in Cairns and looked very lifelike. They gave me one of the first ones that they prepared. Coincidentally, my home was a cattle station called Crocodile and my baby croc's permanent home soon became the wall just over the storeroom door. Its ferocious appearance, with its unbroken row of needle-sharp teeth, very successfully prevented our youngest son from raiding any goodies stashed in the storeroom. He'd heard just how dangerous those crocodiles were.

When they started out, Gordon and his offsiders were possibly the best outfitted shooters in the Peninsula at that time. They came north from a canefarm on the central coast and brought much of their useful machinery with them. The pride of Gordon's collection was his 1961 big Ford Blitz nine-ton truck It was ex-army but was brand-new and fitted with a winch as well. The truck's tray was large enough to carry a 'good solid' wooden boat and a ton of salt. Most of the shooters used the easier-to-carry aluminium dinghies but these were apt to be noisy. As Gordon said, if you put a gun down carelessly, within a split-second there wasn't a croc in sight.

The price for skins from the freshwater crocodiles wasn't as lucrative as that offered for the 'salties' but, living where they did on the western fall of the Peninsula, the Raymonds found that the freshies were there in great numbers, more than enough to make up for the lesser price. The salties were also too big and dangerous for Gordon, Belle and their young helpers to handle. Besides that, the salties were closer to the river mouths where the skinning and handling had to be done most uncomfortably, 'in the mud'. On a good night the Raymonds could shoot up to forty crocodiles. Their ton of salt would last them for three nights' shooting — three days' salting.

The size of the blitz also permitted them to carry a 400 gallon steel tank. This was filled with water and the young stuffer crocs were carried in it. It was a ticklish job netting them as they surfaced chasing moths. Any small damaged crocs were held in a creek at the homestead until they recovered. The two oldest girls usually did the skinning but were also shooters as required. The small crocs could be kept in the tank until time permitted for them to be stuffed. They were about a foot (30cms) long and returned the girls five pounds ($10) for their trouble. The skins were sold mainly to European buyers through local agents. Dutch and French buyers were very active but quite a lot were sold to Singapore.

There had been a crocodile population explosion in those days. Aborigines were no longer hunting them or their nests of eggs and the numbers multiplied accordingly. Eggs were normally laid just before the storms in September or October. They were deposited in a hollow and covered with a layer 30 to 45 cms deep of sand where the heat would cause them to hatch. The Aboriginal women knew where they were usually found and prodded likely sites with a stick to locate them. The crocs had eaten up the fish reserves in the rivers and waterholes. Many of them were in poor condition and looked, as Gordon Raymond said, 'half-starved'. They still had enough life in them to put up a fight when things got desperate. One such time was when the young Bill had shot a croc and was dragging it up the bank by its nose. The croc, in retaliation, did a roll. It pulled Bill back into the water and pushed him under. Fortunately Gordon was on the spot and quickly dispatched the crocodile — permanently this time.

Bill was an excellent shot and used to compete against Henry Hanush at the shooting gallery that often visited Laura during the week of the picnic races. Nothing gave Bill more pleasure than to have his occasional win over the acclaimed champion. It was claimed that Henry could shoot the ash from the end of a smoker's cigarette.

Courtesy Tom Braes

The Braes family and John Baxter with a large skin from a croc caught in Vanrook Creek

There is no doubt that the crocodiles accounted for losses among the domesticated animals in the area. Lakefield Station was a particularly dangerous place as it was a working cattle run and mustering was carried on regularly. On one muster local Aboriginal stockman, Jerry Bob, who was riding in the lead to coach a mob of mustered cattle across a waterhole, had his horse taken from under him. Other horses came up to the camp with the marks of deep wounds from tooth or claw. Jerry Bob's wife, Emily, had a lucky escape. She came out of an unprovoked attack with badly gashed legs. Working dogs led a dangerous life as well. Bowie Gostelow walked out on a log to get a clean drink from the deeper water, felt a sudden movement under his feet and rapidly made it back to the bank. His dog, Skipper, waiting patiently on the bank for Bowie's return wasn't as lucky.

Some shooters preferred to shoot crocodiles by day — early morning was a favoured time — and others by night. Spotlights were used and illuminated the saurians' eyes to a scary degree. The freshwater crocodile's eyes were reputed to be a dull red while their saltwater cousins' eyes glowed a brighter, shinier and more vibrant red. Many of the guns used by the early shooters were ex-army, .303 calibre, but occasionally the smaller .22 Hornet was used. Head shots were the ones usually attempted but if for some reason a head shot wasn't possible, and for all its wiliness the croc only has a comparatively small brain, spinal shots were tried. The spinal cord is of a reasonably thick diameter but the hide along the croc's back is extremely thick. The best place to aim for a spinal shot was just in front of the hindlegs. A good shot to the spine would stop a croc as quickly as a shot to the head.

Sometimes, to prevent a mortally wounded croc from escaping he was harpooned, but this took great skill. Usually the saurian objected strongly. They were extremely powerful and could easily overturn the boat or pull a hunter into the water. Damage done to the hide by a harpoon would considerably downgrade the value of the skin. Grappling hooks were also used at times to retrieve crocodiles from the bottom. Some of the more daring shooters captured their wounded crocs by reaching out of the boat and pulling a front leg up over the boat's bow. They claim that by holding it this way up to the armpit, a relatively large crocodile could be secured, thereby allowing the shooter a second close head shot. With the head and the body in the water, this could be achieved without the risk of blowing a hole in the boat. I haven't tried it though I'm sure Henry Hanush wouldn't have given it a second thought.

Most shooters marked with a float the place where a croc dived. Experienced shooters had a very good idea of just where a wounded croc would attempt to surface, not on top of the water but lying underneath close to the surface. The small boats were usually only four to five metres in length and powered by an outboard motor. However, when the shooters came close to their quarry, the motor was exchanged for oars as the very slightest sound was enough to alert the big creatures to danger. Shooters usually worked in pairs with one attending to the positioning of the boat while the other had the gun in one hand and the spotlight in the other. The man with the gun needed to have faultless aim as second opportunities were rarely on offer. Telescopic sights were standard equipment. At least one croc shooting party, Bob Plant and Bill Weare, used a larger boat in conjunction with the outboard. In their case, they had the specially-designed *Heatherbelle*, eight metres in length, as a tender, much in the same way as a mother ship served the smaller pearling luggers.

Croc-shooting Terminated — 1972

The shooters themselves were the first to notice the declining numbers of crocodiles in the mid-to-late 1960s. Some went as far to campaign for the protection of these creatures for whom, despite the hunter/hunted relationship, they felt an affinity. The Pawlowskis, a husband and wife team of shooters, set up a crocodile farm near Biboohra reputed to be the first in Australia, in an effort to conserve the species. Under the Labor Government of Gough Whitlam, crocodile shooting was legally terminated in 1972.

In recent years a pair of specially made crocodile skin cowboy boots was presented to the once U.S. President, Bill Clinton, on a visit to Port Douglas by the local Federal Member, Warren Ensch. The President was said to have been extremely taken with the gift.

Since the shooting ban, numbers have been building up again and we now hear reports of people, often unwary overseas tourists, being attacked. In some cases the attacks have been fatal.

Courtesy Tom Braes

Barry Braes with a couple of 'freshies' he shot

13

Cattle Pioneers and the Archer Report

A hard choice between completing the 'Missing Link' down the coast & building the Mulligan Highway inland along Mulligan's route · The Mulligan Highway wins out · Pre-road auto adventurers . A pair of New Zealanders drive a Baby Austin to Cape York, 1929 · Cook Shire goes broke and is placed under the control of an Administrator · Archer Report commissioned by the State Government to assess the future of the Cook Shire · Archer's favourable report generates optimism · The Peninsula gets its road and hopes are high for its future prospects

Eventually an inland road from Mareeba and Mt. Molloy won out over the concept of a shorter coast road from Daintree to Cooktown, even though the colourful local Member of Parliament, Bunny (H.A.) Adair, walked the proposed route from Cooktown to Daintree. He tramped through the wooded ridges, crossing the central 'Missing Link', as the eighteen miles (29k) without any form of wheel-track 'road' was called, to prove his point. Hopes for the benefits that the new road would bring were high. The thoroughfare was optimistically named the Mulligan Highway in honour of the prospector James Mulligan whose gold find started it all.

Although local Cooktown identity, Stan Boyd, was jokingly said to have been against building a road to the south — how'll we keep the people here? — the road did eventually come. There had been vehicles following the wagon ruts and pack tracks of the miners. Two intrepid New Zealanders, Hector MacQuarrie and Dick Matthews made the trip from Sydney to Cape York, reaching their destination after a series of adventures 'on the night of 31st October, 1928.'[1] They successfully managed to keep the little car in top running order and in pristine dentless condition as they had to sell it to finance the trip. Mrs. Vidgen, descendant of the famous Jardines, bought it at Thursday Island.

First Car Overland to Cooktown

On their way, they detoured to Cooktown when Ned Earl at Butcher's Hill told them that there could be a reward on offer for the first motor vehicle to make the overland trip from the south. There wasn't, but they enjoyed their detour and made up for a little of the lost time by buying tickets for themselves and their car, a tiny Baby Austin, on the Cooktown to Laura railmotor. As well as not having any visible road to follow, obtaining fuel was another of their problems. Some was obtained in Cooktown but, because of the Baby's very small size, no appreciable quantity of fuel could be carried.

Providentially they were able to replenish their supply again at Weipa Mission where the Flying Missionary — an allusion to his driving ability — had another, much larger car. The New Zealanders were told of the missioner's offer of fuel when they arrived at the Mein Telegraph Office near the then State-owned Merluna cattle station. There was, they were told by the station manager, a wagon road leading to the Mission but they were also cautioned to be careful not to frighten the 'quadrupeds' ahead of them and pulling a wagon. The 'quadrupeds' were unused to vehicles. The motorists soon found why the manager had used the word 'quadruped'. The wagon was drawn by '4 donkeys, about 6 mules, and 20 horses, all harnessed together.' The mules generally ignored the little car, the horses were 'obviously very much frightened' but the donkeys 'were very naughty indeed' and played up badly. Fortunately, the wagon wasn't overturned and the motorists reached Weipa Mission and the extra fuel supply. The Missionary also advised them to take some of the local Aborigines with them to assist getting the car to the Tip. This they did and a good time was had by all, with the motorists exceedingly grateful for the extra muscle power of their helpers.

They nearly ran out of petrol again just short of Cape York. The fuel gauge was very close to reading empty. When they called at the slaughter yards at Red Island Point they mentioned this in passing to the woman, Mrs. Gibson, who lived there. They were amazed when she offered them six bottles of petrol. She had just received her Wet Season stock of fuel for use in her petrol iron. They thought it a 'miracle'. Petrol irons were the modern woman's alternative at that time to Mrs. Potts's irons, which had to be heated on the top of a roaring wood stove. The irons had a small elevated reservoir for the petrol which led to a hollow loop with minute pin-holes, in the body of the iron. Methylated Spirits was poured on the loop and lit. When the ironer considered that the loop was hot enough to convert the liquid fuel to a gas to power the iron, she carefully turned the fuel on. They were certainly a cut above Mrs Potts's offering but they did possess at times the attributes of incendiary bombs. No one mourned their passing when the use of electric irons became possible.

With fuel today giving not much change from a dollar for a litre, it is interesting that the economic Baby drove from Cairns to Cape York for a fuel cost — petrol and oil — of just under today's $26. The Shell Company asked the motorists to contact them when they reached Cape York. They were interested if the little car could actually do the trip and to know what fuel it used. On arrival Hector wired Shell and the latter promptly sent them a refund cheque for the fuel used. 'We did not return it,' wrote Hector in his book, *We and the Baby*.

Captain Appleby Tries to Survey Wartime Road

Over a decade later, during the War, Captain Sid Appleby led 80 'hand-picked military bushmen'[2] and 20 vehicles on a survey trip along the eastern side of Cape York Peninsula. It was 1942. The Captain was cognisant of Japanese landings in the recent past in an area from Cooktown to north of Coen and hoped to improve road communication for the Allies should that happen again. His recommendations weren't all that optimistic, even allowing for the greatly increased difficulties compounded by the Wet Season. 'It is seriously recommended that horses be made available, or the means of quickly procuring horses, to any commander assigned to an active role in Cape York. Even in the Dry Season horses can *walk* faster than motor transport can push through the sandy forest. Unless some sort of road is made, pack horses following at 4 miles per hour or less, can easily beat motor transport.'

The Allied armies did make roads in the far northern part of the Peninsula, but it wasn't until the Mulligan Highway was pushed through to Cooktown, a branch road turning off at the present Lakeland constructed to Laura and then gradually extended to its furtherest limit, did the Peninsularites get their road. This roadless state, as well as making it almost impossible to get supplies for station improvements like fencing and water points, also made it hard for parents to educate children. With no regular mail service Correspondence lessons weren't an alternative. Irene Taylor of Coen told how, to attend boarding school at Herberton on the edge of the Atherton Tableland, she first rode for two days on a horse to Port Stewart. A pearl lugger picked her up from there and took her to Flinders Island from where she could board a coastal steamer on its way south to Cairns. From Cairns she travelled by train to her school. The alternative to this was a five-day ride to Laura to catch the railmotor to Cooktown, another boat trip to Cairns and then up to Herberton by rail. To have a road of almost any sort was considered little short of a miracle.

When the road to Cooktown was finally completed it was usable only in the Dry season, from the end of the Wet in March or April until the storms which generally heralded the onset of the monsoonal rain at the end of the year. At first there were no bridges. Gradually, primitive log bridges and a few concrete causeways were put in place. Travel on the road was slow, but even at a mere 25 miles per hour (40k) it was five times quicker than travelling the same route by horse. As the road continued to improve, small cattle trucks made their appearance to at least as far as Laura. The intrepid Burton brothers were pioneers of this enterprise and George Burton was himself killed in a truck accident at the McLeod crossing. George was not driving at the time. The speed with which cattle could be transported to the relatively new saleyards in Mareeba, the meatworks in Cairns and the paddocks of coastal fatteners filled the Peninsula cattlemen with almost boundless optimism. Even the dream of a local meatworks took second place for a while.

The cattle not only arrived at their destination in a fraction of the time droving took, but they were usually in much better condition when they arrived, though some drovers claimed, quite truthfully, that they often fattened cattle on the long trip down. The cattlemen looked forward to better prices which in turn would lead to some small profit. The better return could then be invested to buy tick-resistant bulls, the hump-necked Zebus (Brahmans), to improve the robustness of their herds. Wire could be bought to erect fences and possibly there might even be some money left to provide for the installation of much-needed watering facilities. The future looked good.

With Small Rate Base, Cook Shire in Difficulties

Over 20,000 head of cattle walked down and passed through the Government dip at Laura in the 1950s and 60s. Cattlemen were hopeful this could be increased both in number and in quality with the hoped-for improvements to their herds and properties. Sadly, by the mid-fifties the Cook Shire Council was struggling financially. It had a limited number of rate-payers, mostly cattlemen, to finance its operation. The opening of the road made it necessary for the Shire to purchase machinery for road maintenance, and southern-based governments didn't seem to realise that the country north of Cairns was inhabited. They did manage to get a Federal Aid grant but money was very hard to come by.

The Shire was the largest in Queensland at 48,000 sq. miles (114,938 square kms), just under the area of England [3] and very nearly twice the size of Tasmania. It had a revenue base of $30,000 per year plus the Aid grant of $48,000.[4] The care and maintenance of the road took all of this — and more. The Shire councillors had hoped that the road would quickly lead to development and a rate-base that increased in proportion to the resulting prosperity but their dreams foundered. Finally it came to the stage when the Council had to give up their fight to exist. After some discussion in State Parliament, a man was sent up to investigate the situation and to report back.

The Archer Report

He was Archibald Archer, a retired grazier from Longreach. In 1958 the Archer Report stated that there were then 'some 31' cattle stations in the Cook Shire, ranging in size from 200 to 4500 sq. miles (518 to 11,655 sq k). Cattle numbers, difficult to obtain accurately, were thought to be in excess of 125,000. The State Government levied a fee per head on the annual Stock Returns that owners were required to fill in. This naturally kept the official figures at a 'conservative' level. With the benefit of the road, the cattlemen felt that their greatest handicap was removed. Plans were also back to encourage the establishment of a killing works at or near Cooktown with chilling/freezing capabilities for both beef and fish products. Cooktown, situated almost at the mouth of the Endeavour River, possessed a natural port readily able to be used by large vessels. Market access was the main problem for the stock and it was hoped that the road, once upgraded to all-weather standard, would solve this. The fishing grounds were much closer to Cooktown than to the fishermen's base at Cairns and it was hoped refrigeration facilities would attract many of them to move north.

A report[5]by the Minister for Public Works and Local Government, Jim Heading, himself with a country background, showed that he was as optimistic as the Peninsularites. He believed that cattle numbers could be 'lifted by approximately one third on a short term basis and doubled on a larger term basis.' From this increase in productivity, he predicted, other 'development would follow'.

Archer's investigation, undertaken from the end of October 1958 to 27th November the same year, was as comprehensive as possible, given the time available. During that time, Archer flew 1000miles (1600k), travelled almost double that by vehicle, almost always a 4WD, sailed on the little cattle boat, *Wewak,* and even resorted to walking in the less accessible country. He visited half of the cattle properties, nine of the ten commercial farming operations, five of the six 'towns and settlements', three Missions and a Department of Native Affairs settlement, and, for good measure to round it off, one tin mine. He kept a diary and took notes of his interviews with not only the station owners, farmers and Mission people but with 'timber contractors, miners, fishermen' and Public Servants. Widening his horizons, he consulted with the adjoining Shires of Mareeba and Douglas, the Cairns Harbour Board, Meatworks and Main Roads executives, Engineers, Irrigation and Water Service and Agriculture Department officers as well as representatives of a variety of local industries. Mindful of the benefits improved pastures could bring to the Peninsula's grazing industry, he also consulted the staff at the Pasture Research Station at Parada then flourishing between Mareeba and Dimbulah.

Archer considered that the industry with the more immediate future was the cattle industry. Although most of the annual rain fell in a few short summer months, it was considered 'safe' country not prone to regular droughts. The 'disadvantages be rather in marketing problems and shortage of improvements.' Since the opening of the grazing lands to trucks in 1951, cattle numbers had risen, as had the branding figures for the natural increase. In addition to the 'conservative number of 125,000 head plus' running on the stations, the Mission Settlements ran over 10,000 cattle on their own account and which were not included in the general total. He estimated that the nett return to cattlemen, less selling costs and freight/droving was $32- $34 per head.

On the agricultural side, he was also optimistic. While a much larger area had been farmed 'at one time or another', the number of farms left in production were managing to pay their way. The growing of tropical fruit was an outstanding success if the problem of marketing were overlooked. 'Sugar, tobacco, cotton, coffee have all been grown successfully'. Other farmers had gone in for improved pastures for cattle fattening, with the sale of hay and pasture seed as a sideline.

'Much timber' had been milled and a 'good deal' remained to be marketed, Archer reported. Cooktown had, only in the August of 1957, the year prior to Archer's visit, closed its sawmill which had employed 32 men. Bloomfield's plymill was still operating with a staff of fifteen, and two men using a portable saw contracted bridge timber for the little railway line to Laura. Several Missions and one Settlement also operated their own sawmills. Archer considered that improvements to the roads would encourage both the Cooktown mill to re-open and the Bloomfield mill to 'expand its operations'.

While acknowledging that he had 'little knowledge' of mining, he noted that gold production for the preceding five years had shown a steady rise but that the production of both tin and wolfram was declining. Again, he considered that the availability of reasonable access roads would stimulate both exploration and production. He noted that a 'Canadian show' was optimistically prospecting for alumina with headquarters near Mapoon. The value of Weipa's 'Remarkable Red Cliffs'[6] was still to be commercially recognised.

Archer considered that tourism also had a bright future and again recommended the 'speeding up of the construction of the Mulligan Highway' and extending it as a road trafficable for cars, to Portland Roads and Coen. In addition, he considered that the completion of the eighteen miles (29k) of Missing Link over the McDowall Range between the end of the existing road to Baird's Crossing on the Daintree River and Timber Camp, be carried out.

From Timber Camp a road, trafficable by 4WD and with 'safe steep grades', led to Bloomfield which was connected to Cooktown by way of Rossville and the tinfields. However, he gave financial preference to hurrying the development of the Mulligan Highway.

In Archer's opinion — and I daresay the cattlemen agreed — as subscribers to over 70% of the Shire's annual finance, cattlemen were paying rates in excess of what they could afford and of what they received in return. High rates and high freights were frustrating the cattlemen's hopes of property improvement. 'Bulls, wire and water' were needed, he stressed and told of one property out from Coen that paid over $3000 in rates while a smaller one, '150 miles (240k) from the nearest Shire road' was still asked to pay $100 per year in rates. Archer was tempted to wonder what the property owner received in return for his contribution to the Shire's expenses. High freight charges were a severe deterrent to making the necessary improvements to increase both the number and the quality of stock able to be de-pastured safely.

In addition, many cattlemen had not erected additional fencing to upgrade stock management as, never having been surveyed, the properties' boundaries were in doubt. Archer considered this could be alleviated and 'reasonably accurate boundaries' be established using aerial surveys.[7] For the cattle industry he advised the provision of 'long term, low interest loans' for the purchase of ' bulls, wire and water'. Brahman bulls should be introduced to the herds to promote tick tolerance, the erection of cattle dips, yards and paddocks encouraged as well as the purchase of pasture seeds, plant and building materials. He also suggested taxation concessions to try to equalise the very high cost of living. His general idea was to breed cattle on the existing but upgraded runs for fattening on improved pasture blocks. A stylo, Townsville lucerne, was widely established in the Peninsula and trial plots of newer legumes were looking promising. The establishment of improved pasture blocks along the higher rainfall coastal section would aid cattle fattening and the finished stock could be transported from the coastal landings by cattle boats larger and more efficient than the valiant little converted landing barge, the *Wewak*. One property owner near Cooktown, in a drier than average year, was fattening a beast to the acre.

A case was made for the establishment of 'some form of meatworks within the Shire, preferably at Cooktown' which had the best port and was already used by vessels of 5000 tons. An annual flow of 10,050 cattle was estimated to be immediately available for slaughter in varying mob sizes. Laura and Lakefield, with an annual turn-off of 1400, was the largest producer and Aurukun Mission proposed a turn-off from there of 500 head. Mission and Settlement cattle hadn't been included in the estimated count. As well as having a good port and an adequate supply of cattle available, Cooktown also had the back-up of potential dry and irrigated farming land.

Archer considered that the 'provision of cold storage' could interest professional fishermen 'now operating from Cairns' to change their base to Cooktown which was much closer to the fishing grounds. Another 'long-term view could be the development of the works to can both fruit and meat' as the area grows tropical fruit 'profusely'. A short four-month, 'winter', operating season was suggested for the beef part of the operation. Coen people favoured a local airbeef scheme similar to one that was operating in the Kimberley, where refrigerated meat could be air-freighted from Coen to markets in New Guinea and the islands. Mr. Archer considered that this scheme was unfortunately 'at present impracticable'. At one period Cooktown had sent unfrozen meat to Cairns and to Thursday Island but the scheme, though successful at its onset, didn't continue.

Emphasis was placed on the method of transport of cattle to Queerah Meatworks in Cairns. The average weight of a run of 2000 head from the Peninsula killed there was 452 lbs dressed (a little over 200kgs) for steers and just under 200kgs for cows. Only 12% graded first quality. A draft from a 'well-improved' property closer in showed what could be achieved. The cattle, brought down by the *Wewak* from Cooktown graded as 'high as 78% first'. Archer considered that the annual subsidy for operating cattle boats would be less than half of the costs of the Laura to Cooktown railway ' which has little significance in the development of the cattle industry'. *S.S.Waiben*, which serviced the population of Thursday Island was liberally subsidised and 'rarely calls at any Peninsula port.'

Until road transport of stock could be up-graded in load-size as well as travelling conditions, 'more water facilities should be provided along the route for travelling stock'. Supplies of penicillin (refrigerated) should also be kept at 'Musgrave Station, Laura township, Butcher's Hill and Maitland Downs stations' and supplied to drovers at cost to reduce losses from Foot Rot. Agriculture suffered from the same difficulties as grazing. Markets and access to them, high freight both in and out, isolation and lack of finance, all worked against it. Peanuts and maize continued to be grown with some financial success around Cooktown. There were good possibilities for the irrigated farming of tobacco at Laura and at the Hann River to the north. Cotton could also be successfully grown as well as the crops already planted along the Endeavour River. Archer foresaw Foyster's dream of the Lakeland farms and suggested 'dry-farming on the Basalt country south west of Cooktown'. The Lockhart River /Portland Roads area was also worthy of agriculturists' attention and port facilities could be established there without trouble.

However, Archer summed up by saying, ' It is recommended that no action be taken other than to apply such encouragements to pasture grazing and agriculture as may be applied to the cattle industry generally.'

The Cook Shire Council was 'heavily in debt and virtually bankrupt'. Archer advised that they sell off some of the newly purchased road maintenance plant 'to liquidate outstanding loans' and for contractors and 'very stringent economics' to be used. Then came the crunch. He advised that it would be better to 'disband the Council temporarily' and to appoint an Administrator. This bombshell severely shocked the local population. Only little Thursday Island, of all the districts in Queensland, had an Administrator and not an elected council. A practical man to the end, Archer recommended that the Administrator preferably be an engineer cognisant of the difficulties faced in the Shire[8]. When the Local Authority was 'on its feet again,' a new council could be elected to carry on. The Administrator was appointed on the 15th January 1959.

Archer succeeded in acquiring his practical engineer to take charge. W. Hansen, the Department of Development's northern director was chosen for the task. He quickly learned firsthand of what difficulties had to be surmounted and set about making improvements to the road system. His place was later taken by a man whose name is synonymous with Cooktown and its Mulligan Highway — Rollo Gallop. Contractors, more eager to tender now that conditions were improving, were used rather than the expensive Shire machinery, and the services of Consulting Engineers, a major expense hitherto, were dispensed with. Rollo Gallop was also a more than competent engineer. He was also a man who could use his boundless stock of ingenuity when required. I had heard a story that, unable to obtain sufficient blasting explosive, he had used ex-army hand grenades to blast the road up the Byerstown Range. After meeting Rollo's son Darcy, I thought I had better corroborate the story. "Did he really use hand grenades," I asked. "No," was the reply. For a few moments I was sadly disappointed. It had been a good story. I was quickly cheered by Darcy adding, "They were land-mines."[9] They had been railed up from old army supplies in Brisbane. Archer rounded off his report by saying that, after the establishment of good roads, 'other developments can follow'. The Peninsularites heartily agreed.

14

A Road from Cooktown to the Daintree

Rollo Gallop in charge of construction · Seeing possibilities in the cattle industry, new owners buy properties · Professor Skerman reports on future agricultural and pastoral enterprises · Truckies take advantage of the road to capture new business · Toots Holzeimer and her truck 'Little Toot' · Road access makes possible improvements to herd quality by the introduction of new bulls and to management tools like fencing and water-facilities · Availabilty of Sea Beef adds to cattlemen's choice of transport for stock · Machinery for hay-making brought in, kerosene refrigerators and lighting plants improve living conditions at the homesteads · New station airstrips pave way for Aerial Ambulance Service · Purchases of prime cattle stations by U.S. interests · Weipa's success story. Royal and vice-regal visitors · The road makes for easier access to the annual picnic race meetings

The road would have probably taken a lot longer to become a reality if it weren't for the skills and enthusiasm of R.D. (Rollo D'arcy) Gallop. Though badly gassed in the First World War at Ypres in France, Rollo played a leading part in the contruction of many very difficult roads and other projects in north Queensland. As far back as July 1947[1] Gallop, with his offsider Horrie Moon, set off in an old Army jeep to map out a road to connect Cooktown to Cairns. The road went through Mareeba and Mt. Molloy to the small mining settlement of Mt. Carbine. From there a track of sorts snaked its way to the Roberts' family property, Curraghmore. At the Cooktown end, a build-as-you-go route connected Cooktown and Helenvale with Butcher's Hill station. As Rollo and Horrie tried to follow the old wagon road from Curraghmore over the miners' Cooktown Crossing of the Mitchell to Butcher's Hill, they came to a battered sign with COOKTOWN outlined in 'punched nailholes' and 'spiked to an old stunted box-tree.'[2] At least they were on the right track. They followed the drovers' route to the Byerstown Range where the wagon road, built over a half-century earlier, took them, even in a four wheel drive as nippy as a jeep, two hours to negotiate the three miles (just under five kilometres) from the top to the bottom.

After getting directions (and tea and scones) from Doreen Wallace at Butcher's Hill, the two pathfinders proceeded through Springvale and King's Plains stations to the Annan River on the way to Helenvale. 'Fortunately the water level at the Annan was not over two feet (60cms) so the crossing was effected without incident.' It took two hours after they left the Lion's Den hotel at Helenvale to reach the Commercial hotel, twenty miles (32 k) away in Cooktown.

This was the start of the road. Funds were found to bulldoze the track from Curraghmore to Butcher's Hill and Archie Elmsley was placed in charge of the heavy machinery needed for the job. Archie was known for his trusty 4WD high clearance command car, a weapon carrier, another U.S. army vehicle. Within three months, four wheel drives were able to use the 'road' with care. In 1950, after an inspection by Commissioner Crawford, the road was declared to be the Mulligan Highway, in memory of the prospector who blazed the way. Sadly, Mulligan's association with the road is no longer acknowledged. It's now the Cooktown Development Road. The 'highway', which it didn't really resemble, came about because roads coming under that description were 'free of cost to local authorities'. Other road categories were the complete financial responsibility of the shire or shires involved. It achieved its highway status because it was considered to be a road of 'national importance'.

The road to be constructed was divided into three sections with two-way radio contact with Cairns Aerial Ambulance Base, VKA, at each camp. Apart from the emergency ambulance service, VKA also provided a means to send and to receive telegrams and, more importantly to the road gangs working to outwit the Wet, useful daily weather reports.[3] It was the first radio system operated by the Main Roads Department in Queensland and proved to be very successful. Within twelve months of the start of the road upgrade, intrepid cattle truck drivers were already making use of the road.

Gallop and Moon also made a preliminary inspection of a road survey from Butcher's Hill, through Laura to Portland Roads. As MacQuarrie and Matthews had railed themselves and The Baby from Cooktown to Laura, Gallop and Horrie Moon were the first to drive a motorised vehicle from Butcher's Hill to Laura. Consideration was given to using the course of the railway to Laura for the proposed road but the presence of the eighty-seven narrow bridges along the route dampened the enthusiasm for that idea. It is to be regretted that Rollo Gallop's name is not perpetuated anywhere along the road on which he spent so much of his energy and enthusiasm. One road name has some association with him but that is probably remembered only by the old-timers. Capsize Gully commemorates an occasion when Rollo's faithful weapon-carrier badly let him down — and not very gently. It was some time on that lonely stretch before Rollo was discovered, rescued and taken to Cairns to have his injuries treated.

Increased Interest Leads to Property Sales

With the road at last a reality, interest was generated in purchasing Peninsula cattle properties. In the mid-1950s, one of the largest properties, Rokeby, north of Coen, was sold to H.E. Corbould from Tenterfield in New South Wales. Rokeby had been in the hands of the Massey family for generations and was only sold to wind-up an estate. The earliest of the Rokeby Masseys, Charles, was speared. He climbed onto his horse to ride for help — a mere 400 kilometres away. Seriously injured, he fell from his horse, dead, after traversing but a third of the distance. Glenville Massey was the last of that family to own the seven thousand square kilometre block.[4] With Rokeby, Corbould also became owner of South Edge, the smaller bullock depot situated between Mt. Molloy and Mareeba. For many years, mobs of Rokeby bullocks made the trip down to be grown-out and fattened at South Edge. Corbould was keen to keep up the same practice and planned also to establish a small stud herd at South Edge to provide herd bulls for Rokeby. He was attracted to the idea of sea transport for cattle but the price difference won the day for the drover. The cost per head for droving two year old steers from Rokeby to South Edge was $3 per head. The rate for sea transport to Cairns from Marina Plains was $8 per head in addition to the cost of droving them down to the landing.

Corbould was quite happy with his purchases. Rokeby was watered by the 'Coen, Archer, Holroyd and Kendall — in addition to over a hundred permanent lagoons.' He certainly had no problems with water, and was confident that road conditions would only continue to improve.

During the War, people had been evacuated from cattle stations north of Wenlock. A few had been able to take some of their herd with them but most of the cattle were abandoned to their own devices. With no one to brand the resulting calves, cleanskin bulls reigned in profusion, escaping contact with humans by hiding in the turkey bush and nearby scrubs. During the War, the U.S. forces took advantage of the wild cattle to obtain a real treat, 'fresh beef on the hoof'. Being chased by armed personnel made the cattle rather wary of humans but gradually the cattlemen returned to restore order once more.

Ron Heineman was at Bramwell and another New South Welsh family moved up near him. Rennie Bornholt took over the Locherbie/Laradeenya lease from the pioneering Holland family who had been evacuated further south. Mrs. Bornholt must've noticed a great difference between life in the far north and her previous life on the Tweed but she soon settled in.

About this time, the Senior Lecturer in Agriculture at the University of Queensland, P.J. Skerman, decided to take advantage of the new road and to look into the remote cattle country management at first hand. Inspired by the optimism induced by the relatively recently-established saleyard complex at Mareeba, the new road and Sea Beef, many men from the Department of Primary Industry were beginning to visit the area previously unknown to them. Professor Skerman found the isolation a little overwhelming at first. There were then, he wrote, 'only *four* white women north of Coen'.[5]

Skerman also commented on the ever-present problem of stock and station water supply. There were shallow wells but only one 'successful bore'. This was at Olivevale on the northern outskirts of Laura township. Skerman accurately predicted that the road would encourage the entry of boring contractors. Primarily their machines were the old, slow Southern Cross percussion rigs but they did provide welcome water on several properties.

Olivevale, held by Porter and Turner for many years, was put up for sale after Rupe Porter's untimely death. The sale advertisement advised would-be buyers that 'stock have not more than three miles (5k) to walk to any watering facility'. Quite a lot of outside interest was aroused but, much to Mrs. Porter's satisfaction, the buyers were locals, the Elmes family of Springvale and Cooktown. A new era had well and truly dawned. Instead of the property being offered for sale at the traditional three pounds ($6) a head for the cattle and the property 'thrown in', the price was 50,000 pounds ($100,000) for the station with '6200 Devon/Shorthorn cross mixed cattle' available for an extra three pounds per head.

With the opening of the road, primitive though it was at first and trafficable only in the dry months of the year, optimism was rife. Even the 'old' station owners and their ringers began to take driving lessons and most properties bought at least a four wheel drive. These were usually ex-Army jeeps or the new Land Rover, Britain's answer to the go-anywhere jeep. Toyotas hadn't yet migrated to the north. Some property owners invested in a station truck, nothing very big, unless it was an ex-Army four wheel drive Blitz. They were usually only thirty hundredweight (a bit over a tonne) but were expected to carry as much as could be stacked on the tray, with sturdy greenhide ropes aplenty to keep the load there.

Mechanical knowledge also had to be acquired, often in stressful situations, as mechanics and garages were few and far between. Cooktown did have a mechanic and when George Nankervis came down from further north, he set up a mobile motor repair service which was greatly appreciated. George's services were so much in demand that his own vehicle was possibly in greater need of attention than many of his clients.

As the roads improved, intrepid truckies extended their suburban services to cart cattle down, and goods up, the Peninsula. It was an excellent opportunity for cattlemen to obtain those new bulls and the fencing materials they had so badly needed. There was even a lady truckie, Toots Holzeimer, who made the arduous trip regularly for years in her 'Little Toot' until she lost her life, crushed against her beloved truck, in a tragic loading accident at Weipa.

The third part of the cattleman's wish-list, 'water' was also speeded up by the advent of the road. Any man-made water supplies and storages prior to the coming of the road were either small weirs laboriously placed across creeks or wells dug by hand with pick, shovel, bucket and windlass, a modicum of explosive and a lot of determination. If water couldn't be found at a reasonably shallow depth, the well-sinking was abandoned and another site, usually divined, checked out. On arriving north to set up their home at Kimba, Gordon 'Pop' Raymond and his family put down a number of wells for Charlie Wallace at Butcher's Hill and for other cattlemen. As in everything the Raymonds did, the whole family participated. Pop 'laid the charges' but the girls did more than their share in excavating the loosened dirt.

Boring plants and bulldozers began to appear under the control of contractors not afraid to have a go. The success of their operations inspired locals to buy their own machinery. Bill Wallace of Crocodile was so impressed with the bores Ed Marsterson had put down next door at Butcher's Hill that he bought himself a Southern Cross percussion plant. His operator, Bill Raymond

From Melbourne Zoo — the Robbins Bull as a 2 yr old — ancestor of many Zebu's still in the North.

from Kimba, quickly learned the art and put down many welcome bores in the area. Some of the old discarded well sites were tried, and yielded good supplies at an increased depth. Ronnie Solomon of Yarraden invested in a bulldozer and soon had more than enough dams and earth tanks to ensure a permanent stock-water supply in all but the extremely exceptional year. The dozer was also used for the making of roads on the station and in the construction of an airstrip.

New bulls purchased were almost without exception Zebu or Zebu-cross as Brahmans were then called. They were hardier, more heat tolerant and tick resistant than the British cattle breeds and had been put to the test by some forward-thinking cattlemen since the first Zebu made his way north to Mowbray near Port Douglas from the Melbourne Zoo in the early 1900s. Before you laugh at the place of origin of the zebu or Bos Indicus in Australia, the well-credentialled American Brahmans can trace their roots back to a bull from a circus — Hagenbecks.

The little Sea Beef boats also helped to make life easier by carrying freight to the Endeavour River, Marina Plains, Lockhart River, Catfish and other small landings on their way north to pick up cattle. The legume, Townsville Lucerne, a stylo, hardy and with a high protein content, was rapidly spreading through Peninsula pastures. Some station-owners used it to make hay for use in the dry weather and for feeding weaners. At first it was laboriously cut by scythe or reaping hook until the first mowers and balers became available. The early balers had very little in common with their latterday counterparts except for the end result — the small 'square' bale. Hay was cut, windrowed and dried and then forked into the early balers which compressed the dried pasture into the required shape as they were drawn along the length of the windrows. Even the baler twine had to be applied and tied manually until the newer models arrived. Haystacks, stored in bush timber framed, galvanised iron roofed sheds, were also admirable for use in the dry months to keep lactating cows in strong condition.

Much of the early freight was destined for the running of the properties but gradually there was room for 'luxuries'. Kerosene fridges and lighting plants replaced the old Coolgardie safe coolers and the temperamental carbine lights though, it could be said, kerosene refrigerators were not without their share of temperament. Airstrips were put down, large enough to accommodate the small planes flown by the wonderful Cairns Aerial Ambulance Service. With two-way radios on most of the properties, each with a link to the Ambulance's base, VKA, in Cairns, speedy evacuation was possible for most of the year. Medical — and at times other non-medical but very helpful — advice was readily given over the radio network. This provided the Mantle of Safety John Flynn had in mind when he founded the Royal Flying Doctor Service. The

Aerial Ambulance finally gave way to this service but the little ambulance planes will always be remembered for their ability to land — and take off — from just about anywhere. They never missed a call for help.

As well as the road making it easier to muster and to sell cattle, prices for cows and bullocks rose with expanding world markets — as did the price of herd-improving bulls. Probably for the first time, cattlemen were finding that they could make their hoped-for improvements and buy bulls out of their cattle sale proceeds. Reliance on finance from the pastoral houses wasn't quite as necessary to tide them over. During this euphoric state of affairs, others began to notice the potentials of the Peninsula. The country was reasonable grazing land and less prone to drought than many areas. With suitable pasture grasses and legumes it could be improved to carry larger herds in safety. The annual rainfall, though falling mostly in the monsoonal summer months, was for the most part, reliable. Above all, property values, compared to those in less remote areas, were low. It wasn't long before new owners moved in. The most conspicuous of these were the American investors.

U.S. Investment in Cattle Properties

Then chairman of the Australian Wool Board, Sir William Gunn, who had interests in both sheep and cattle, acted as Australian agent for many of the American purchasers. He was go-between for a syndicate headed by Texas oil-magnate, Bob Leibock.[6] On his advice, the consortium bought what was possibly the top property in the Peninsula, Lakefield, with its rolling marine plains and abundant (croc-infested) rivers and waterholes. With Lakefield, they also bought the adjoining property to the south, Laura Station. Lakefield had easy access to Sea Beef's landing facility at Marina Plains and Laura Station was all but in the outer suburbs of Laura township.

An immense development program of fencing, water management, and pasture and herd improvement was quickly undertaken. Finance did not seem to be a problem. Staff was brought in, mostly from the south, many with agricultural and animal husbandry qualifications to aid in land development and herd improvement programs. For a time, local knowledge was brushed aside until the value of that hard-won experience was realised.

Andrew, John and Ferdinand Duda, successfully involved in the canning industry in Alabama, followed up by acquiring Merluna and York Downs near Weipa. This purchase was increased by the later addition of Batavia Downs and Bertiehaugh in the same area. Wylie Fancher, another American from Alabama, purchased Mount Mulgrave in the Mitchell River catchment, followed by Yarraden, Ron Solomon's property on the old Ebagoolah Goldfield. Further north again, Richard Rand, an American who also had interests in Hawaii, became the new owner of Silver Plains near Coen. It was estimated that the turn-off from the American-controlled properties at that time roughly approximated half of the Peninsula's total of just under 20,000 head. The American syndicates also discussed their interest in opening their own meatworks to treat the increasing cattle numbers, probably in Cairns.

The future looked rosy. Mineral exploration was coming back into the picture with the development of the bauxite deposits at Weipa at the foremost. All this was expected to lead to even better roadworks and increased amenities to the benefit of all living in the area. The Minister for Lands, Mr. Fletcher, was very supportive of the American purchases. While freight was much easier to arrange and considerably cheaper in cost, large-scale development such as that planned by the U.S. syndicates, was still largely beyond the financial capacities of local producers. They took a slower course.

Kalpower, held by the Watkin family and Jack Dwyer for many years, also went over to U.S. ownership. It adjoined Lakefield on the eastern boundary, sharing with it part of the Princess Charlotte Bay coastline. While all the properties invested in herd-improving bulls, Kalpower went a step further and established a Brahman stud. Greg Webster, a practical cattleman with experience gained on his parent's stud in southeast Queensland, was in charge. For some years Greg took a small team of the Kalpower Brahmans to compete in the Cairns and Atherton Tableland shows and for sale at the Mareeba Bull Sale.

Unfortunately, things didn't work out as well as the U.S. investors hoped, and some quickly accepted offers for their leases. Lakefield, Laura Station, Kalpower and Marina Plains all became National Parks as did part of Silver Plains. Other properties returned to Australian ownership.

Prominent Visitors go on Tour

By 1960, the road was good enough (if graded specially for the occasion) to permit quite influential visitors to use it. The Governor General, Lord de L'Isle traversed the route in style and broadcast a greeting to all over the VKA radio at Rokeby station. The Ambassador of Switzerland, Mr. Gayar and his wife, drove up the Mulligan Highway to be entertained in Cooktown on the banks of the Endeavour River.[7] Not to be outdone, Sir Charles Lathbury, the Governor of Gibraltar and a keen bird-watcher, was taken on a trip up the Peninsula. He was ecstatic over the outcome. In the short time he was engaged on that trip, he recorded over fifty species of birds, more than he had seen in a similar three-week long trip down south.

Lord and Lady Casey were guests at the A.I.M. hostel in Coen when they, too, travelled up the road. Lord Casey gave the children a school holiday to mark the occasion before the party left by plane from Weipa, an action that ensured his popularity with the children. The then Governor of Queensland, Sir Henry Abel Smith and his wife the Lady May, went to Butcher's Hill from Cooktown in a Main Roads vehicle. They set out again the next day, equipped with folding tables, stools and even a battery operated refrigerator, for Musgrave and then Coen. Again, they visited the A.I.M. hostel cum hospital before leaving for Aurukun. Lady May was a keen rifle shot and had done some big-game shooting in Africa. On their trip from Coen to Rokeby and then to on Aurukun, she bagged quite a few big Peninsula Captain Cookers — wild pigs.[8] Their stay at Aurukun was short, as Sir Henry had to return to take up the duties of acting Governor General, but leaving by boat to a school children's chorus of *Will ye no come back again* and *The Maori's Farewell*, the vice-regal couple heartily wished that they could return. The Queen and her entourage landed in Cooktown in 1970 to mark the two hundredth anniversary of Cook's landing and to open the newly-restored Convent, now the Museum, but she didn't try out the road. In fact she even walked most of the way from the wharf, meeting and greeting the townsfolk as she went.

Contemporary female ringers — Shirley Porter, Ruth Shephard and Connie Gostelow

For the Peninsularites, the optimism that came in with the road soon spread to other fields. The traditional picnic race-meetings held each year at Cooktown, Laura and Coen felt the good effects. Horses and camping gear could now be brought to the meeting in vehicles rather than the old laborious and time-consuming way of riding and driving the horses, with the camp requisites and the race finery on the accompanying packhorses. Although new bloodstock were introduced to upgrade the station horses, it was the stationbred horses that provided the race entrants for many years. These were horses that were not only fleet of foot but were also accustomed to earning their keep as stockhorses. Many of them competed as well in the annual sports day held the day after the two-day racemeeting.

Because most of the jockeys were workaday stockmen, the minimum weight was considerably higher than that carried on urban tracks — ten stone (about 63kgs). As the ten stone also included the jockey's gear and racing saddle, some ringers (stockmen) couldn't even ride at that weight. A special race was programmed, the Stockman's Purse. Here the minimum weight was twelve stone, seven pounds (79kgs) and, as in the race for Aboriginal riders, it was a sure bet that every starter was a genuine go-er. Competition was very keen. Although lady jockeys didn't ride in the races at that time, many participated in the training of the horses once they came out of the 'paddock'. The races, with the exception of perhaps a 'cornfed' race each day for 'open' or non-districtbred animals, were for horses 'off grass', with no supplementary feeding. To ensure all grassfed horses were treated equally, the starters had to be paddocked at a place nominated by the Club for a set period of weeks. On their release prior to the races, supplementary feed was an option, as horses had to be kept either hobbled near the camp or restrained in a yard. The 'ladies' had some concession made for them. The Ladies Bracelet, one of the most coveted trophies, was a race in which all horses had to be nominated in the name of a 'lady' present on the track. The trophy was usually not a bracelet but a rather fancy wristwatch.

The advent of the road also made it possible for travelling showmen to ply an extended Far Northern circuit. Before that, night-time entertainment was limited to the pub, listening to old vinyl records or local singers and guitarists around the campfires or in bull fighting. This was not the Spanish variety of the art. It was a Peninsula special. Two competitors took part on all fours in a head-butting competition that aped two bulls fighting. One of the regular pilots, John Duffy, was rather good at this but most competitors had to be well-primed first at the bar. Jim Sharman came along with his boxing troupe and found no shortage of local amateurs ready to spar with his professionals. Buddy Williams gladdened the hearts of all with his Hillbilly Show and there were even, most years, a shooting gallery and knock 'em downs. No wonder visitors remarked that we thought our local picnic event was The Melbourne Cup. It was just as important.

Cooktown and Coen had suitable venues for staging the race ball but the Laura Club built its own dance hall. For a start it had no walls, but the roof kept off the occasional shower and the dance-floor was as smooth and as fast as that of its two rivals. Many a long and happy night was spent there to the music of a live bush band.

Queen Elizabeth inspecting participants in James Cook's Cooktown Landing re-enactment — 1970

15

The Great Blockade and Wilderness Conservation

Ups and downs of pastoral life with crashing of export prices for beef · Prices recover but other difficulties arise · Brucellosis and Tuberculosis Eradication Campaign reduces stock numbers · Experimental station set up at Heathlands to trial pastures and cattle fattening — Meat supplied to Weipa · Devastating loss of legume Townsville Stylo to Anthracnose · Government policy of non-renewal of Pastoral and Mining Leases · Government 'buy-back' of properties to form National Parks

While the coming of the road was justifiably cause for jubilation, it also brought some rather unwelcome side-effects. With reluctance on both sides, many Aboriginal stockmen (and their families) had been made redundant when Award wages and conditions became mandatory. The Aborigines moved on to take their chance in the towns and the cattlemen tried to convince themselves that, with the new fencing and improvements, mustering would be easier — even with a much-reduced mustering camp.

Slump in Cattle Prices

Then came the Cattle Crunch. Oil was again at the bottom of it and manufacturing nations like the United States of America and Japan were drastically effected by the price rises. Unfortunately, the U.S. and Japan were north Australia's best cattle markets. Prices plummeted back to below the cost of production. This wasn't helped by a Prime Minister who promoted a sale of beef to Russia at 3.5c per pound for cow meat and 9.5c for bullock beef. This translated to a return of about $14 for a four hundredweight cow and a bit over $55 for a good bullock. Naturally, in a buyer's market where only a few export meatworks controlled the price offered to producers, this set a benchmark for their future purchases.

The market did recover but it took some years during which time the gains which had been made by the producers were replaced by debts. Then Mother Nature stepped in. The highly valued Townsville Lucerne (a stylo), which, though seemingly not palatable to stock when green, produced high-protein and irresistible feed in the dry weather when it was needed the most, was fatally stricken with the disease Anthracnose. Stock not only grazed the little stylo to ground level, in some places they even licked up the seed from the ground. On a Townsville stylo diet, breeder cows could well hold their condition until the summer storms rejuvenated the grasses.

Townsville 'lucerne' came into the port of Townsville as a plant 'illegal immigrant'. It quickly became naturalised and spread rapidly north, especially into the poorer sandy country where it thrived. Its value was very soon apparent but all good things come to an end and Anthracnose came into the picture. It wiped out all the stands of Townsville 'lucerne' practically overnight. Newer, 'improved' stylos were introduced (legally) by the Department of Primary Industries but though very useful, they failed to adapt to the same conditions the old stylo had so readily claimed as its own. Decades later, Townsville stylo is beginning to re-appear but, remembering the earlier disaster, cattlemen aren't over-optimistic, although, with fingers crossed, they hope the little stylo will have picked up a resistance.

To keep breeding cows in the same condition as the Townsville stylo had achieved, cattlemen found that they had to feed supplementary licks from almost after the cessation of the Wet season until the flush of growth brought on by the storms. It was a considerable unbudgeted cost which eroded their returns.

Increasing Influence of National Parks

With the road to Cape York available, many people were beginning to realise that Queensland extended for a considerable distance beyond Cairns and the Tablelands. The Green Movement was gaining strength and National Parks and Conservation Areas were rapidly becoming popular. By this time, the owners of Lakefield had become disillusioned and readily accepted an offer from the State Government to acquire the lease for a National Park. This caused some local unrest especially in the many stockmen who had worked on Lakefield and knew its potential for cattle. It used to be Government policy to subdivide larger pastoral leases when their term of tenure ended. The old 'ringers' (stockmen) hoped this would happen in the case of Lakefield so that they could apply for a block of their own but times had changed. Closer settlement was no longer in favour.

Decline in Cattle Numbers and Closure of Meatworks.

Rokeby, one of the larger cattle properties, was also converted to National Park. Both of these runs had depastured very extensive cattle herds and the effect of the cessation of the annual turn-off from these two major producers severely effected the throughput at both the Mareeba Bacon Factory (which killed mainly cattle) and the Queerah Meatworks in Cairns. Other cattle stations were bought for National Parks as leases came to an end, and others reverted to Native Title or came under Aboriginal ownership. This reduced the commercial cattle herd numbers almost by half.

Next came B.T.E.C.,[1] the Brucellosis and Tuberculosis Eradication Campaign. The Peninsula had very few sources of T.B. infection and the number of infected beasts found at the abattoirs was extremely low, but the U.S.A. had conducted a stringent campaign to rid itself of the two diseases and, naturally, required its trading partners to follow the same course. An extensive and expensive operation was set in motion. Cattle were yarded, tested by D.P.I. officers and any reactors were destroyed. Compensation was paid for cattle shown to be positive for either test. With labour shortages on many of the larger properties, a considerable amount of cattle could not be yarded in time to be tested. These were automatically treated as reactors, and were shot from D.P.I. controlled helicopters. Some cattle were captured by use of specially made enclosures called trap-yards and these were able to be tested. However, many thousands of cattle were slaughtered in case they carried the disease. A large number of these were good quality cattle, but although grants were made available to some for re-stocking, very little was done to rectify the situation.

The two meatworks, estimating that it would take ten years to increase the herd numbers to a figure which would ensure a normal turn-off, decided that they couldn't afford to wait. They needed to operate at full capacity to pay their way. Both works closed down, never to re-open. The nearest export abattoir available after their closure was at Innisfail.

The smaller properties, run mostly by families with almost a century's experience behind them of breeding stock to suit the area, persevered and rose again, phoenixlike, from the figurative ashes. Cattle prices rose to profitable levels and, once again, the future looked rosy.

Optimistic Start to Heathlands

An interesting experiment was carried out at Heathlands, a lease near the site of the old McDonnell Telegraph Station. During the B.T.E.C. when cattle were slaughtered in case they may have had either disease, the case was put forward for a 'demountable' killing facility in the northern parts so that 'clean' cattle carcases need not be wasted. The idea wasn't taken up but, some time later, the C.S.I.R.O., a Federal Government research organisation, in conjunction with Comalco at Weipa, came up with another proposal.[2] Heathlands, the area chosen for the project, had historical associations. Kennedy and Jackey Jackey (Galmarra) had camped there, one hundred and twenty years previously — in 1848. The 'port' for Heathlands was Captain Billy Landing which took its name from an Aboriginal or Islander man whom prospector Crosbie met there unexpectedly in the early days of mining in the area. To Crosbie's surprise, Captain Billy spoke excellent English and proved to be a great help to the expedition, freely giving the benefits of local experience.

The man on the ground at Heathlands was Bob Loudon. He had a sound pastoral and a stock and station agency background before he attended both C.S.I.R.O's Lansdowne Research Station west of Townsville and an artificial insemination college, to widen his knowledge. He came out of this training with the title of Technical Assistant and was well-versed in the necessary laboratory procedures. Various grasses and legumes were tested at Heathlands where cattle grazed under trial conditions in segregated paddocks. Green Panic, Guinea grass and Brachiara were the favoured grasses with the vine Glycine, Dolichos Lab Lab and the stylos the most favoured legumes.

Courtesy Bob Loudon

Heathlands abbatoir

Cattle were blood-tested regularly for mineral and trace element deficiencies. The most serious mineral deficiency, cobalt, was supplied as commercial stock-lick blocks. C.S.I.R.O's Bill Winter oversaw the project and maintained a keen interest. As the herd became established, it was decided to provide beef from Heathlands to Welch's butcher shop in Weipa and a small, modern abattoir was erected. Steers came from local properties. Bill and Dawn Jackson of Wolverton, the Duda brothers at Merluna, John and Vera Harris, veterans Ted Youngman and Rod and Theresa Heinneman, all supplied steers for fattening on the trial pastures. Paddy Shephard even sent cattle from his block near Coen.

The cattle put on weight quickly and could be turned off within six months at a 200-250 kgs weight range to suit the Comalco market. They were ideal for barbecue steaks. Heathland began by killing two bodies per week but this was soon increased to nine or 450 steers per year. This was quite a substantial saving to the breeders who would otherwise have been faced with high freight costs to get their cattle to Mareeba and beyond. Cattle were later also bred at Heathlands with bulls coming up in style by sea on the *Weipa* or the *Dundas*. Veteran Stock Inspector Neville Copeman took a keen interest in the sea transport of cattle but was concerned about a condition which, at times, affected cattle sent by sea. A few died and some 'went mad', acting in an 'unsocial manner'. The short-coated Brahman cattle seemed more prone to this complaint. With Bob Loudon's help, Nev Copeman conducted 'practical research'. The culprit turned out to be the absorption of excess salt from the sea spray. Once the cause was found, it was simply counter-acted with an 'instant and miraculous cure'- a dose of liquid glucose. Cattle were also kept away from sea-spray.

Like most of the projects proposed for the Peninsula, the good progress made at Heathlands couldn't be maintained. Bob Loudon had to resign for health reasons and the plans introduced after he left didn't quite fulfil the earlier requirements. The undertaking was abandoned.

As cattle prices maintained a reasonable rate for some years, the cattlemen's natural optimism for the future was rekindled. Even the seasons were working co-operatively, with very few really heart-breaking droughts. With a large area taken up by National Parks and other erstwhile working properties no longer being used to graze stock, bushfires were more prevalent but most graziers managed to stick to the long-held practice of burning breaks to halt their progress. The farmers at Lakeland had other fire problems. Many of these were caused by birds in flight hitting the power lines, shorting out, and plunging in flames to the ground.

Weipa and *Dundas* at Captain Billy Landing

Farming at Lakeland

It took more than these fires to lower the enthusiasm of the Lakeland farmers. New crops, including one of the largest coffee plantations in Australia were introduced and prospered. The coffee was watered from one of the big irrigation dams constructed by the visionary Clive Foyster. I was told that if all the polythene pipe used to water the coffee trees was joined together, it would reach from Lakeland to Mt. Carbine, 120 kilometres away. The coffee is delicious, so the polypipe is doing a great job where it is.

The Lakeland success spurred on the farmers along the Endeavour and McIvor Rivers north of Cooktown. Here, too, there was a slight move away from the more traditional corn and peanuts. Tropical fruit, including the more exotic varieties, grew extremely well and plantation timber projects were successfully trialled.

The cattlemen's complacency was again shattered in 1995 when, watching T.V. at the Laura pub during race week, they saw a proud Premier Goss announce his plan to turn all of the Peninsula not under Native Title or Aboriginal ownership, into a colossal conservation area that would be the envy of the rest of the world. This was the first that the lease-holders had heard of the Government's intentions. They were surprised, to say the least. As soon as the Lands Department office opened in Cairns after the weekend, they attempted to find out where they stood in the Premier's scheme. Unfortunately, the officers there either knew nothing, or weren't prepared to speak. It wasn't until the end of the week that the cattlemen received any reply to their inquiries.

Lakeland Blockade 1995

By this time, the lease-holders and their supporters came up with a reply of their own. They'd 'blockade' the road junction at Lakeland and try to get their message across to the tourists. The dates set were for Monday and Tuesday, 10th and 11th July 1995. The 'blockade' was anything but violent. The cattlemen were confident that other people would understand their predicament. Decked out in an 'Enough is Enough' T-shirt, I was one of Joy Marriott's offsiders on the Laura road. Bill Raymond and his helpers covered the Cooktown turn-off. Off the road, two cattle trucks were parked to form the 'walls' of a 'refreshment room'. Tarpaulins, reaching across from the tops of the high sides of the stock crates, formed the roof. In the shade thus provided, were tables with cakes, bikkies and the requisites for making hot or cold drinks. The children from the local Lakeland school provided posters they had done to illustrate their side of the story and these were displayed on the cattle crate 'walls'. Some pro-industry literature was available, as were the blockade T-shirts with the Eureka flag as logo.

All vehicles were stopped and the occupants asked to come in for refeshments. Most accepted and also seemed sympathetic to the farmer, miner and cattleman's cause. Many even purchased the T-shirts. There was also a petition. Of the hundred or so people I asked to sign the petition, only one woman took umbrage and rather vehemently refused. However, some travellers asked for spare copies of the petition so that they could gather more signatures for us. The other 'blockaders' reported in a similar way. The majority of the travellers were on side and most accepted the offer of refreshments in the 'tea room'.

A group of Aborigines who had learned to make their own way in life, came out from Hopevale way to support the blockaders. Many had previously worked on the stations and in the droving camps. Their presence was heartening.

The effort wasn't in vain. Premier Goss lost the next election and the great Wilderness Area idea was shelved. For the time being, at least. Some properties changed hands. Small tourist ventures started up along the road to the Tip and proved popular with the travelling public. New impetus was given to the cattle industry by the re-appearance of the live cattle export market. With the encouragement of Janet Holmes a Court of Heytesbury Pastoral Co., which had a business venture in Malaysia with the R.M. Meat Groups, Doreen Quartermain of Watson River stirred life again into live exports from Weipa. Cattle came from as far south as Olivevale near Laura to fill one shipment. With freight charges to Mareeba and beyond continually on the rise, the re-opening of the trade in live cattle was a profitable alternative. But, once again, problems came from Government decisions. Pastoral and mining leases failed to gain renewed tenures. The Nixons at Shelburne Bay, on Kennedy's route to Cape York, lost the lease to their property but have persisted in staying on as 'squatters', using the term in the contemporary, rather than the traditional way. Other leases were not renewed and some of these stations were purchased by the Government. A few were sold as working cattle properties to Aboriginal interests. Uncertainty of tenure was a strong disincentive to making further improvements to the cattle runs. Not much less than half of the entire Peninsula is taken up by Parks and Aboriginal lands which do not have to pay Council rates. This has a rather deleterious effect on those trying to balance the Council's books.

In early 2003, the State Government announced the purchase of Lilyvale near Princess Charlotte Bay, and Green Hills/ Archer Point to the south of Cooktown. The Shephard family at Lilyvale, whose forebears came to the

Joy Marriott, Lennie Wallace and Debbie Bennett at the Lakeland Blockade — 10th & 11th July 1995

Peninsula in the days of the Palmer Goldrush, were advised that the request for renewal of their pastoral lease would not be granted. They had no alternative but to take up the Government's offer to buy them out. Archer Point was Cooktown's hope for a deep-water port. It had already been used successfully in Foyster's time at Lakeland to ship grain overseas, and had resulted in a great savings of the freight required to send produce overland to Cairns for export from Cairns harbour. Recent surveys done for the Cook Shire Council reinforced their contention of Archer Point as a safe anchorage for larger vessels.

Perhaps Premier Goss's dream of a Wilderness Conservation Area may still come true.

Endnotes

Chapter 1

1 *Historical Geography of the British Colonies,* J.D. Rogers, Clarendon Press, Oxford. 1907

2 *Ships in the Coral,* Hector Holthouse MacMillan, Sydney. 1976

3 *Ships in the Coral,* Hector Holthouse MacMillan, Sydney. 1976

4 *Islanders and Aborigines at Cape York Peninsula,* David R. Moore Aust. Institute of Aboriginal Studies. Canberra. Humanities Press. New Jersey, U.S.A. 1979 p76

5 *Islanders and Aborigines at Cape York Peninsula,* David R. Moore Aust. Institute of Aboriginal Studies. Canberra. Humanities Press. New Jersey, U.S.A. 1979

6 *Kennedy of Cape York,* Edgar Beale, Rigby 1970 p238

7 *Islanders and Aborigines at Cape York Peninsula,* David R. Moore Aust. Institute of Aboriginal Studies. Canberra. Humanities Press. New Jersey, U.S.A. 1979

8 *Islanders and Aborigines at Cape York Peninsula,* David R. Moore Aust. Institute of Aboriginal Studies. Canberra. Humanities Press. New Jersey, U.S.A. 1979

9 *A Mother's Offering to her Children,* By a Lady long resident in N.S.W., Gazette Sydney 1841

10 *Northmost Australia,* R.L.Jack, George Robertson, Brisbane. 1922 p 155

11 *Northmost Australia,* R.L.Jack, George Robertson, Brisbane. 1922 p 155

12 *A Mother's Offering to her Children,* By a Lady long resident in N.S.W., Gazette Sydney 1841

13 *A Mother's Offering to her Children,* By a Lady long resident in N.S.W., Gazette Sydney 1841

14 *A Mother's Offering to her Children,* By a Lady long resident in N.S.W., Gazette Sydney 1841

15 *Across the Years,* Charles Barrett, The Hawthorne Press, Melbourne 1948.p 83

16 *Aust. Dictionary of Dates and Men of the Time,* J.H. Heaton, George Robertson, Melbourne 1879

17 *Aust. Dictionary of Dates and Men of the Time,* J.H. Heaton, George Robertson, Melbourne 1879

18 *The Mutiny on Board H.M.S. Bounty,* Wm. Bligh

19 *The Missing Coast,* J.C.H.Gill, Qld Museum, Brisbane 1988

20 *The Missing Coast,* J.C.H.Gill, Qld Museum, Brisbane 1988 p 151

21 *The Missing Coast,* J.C.H.Gill, Qld Museum, Brisbane 1988 p 160

22 Bev and John Shay, Cooktown Historical Society 2001

23 *Some North Queensland Mysteries,* Writers in Townsville, Y. Crossan. Townsville. n.d.

Chapter 2

1 *Kennedy, the Barcoo and Beyond* Edgar Beale, Blubberhead Press, Hobart. 1983
2 *Kennedy of Cape York* Edgar Beale, Rigby 1970
3 *Kennedy of Cape York* Edgar Beale, Rigby 1970, p 143
4 *Kennedy of Cape York* Edgar Beale, Rigby 1970
5 *Jardine's Journal* F.J. Byerley, Buxton, Brisbane 1867
6 *Jardine's Journal* F.J. Byerley, Buxton, Brisbane 1867
7 *Jardine's Journal* F.J. Byerley, Buxton, Brisbane. 1867, p73
8 *Northmost Australia* R.L. Jack, G.Robertson and Co., Brisbane 1867, p342
9 *Queenslander* 9th November 1878, p 185
10 *Cooktown Courier* 19th July 1892
11 *The North Queensland Beef Cattle Industry* Dawn May, J.C.U. Townsville 1984, p134
12 *Evening Advocate* 18th May 1970 and letter from W. Armbrust, Cairns.

Chapter 3

1 *'From the Gulf' Fair Girls and Gray Horses* Will H. Ogilvie, Angus & Robertson, London 1913.
2 *Chasing the Rainbow* Glenville Pike, Pinevale Publications, Mareeba 1993, p32

Chapter 4

1 *Telegraph* Brisbane. 28th December 1925
2 Australia Post and Telegraph Historical Society, Brisbane
3 *A Century at the Top 1887-1987* Don Sheehy, Telecom, Cairns 1987
4 *A Century at the Top 1887-1987* Don Sheehy, Telecom, Cairns 1987
5 *Northmost Australia* R.L.Jack, George Robertson and Co., Brisbane 1922, pp 662/663
6 *Northmost Australia* R.L.Jack, George Robertson and Co., Brisbane 1922, p 666
7 *Northmost Australia* R.L.Jack, George Robertson and Co., Brisbane 1922, p669
8 *A Century at the Top 1887-1987* Don Sheehy, Telecom, Cairns 1987
9 *Northmost Australia* R.L.Jack, George Robertson and Co., Brisbane 1922, p 675
10 *A Century at the Top 1887-1987* Don Sheehy, Telecom, Cairns 1987
11 *A Century at the Top 1887-1987* Don Sheehy, Telecom, Cairns 1987
12 Records from the Australia Post and Telegraph Historical Society, Brisbane
13 *A Century at the Top 1887-1987* Don Sheehy, Telecom, Cairns 1987
14 *The Cooktown Railway* J.W. Knowles, Australian Railway Historical Society, Queensland Division, Brisbane 1966

Chapter 5

1 Australian Post and Telegraph Historical Society, Brisbane

2 *The Cooktown Railway.* J.W. Knowles. Australian Railway Historical Society, Queensland Division, Brisbane 1966, p4
3 Australian Post and Telegraph Historical Society, Brisbane
4 Conversations with Bowie Gostelow and Jim MacDowell Jnr.
5 Conversation with Bowie Gostelow 2002.

Chapter 6

1 Baron Ferdinand Von Mueller *Select Extra Tropical Plants* Thos. Richards, Sydney 1881 pp 305-6
2 Dorothy Jones *Cardwell Shire Story* Jacaranda Press, Brisbane 1961 p26
3 Sam Elliott *The Lone Wolf* John C. Hay, J.D. & R.S. Kerr, Mareeba 2002, p 112
4 *History of Burns Philp* K. Buckley and K. Klugman, B.P. Co. Ltd 1981
5 *History of Burns Philp* K. Buckley and K. Klugman, B.P. Co. Ltd 1981
6 *With the Cape York Prospecting Party* M.W. Sheehan, *Queenslande*r 19th September 1896
7 *Northmost Australia* R.L. Jack, George Robertson and Co., Sydney 1922, p 724
8 *Ion Idriess* Beverly Eley, Harper Collins, Sydney 1995, p 108
9 *Onward Australia* Ion Idriess, Angus & Robertson, Sydney 1945, p 250
10 *Thirty Years in Tropical Australia* Rev. Gilbert White, Angus & Robertson, Sydney 1918
11 Ion Idriess *Walkabout* 1 October 1937
12 *Thirty Years in Tropical Australia* Rev. Gilbert White, Angus & Robertson, Sydney 1918
13 *Some Experiences of a New Guinea Resident Magistrate* C.A.W. Monckton. John Lane, London 1921 pp1-2
14 *History of Burns Philp* K. Buckley and K. Klugman, B.P. Co. Ltd 1981
15 *Lizard Island* Jillian Robertson Hutchison, p162

Chapter 7

1 *Cairns Post* Alec Martin, 12th June 2000
2 *N.Q. Register* Sundowner, 3rd December 1998
3 *N.Q. Register.* Sundowner. 3rd December 1998
4 *Northmost Australia* R.L. Jack, George Robertson and Co., Melbourne 1922, p554
5 *Queensland Frontier* Glenville Pike, Rigby 1978, p 239
6 *North Queensland Register* Sundowner, 13th November 1981
7 *A Flower Hunter in Queensland and New Zealand* Ellis Rowan, John Murray, London 1897 p112
8 *Northmost Australia* R.L.Jack. George Robertson & Co., Brisbane 1922, p568
9 *North Queensland Register* Sundowner, 13th November 1981
10 *Qld. Govt. Mining Journal* E. Cecil Saint Smith, August 1915

Chapter 8

1 *The History of Burns Philp* K. Buckley and K. Klugman, Burns Philp 1981, p3
2 *The History of Burns Philp* K. Buckley and K. Klugman, Burns Philp 1981, p111
3 *More About Cairns* J.W. Collinson. Smith and Paterson, Brisbane 1942, p16
4 *Paper Power in North Queensland* J. Manion, N.Q. Newspaper Co., Townsville 1982 p7
5 *Paper Power in North Queensland* J. Manion, N.Q. Newspaper Co., Townsville 1982, p33
6 *Paper Power in North Queensland* J. Manion, N.Q. Newspaper Co., Townsville 1982, p189.
7 *The Most Amazing Story* Geoffrey Maslen, Angus and Robertson, Sydney 1977, p152
8 *The Most Amazing Story* Geoffrey Maslen, Angus and Robertson, Sydney 1977, p119
9 *North Queensland Register* Hugh Borland n.d.

Chapter 9

1 Correspondence with Canon John Warby November 2002
2 Correspondence with Canon John Warby November 2002
3 *Speak You So Gently*, Kylie Tennant, Victor Gollancz, London 1959, P16
4 *Northmost Australia*, Robert Logan Jack, George Robertson, Brisbane 1922, p681
5 *Northmost Australia*, Robert Logan Jack, George Robertson, Brisbane 1922, p682
6 *Coasts of Cape York*, Coralie and Leslie Rees, Halstead Press, Sydney 1960, p102
7 *Aurukun Diary*, Geraldine MacKenzie, The Aldergate Press 1981 p105.
8 *Aurukun Diary*, Geraldine MacKenzie, The Aldergate Press 1981, p55
9 *Aurukun Diary*, Geraldine MacKenzie, The Aldergate Press 1981, p171
10 *Coasts of Cape York*, Coralie and Leslie Rees, Halstead Press, Sydney 1960, p102

Chapter 10

1 Labour in Politics Convention 1898
2 *Labor in Power*, D.J. Murphy et al., U.Q. Press, Brisbane 1980, p155
3 Summary of Various Administration Actions 1915-1918
4 *Labor in Power*, D.J. Murphy et al., U.Q. Press, Brisbane 1980, p143
5 *A Handbook for Nationalists. State Enterprises*, M.H. Ellis, Brisbane 1918, p41
6 *Northmost Australia*, R.L. Jack, George Robertson and Co., Brisbane 1922, p738
7 Sales brochure, Qld Govt. Printer, Brisbane 17th September 1929
8 *A Handbook for Nationalists. State Enterprises*, M.H. Ellis, Brisbane 1918, p42.
9 *Queensland Country Life* Brisbane, 2nd January 1992, p11
10 *Results of the Archbold Expedition No. 68*, L.J. Brass, American Museum of Natural History, New York 1953, p204.
11 *A Handbook for Nationalists. State Enterprises*, M.H. Ellis, Brisbane 1918, p45

Chapter11

1 *Moreton Bay Courier to The Courier Mail 1846-1992* Brisbane 1992, p201
2 *Queensland Airfields WWII — 50 Years On* , R.R. Marks, Mansfield, Queensland 1994, p14
3 *Queensland Airfields WWII — 50 Years On* , R.R. Marks, Mansfield, Queensland 1994, p14
4 *Queensland Airfields WWII — 50 Years On* , R.R. Marks, Mansfield, Queensland 1994, p19
5 *Aurukun Diary*, Geraldine MacKenzie, The Aldersgate Press 1981, p112
6 *Battlers in the Bush*, Joe Fisher, Darwin 1998, p71

Chapter 12

1 *Northmost Australia*, R.L. Jack, George Robertson and Co., Brisbane 1922, p394
2 *Trinity Phoenix*, Dorothy Jones, Cairns Post, Cairns 1976, p105
3 *Cairns Post* Cairns, 3rd September 1885
4 *Crocodile Men*, Bryan Peach, Universal Enterprises, 2000

Chapter 13

1 *We and the Baby*, Hector MacQuarrie, Angus and Robertson, Sydney 1929
2 *The Sunday Mail* , Joan Starr, Brisbane 24th March 1974
3 *N.Q. Register* 10th January 1985, p16
4 *Local Govt. Journal* December 1958 p35
5 J*Review of Archer Report*, A. Heading, 2nd January 1958
6 *A Voyage to Terra Australis Vol.2*, Matthew Flinders
7 A. Archer Conversation Harvest Home, 1958.
8 Queensland State Archives 15th January 1959
9 Conversation, January 2003

Chapter14

1 *Bush Engineer*, Alexa Gallop 1979
2 *Bush Engineer*, Alexa Gallop 1979
3 *Bush Engineer*, Alexa Gallop 1979
4 *Queensland Country Life* Brisbane 20th December 1956
5 *North Australian Monthly*, P.J. Skerman, February 1956
6 *Sydney Sun*
7 *Bush Engineer*, Alexa Gallop 1979
8 *Bush Engineer*, Alexa Gallop 1979

Chapter 15

1 Information for much of this chapter was given in conversations with Peter Marriott and Graham Elmes both of Lakeland

2 Conversation with Bob Loudon, Mareeba 2001